Alternatives for Growth:
The Engineering and Economics of Natural Resources Development

NATIONAL BUREAU OF ECONOMIC RESEARCH

Edited by,
HARVEY J.
McMAINS
*Institute for
Computing Science
and Computer
Applications
The University of
Texas, at Austin*

and

LYLE
WILCOX
*Dean, College of
Engineering
Clemson University*

Alternatives for Growth:
The Engineering
and Economics
of Natural
Resources
Development

A Conference of the
National Bureau of
Economic Research

Published for the
NATIONAL BUREAU OF
ECONOMIC RESEARCH, INC.
by
BALLINGER PUBLISHING COMPANY
A Subsidiary of J. B. Lippincott Company
Cambridge, Mass.
1978

This book is printed on recycled paper.

International Standard Book Number: 0-88410-480-x

Library of Congress Catalog Card Number: 77-11870

Printed in the United States of America

Library of Congress Cataloging in Publication Data

Main entry under title:
   Alternatives for growth.

   Includes index.
   1. Natural resources—Congresses. 2. Environmental policy—
Congresses. I. McMains, Harvey. II. Wilcox, Lyle.
HC55.A37   333.7   77-11870
ISBN 0-88410-480-x

Relation of the National Bureau Directors to Publications Reporting Conference Proceedings

Since the present volume is a record of conference proceedings, it has been exempted from the rules governing submission of manuscripts to, and critical review by, the Board of Directors of the national Bureau.

*(Resolution adopted July 6, 1948,
as revised November 21, 1949,
and April 20, 1968)*

Contents

Preface

No event can be beyond expectations,
Fear contradiction, or compel surprise, for Zeus,
Father of Olympians, has made night at full noon,
Darkness mid the brilliance of the sun—
And pale fear has seized men.
Henceforth nothing for them is certain:
One may expect everything,
And none among you should be astonished to see,
One day, the deer, preferring the sonorous tides
Of the sea to the land,
Borrow from the dolphins their sea pasture,
While the latter plunge into the mountains.

—Archilochus, 700 B.C.

Future historians will probably describe this time in our enlightenment as the age of conscious social change—a time when we take into account what we as humans have done and are doing to our planet earth and what we must do if we are to continue to improve our conditions and not return to a less abundant existence. The Charles Carter Newman Symposium on Natural Resources Engineering provided the opportunity to convene a group of concerned and interested scholars, scientists, educators, and policymakers to review and discuss a set of original and useful papers in the areas of natural resource use, development, and shortage. It was the feeling among those of us responsible for the planning and organization of this meeting that too much has been written about the limits of the world's future and the troubles that lie ahead for all mankind, and that not enough consideration has been given to the more positive aspects of alternatives, which surely must exist.

During the last quarter of the twentieth century all peoples have been told over and over again that we face an uncertain future because of unanswered fundamental questions such as: How do we control human population? Can we permit increasing consumption of energy and natural resources? Should we allow technology to continue its exponential growth? How do we produce an ever-increasing supply of food and fiber? Can the leadership of the world continue to plan for the improvement of the quality of human life, or must it be content to regress because of finite supplies of essential natural resources? What is the one predominant factor underlying any possibility for answering these questions in a satisfactory way? It is surely the assessment of where we are, where we want to go, and the focusing of the advancement of our technology in a more meaningful way. Will mankind continue to improve the quality of human life and make technological progress? Or will we regress because of misuse of our current essential natural resources?

This debate was, in a way, initiated by the "limits of growth" controversy. Along with carefully documented studies of the topic came an assault of emotionally charged reports and discussions. On the one side were advocates of a total moratorium on economic growth; on the other, proponents of unlimited industrial and technological advancement. On both sides there has been a proliferation of experts eager to tell us in the most explicit detail just what the impact of shortages in natural resources, or a slowdown in exploiting all resources, will be, and as a rule, predicting the demise of Western technological civilization because they are not being taken seriously. There is nothing wrong with a prediction in itself, provided it is arrived at rationally and founded upon accurate information. This is quite different, as one writer put it, "from the torrent of soothsaying that pours over us, predominantly emotional, frequently verging on the hysterical, and displaying ignorance of technology, science, economics, or history."

Out of all this heat has come some light with the dedication to obtain better data, develop plans, and move toward a reasonable synthesis of positions on the "growth" issue. Other economic alternatives have been added to those of "no growth" and "unlimited growth." Some scholars have raised questions about the very concept of natural resources: What is a resource? Aren't people a natural resource? Are resources truly limited? Isn't it *time* that we're really short of? Will our present thoughts about the true constraints on growth used in 1977 be the same as those used in 1997? Others offer resource-use alternatives that emphasize individual action and creativity, the role of economic incentives, market forces, and property rights. Still others suggest studying the interrelationships between natural resources, technological change, and the social system, using systems analysis to formulate action plans.

The future is, of course, uncertain, but it is the natural creativity and genius of the people of all the world that makes it almost certain that there are solutions to all problems. Natural-resources engineering, economic analysis, planning, and management applied to the utilization and conservation of land, natural resources, air, water, and human resources are the crucial aspects of any rational strategy for solving the resource utilization-conservation dilemma, and for determining alternatives for continued growth. An intricate web of fact-finding, education, information and decisionmaking links engineers, scientists, agriculturalists, economists, financiers, government officials, legal experts, representatives of the media, and all people into a fellowship of concerned action.

The power of our technology makes it possible for us to do more than dream. Technology has allowed us to substitute plastics for metals, create a synthetic energy called electricity, communicate by satellite, calculate by computers, program machines to do much of our manufacturing, develop space vehicles and nuclear weapons, and do a host of other "impossible" things. There is widespread public recognition of technology's influences—good and bad—upon every facet of our way of life. It has raised fears and concerns that make us wonder if it has gone too far. Without question, however, it is our hope for the future. To forget what we know is not possible even if it were desirable. All of us who have been a part of technology's science, its management, or its support know that it is not always predictable, nor does it always achieve what we had hoped. But, when treated with respect, concern, and common sense, technology does deliver a fair share of its promise.

It was to this end that the Charles Carter Newman Symposium took place, bringing together specialists of international reputation to generate new thoughts on natural resource development among concerned scientists in agriculture, engineering, and economics. We hope that the papers and comments printed in this conference volume will serve as a series of philosophical and practical points of departure for researchers and policymakers involved in natural-resources management, economics, and engineering, that as a result the problems facing the nation and the world will be in better focus, and that programs will be developed and carried out to ensure that growth and economic well-being can continue. The discussions in these papers deal with the larger issues, the social and economic as well as technological aspects of resources utilization and conservation, and aim at producing the kind of thought and research required to develop alternative plans to cope with these real issues. Above all, these papers embrace a view that humanity is a steward of the future, and that we should plan and act wisely in the use of all resources. Bertrand Russell once said, "If rational men cooperated and used their scientific knowledge to the full, they could now secure the economic welfare of all." This is our hope.

Harvey McMains, National Bureau of Economic Research
Lyle Wilcox, Clemson University

Acknowledgments

We gratefully acknowledge participation by H. Guyford Stever as our program moderator, and John J. McKetta, Jr. and Paul W. MacAvoy as banquet speakers. All are experts in fields covered at the Symposium and all contributed greatly to its success.

In addition, we acknowledge with appreciation the family and J. Wilson Newman, whose gift to honor his father created the Symposium Series.

Part I

Technology

Chapter One

Engineering and the Natural Environment

John R. Pierce

Our concern with engineering and the natural environment stems from human life and from the power of technology. If there were no people, the earth would pass from birth to death without human concern. Species would arise and become extinct, continents would drift through the oceans, tropical ages would alternate with ice ages, but there would be no concern about better or worse. Or, if rational people were destitute of a powerful technology, they might speculate about past, present and future, but one would be little able to influence them. One could farm, wisely or unwisely, until the soil was exhausted. One could in some ways protect oneself and one's possessions from inclement weather. If all else failed, one could perish or migrate.

Humanity does exist, and does have a powerful technology. In some degree we are able to influence our environment. Our concerns about ourselves and our world are more than that of seeking religious or philosophical reasons or values. They are concerns about what we have done and what we may do. In considering engineering and our environment, it seems to me reasonable to discuss three general topics. The first is, What is the actual power of technology and how do we measure that power? The second is, What *is* the natural environment? The third is, What can we do and what should we do?

THE POWER OF TECHNOLOGY

The Apollo program, which took men to the moon and back, was clearly a triumph of engineering. Twenty-five years earlier, no one but Wer-

3

nher von Braun and a few science-fiction writers regarded a flight to the moon as feasible, yet men went to the moon and returned. This proved to be a very difficult and complex undertaking. The more informed one was, the more surprising it seemed that everything worked. Yet the people and the equipment, the space vehicles as well as the many persons concerned, played their complex parts. Six landings were made on the moon, and the only fatalities in the program were on earth, preceding the moon landings.

It is of interest that the Apollo program cost $25.4 billion, and that the total distance covered was 18.1 billion nautical miles. For a crew of three, the man-miles traveled are three times as large. The cost of Apollo travel per man statute mile is about $400. Not many people can afford to pay $400 a mile to travel. I think that Apollo has little significance for everyday human activities.

Apollo is a grand monument to contemporary engineering skill, as the pyramids are a monument to the skills of the Egyptians, and the cathedrals of Europe and the temple Angkor Wat are monuments to the skills of other peoples. Monuments represent only a part of humanity's skilled effort, and usually a small part. Historically, except in favored regions of easy life, people have worked hard just to feed and clothe themselves and to protect themselves from the elements. As a part of this practical work, humanity has accomplished things rivaling the monuments that have been raised.

The Indians of the Salt River Valley of Arizona irrigated 250,000 acres with 1,000 miles of canals and ditches. About 3000 B.C., the Egyptians built a 49-foot-high masonry dam on the Nile at Kosheish to provide water for Memphis. The Tu-kian Dam, built in China about 200 B.C., irrigated 500,000 acres of land and provided water for the 700-mile-long Imperial Canal, built in 589-618 A.D. The Minneriya Tank, a reservoir built in Ceylon in 900 A.D., has surface dimensions of 6 miles by 2 miles. New York City may be a monument to the past, but it was financed and built for housing and commerce. Engineering feats in the pursuit of everyday, practical ends are as astonishing as, and far more extensive than, the monuments we have raised.

Technology today is so extensive and various that one might despair of describing it, let alone giving a measure of its power. Yet a rational measure of the power of today's technology is indeed possible. In order to arrive at such a measure it is best to look at the ends of technology and how well they have been accomplished, rather than at the internal nature of the technology itself. Technology is particularly well adapted to increasing our ability to provide material goods and services. In the early days of our country, most people were farmers. It was hard for people to feed and clothe themselves adequately. Housing and the production of goods took much of the rest of their efforts. People began productive activities early in life, and physical productivity was limited by failure of strength rather than an arbitrary retirement age. Technology has changed all that. All of the population—men, women, children too young to work, those who have retired—all must eat. Today, in the United States, about 1.5 percent of the total population is engaged in agriculture. This 1.5 percent of our population grows a great deal of food for the rest of the world, as well as enough for their fellow citizens.

About 15 percent of the U.S. population provides us with *all* physical goods and services. These include food, minerals, houses and buildings, all manufactured goods, and transportation, communication, electricity, gas and water. The fraction of the population that produces goods and physical services has declined steadily. It was 21 percent in 1950, rather than 15 percent, as it is today. So in 1977 less than a sixth of the population provides, and provides lavishly, all the physical things that they and the rest of the population have come to depend on. We may wonder what all the other people do. Nearly half are deemed to be too young or too old to work. About half of the population is female, but about half of the women with children work, and that fraction is increasing. Further, the very technology that has made it possible for less than a sixth of our people to supply the physical needs of all is a very specialized technology. Few producers sell their products directly to consumers. Hence, a great many people are engaged in distribution and marketing and in advertising. Others work in government agencies, or in schools or in hospitals, or are lawyers busy helping us to sue and to be sued. Some are unemployed. The point is that 15 percent of the U.S. population can now supply the physical needs of the entire population of our nation. This, it seems to me, is a true and valid measure of the power of today's technology. And it is a quantitative measure.

The implications of this power of technology are another story. Our technology of production has made possible an increase in the total national expenditure in health care from about $10 billion in 1950 to about $150 billion in 1977. That this increase in expenditure appears to have affected our health very little is irrelevant to the argument made here. The argument is that a small fraction of our population can supply our physical needs, and the rest are available to do something else, or to do nothing. We should also note in passing that if some country could find a way to employ 45 percent of its population in producing physical goods and services, that nation could have as much per person as we do even if the productivity of each worker was only a third as great as ours.

In terms of producing what people need, or at least what Americans want, our technology is very powerful indeed. Are there other measures of its power? What about measuring it against the power of nature? Measured in this way, common examples show us that our technology is puny indeed. A hydrogen bomb is puny compared with a major volcanic eruption or an earthquake. Some are concerned lest our activities *may* influence the climate. Nature has repeatedly produced ice ages, and even more drastic alterations of the climate. Continents drift while our technology changes the face of the earth scarcely at all. Quantitative measurements also confirm that humanity is puny compared with nature. The energy of sunlight that falls on our country each year is a hundred thousand times as great as our total energy consumption.

We can imagine that humanity may truly alter the face of the earth. During the first atomic test, Oppenheimer feared that the intense heat might ignite the atmosphere, causing the oxygen and nitrogen to burn. Early in the atomic era, people feared that cobalt bombs might destroy all life. Perhaps we *should* fear. People bent on destruction might, wittingly or unwittingly, change our planet in a major way. It hasn't happened, and it might be very difficult to make it happen. Still, we should keep the possibililty in mind.

We can conclude, however, that technology is weak compared with other natural forces, but that it is powerful in altering human life. It is important, however, that we understand a condition. If our technology is to have a major effect on our lives, our lives and our world must change drastically. It is a wonder of technology that 1.5 percent of our country's population can produce food for us all, and a good deal more. It would be ridiculous to imagine that technology could simply have reduced each farmer's labor without changing the nature of farming and without moving people from farms to factories. The increased productivity of agriculture depends on science and technology of plants, fertilizers and machines that could not exist in a primarily agricultural society. Even the computer plays an important role in farming. Agriculture has advanced because the whole world has changed. The changes in agriculture would have been impossible without other changes.

In trying to understand how technology is linked to social change, we can trace particular technological changes, but we must realize that the changing aspects of our world interact in ways so complicated that we can scarcely understand them. Transportation was once largely via seas and rivers, and great cities were thus situated on harbors and rivers. In the early nineteenth century, canals became powerful extensions of rivers and opened access to locations far from natural waterways. By the end of the last century, canals were largely displaced by railroads, which opened up even more remote regions to commerce and settlement.

It is easy to see that these changing modes of transportation had a profound effect on life in this country. We may overlook the fact that they brought with them other changes. In the day of canals, the ownership of canals and barges was separate. This pattern of ownership and operation was tried in the early days of railroads, even before steam locomotives. It proved impractical. Railroad companies came to own both trains and tracks. With the advent of the airplane, some thought there would be widespread personal ownership of airplanes. There is, but not in the sense of widespread personal ownership of automobiles. Not only are new technologies different, but their implications for social patterns are different.

More than canals, railroads and interurban rail opened up new land for business and residence. Indeed, the value of the land opened up was a chief source of funds and profit for those who built railroads and interurban rail. That the appreciation of land values because of rail is a thing of the past may well explain a part of rail's financial problems. California once had 1,200 miles of interurban rail, and interurban rail in the East was even more extensive. In those days, residences and work locations were within walking distance of trolley lines. People could reach work from lakeside summer resorts by interurban. With the spreading of the automobile, people moved beyond walking distance of anything. The whole pattern of settlement changed.

The automobile plays an important part in our lives because our life has so altered that we have become dependent on the automobile. The telephone plays such an important part in our lives because our lives have so altered that we have become dependent on the telephone. What of the fraternal organizations of the days of my father? The very sort of communities in which they thrived are gone, or are so altered by television and easy travel that people seek companionship and distraction in other ways. They seek help from the government, not from lodges.

The power of technology is dependent on its power to change our world. Those who call on technology to ameliorate present conditions are misled about technology's power and effect. Early in this century a person might have asked for a scientific solution to the pressing problem of keeping the streets clear of horse dung. That problem has vanished. Today we are fighting the emissions of gasoline-powered vehicles. It is a secret from only the blindest or most inattentive that the problem of pollution through burning gasoline cannot persist for many decades. We will run out of oil. We must indeed use technology to cope with present problems, but present problems are problems left over from the past. Unless we prevent change, which would be very difficult, the world of tomorrow and the problems of tomorrow will be very different from the world of today and the problems of today.

That technology can be very powerful in people's lives is demonstrated by the ways in which it has changed people's lives. It has made it possible for 15 percent of the population to provide all our material goods and services. This power of technology can be exercised only by changes in our world—in our environment, if you will. With such change, our work, our concerns and our behavior have changed. The power of technology is not a power manifested in our machines only; it is a power manifested in our lives, and in our concept of our world and ourselves.

Yet, when we compare the power of technology with the power of other forces, we find it weak indeed. The history of the earth before people existed exhibits changes in geology, climate and species that make any general changes wrought by humanity insignificant. The changes that we have worked seem so large to us because our technology has changed profoundly those things that we deem important.

WHAT IS THE NATURAL ENVIRONMENT?

The Book of Genesis recounts the creation of the heavens, the earth, the sea and the dry land; of plants, fishes, birds and beasts; and of man all in a week of creation. God gave man dominion over the fish of the sea, and over the fowl of the air, and over every living thing that moveth upon the earth. And of the earth, God told man to subdue it. We need not argue whether the Bible is the word of God or whether it proceeds from the human heart. For many years, Western cultures have accepted nature as it is described in Genesis, a nature of which we are a part and are yet somehow above, a nature which we must subdue in deriving support. Our natural environment includes the stars and the planets, and air and the sea, the land and the plants and animals that dwell in the sea and on land. It is very hard to argue that humanity and its works are not a part of nature.

We flatter ourselves that we have greater and more far-reaching powers than other animals. No other animal has placed things on the surface of the moon or Mars, or has caused satellites to orbit the earth. No other animal has built works so complex as ours, and few other forms of life have spread over so many regions of the globe. We have even worked the extinction of species. The smallpox virus is all but extinct, and this has been a deliberate effort at extinction. The passenger pigeon is gone; that was inadvertent. Other species are endangered. But the number of species that we have extinguished is miniscule compared with those that have perished without our intervention. Where are the many species of dinosaurs, and what destroyed them? It was certainly not humanity.

We are not the only force, or the only life, that causes changes in the environment. But we are the only creature with a conception of change, and with a fear and distrust of change. We continually hearken back to the golden age, the Arcadian myth, the good old times. In the very process of changing our environment, we become distrustful and wish, somehow, that things were still as they were before. Yet it is the nature of humanity, which is a part of nature, to change its environment. Perhaps there is a happiness that does not involve such change—the happiness of our first parents in the Garden of Eden before their curiosity was aroused—the happiness alleged of South Sea islands before contact with the West. In "The Water Babies," Charles Kingsley describes people who lie under the flapdoodle trees, waiting for the fruit to fall into their mouths, and for tigers to eat them.

Most of the environment untouched by humankind is hostile. It is successively cold, hot and damp. It is infested by insects and other annoyances. It will support a very sparse population by hunting and gathering. The life of the hunter can be fun, but game can be scarce or exhausted locally. Commonly, the lives of the hunters and the gatherers involve seasonal journeys, and hardships against which they have no protection.

The environments in which civilized people live can be called natural only if we regard ourselves and our works as a part of nature. Once on a flight over Iowa I took a picture in which the most conspicuous features were the roads, a mile apart east and west and north and south, that bounded the sections. The sections were subdivided into rectuangular fields, and no stream cut diagonally across any. On each quarter section there were a farm house and buildings, or the sites of them, for when the land was first divided, a farm was a quarter section. Around the houses, a few trees grew, planted by the farmers, perhaps on Arbor Day.

The environment that surrounds me today has been drastically altered. Once it was what I, coming from the lush fields of Iowa, would have called desert, though native Californians would have called it chaparral country. Today trees and plants from all parts of the world grow around me, because water has been brought from rivers hundreds of miles away. The houses are fronted by green lawns in imitation of those of the East and Midwest, which in turn, I suppose, derived from the grazed meadows of England. Los Angeles County is a museum of rare nature drawn from all parts of the globe. But is this natural? Would it be natural if we turned the water off? It wouldn't be pleasing to us; we would describe it as a waste, a wreck. To us, the evidence of our intervention would still be apparent. I doubt, however, if the raccoons and coyotes who frequent our Pasadena garden have thoughts on the subject, one way or the other.

We have a vacation place in northwest Massachusetts, in the old township of Buckland. There we fight an unremitting battle to keep the woods from swallowing the house and view. Our meadow is mown once a year; otherwise it would become woods. Down the slope between us and the Mohawk Trail and Deerfield River we spray to keep the trees and bushes from growing. The hillside has been taken over by several varieties of fern, with a scattering of mountain laurel and a few swamp pinks. To us this has a beauty different from the woods, and but for us it would not be the way it is, nor would the meadow.

Still, the woods and the things that grow therein—mushrooms, trillium, indian pipes, and all the things I cannot name—are a delight. We walk through the woods along abandoned roads, between the stone walls that once bounded fields. Nature takes over quickly in Massachusetts. Today the small farmers who once supported themselves from the land could not grow enough to pay taxes. The small dairy farmers are gone; they could not afford to meet today's sanitary regulations. Their farms have returned to nature. The endless stone walls testify to our struggle against adverse forces. Here that struggle with value is almost over, as it is not in the more hospitable fields of Iowa or in the man-made oasis of Los Angeles County.

We have considerable power to modify land by cultivation and irrigation. We have not been able to modify substantially the climate or weather, but we have been able to shelter ourselves from the elements and to light and heat our habitations; today we can even cool them. We can bridge rivers and build roads across treacherous soil. We can travel on these comfortably in heat and cold, and (usually) keep them open in blizzards. I do not think that we have conquered the seas or the air, but we travel them despite their furies.

When we drive across the country on the federal highway system we see that our determined hold on our enviroment spans a huge continent. Towns are recognizably similar from sea to sea. The lives that people live are, despite great diversity, recognizably similar. The technology that has enabled us to live comfortably in the face of the adversity of our environment is similar, coast to coast. But when we pass long miles of untouched grandeur, or of untouched nothing—at least, nothing to us—we realize how little we hold. From the air this is even more apparent. Highways wind through mountains or go straight across barren wastes. A few miles from the highways there is nothing of man's. Even in the declared megalopolitan Northeast Corridor between Boston and Washington there are hundreds of miles of uninhabited pine barrens.

Our reshaping of the land on which humanity lives is extensive in that we live in almost all parts of all continents, but much land remains untouched. We can ruin the environment for ourselves in trying to cope with it, but the effects have been surprisingly local and often transitory. The Greek Islands, or some of them, were once wooded; goats and repeated rapine have rendered them bare and inhospitable. Some say that the classical Mayan civilization failed because their primitive slash-and-burn agriculture failed. Whether or not this is so, the jungle has hidden the Mayan temples. The land below the cliff dwelling of Keet Seel was farmed when that dwelling was inhabited. The fields are now gullied and washed away, perhaps because of that very farming. But Keet Seel and the other cliff dwellings housed few people and are far between.

Sometimes humanity's adverse effect on the environment is more widespread. The Aswan High Dam has changed conditions in the Nile delta. Lake Erie and some American river systems have been seriously polluted. Use and reuse of Colorado River water has raised the salt content where that river enters Mexico. Both hunting and overgrazing have adversely (for people and animals) affected large areas in Africa. Yet it is fair to say that large as humanity's effect on the environment has seemed to us, in a broader context it has been chiefly local and transitory. It is certainly so compared with those changes in the environment that have characterized geological history.

But changes that we can and do work in our environment are essential to our lives. We can live in any numbers and in any comfort only in an environment that we have substantially modified through building, cultivation, and, often, irrigation. Whether or not this modified environment is natural or not must depend on whether or not we regard ourselves as a part of nature. Who worries about this question? We do, of course.

Whether or not we are concerned about the world *natural* in connection with our environment, we are concerned about whether or not that environment is congenial. Sometimes we wish to go to places relatively untouched by humankind. Mostly, we want to live in comfortable and convenient surroundings. Here almost all people express very real concerns. Some of these concerns are about features of the environment that affect health or welfare very directly. Some of the concerns are about preference—preference for the sea, or for skiing, or golf, or crowds and public entertainment, or comparative isolation, or for handsome surroundings and an absence of billboards and garish signs.

Among features of our environment that can affect our health and welfare very directly are danger from intense smog; danger of earthquakes; danger of flooding, especially in low-lying land protected by levees; danger of landslides; danger of fire, especially near some mountain areas; danger of tidal waves; danger from volcanic eruptions; danger of loss of water or fuel, such as natural gas; danger from auto traffic, especially to children; danger of violence from other people; and lack of reasonably priced housing.

Among matters of preference, one of the strongest contrasts in preference is city versus small-town or country living. Other matters of preference are clean air versus excessive soot and dirt, and handsome surroundings versus billboards, junky stores and run-down houses. Access (which means good roads and not-too-great distances) to sea, lakes, mountains, skiing, fishing and other sports is very important to some.

Today, many profess a deep love of nature. Love of nature can mean many things. Hunting and gardens have played a part in the good life in many ages. Forests and parks are important in hunting because huntable game live there. Poachers and development are the enemies of game, as are the hunters, who want the game preserved for them. Gardens have often been as formal and highly developed as palaces.

In Western culture, the love of nature in a primitive state is said to have begun with Rousseau. Certainly, Western romantic landscape painting follows him. In China and Japan, landscape painting was associated with a love of nature that preceded Rousseau by many centuries. In Japan, for over a millenium, nature—and the seasons and the changes accompanying them—have been a subject of poetry, and the observation of nature has been an important part of esthetic experience. This has led to the preservation and embellishment of natural sites. The scenery around Nikko is beautiful, but so are the temples and shrines. As the Japanese consider seals and calligraphy an embellishment of pictures, so they consider temples an embellishment of landscapes.

The Japanese love of nature has led to some of the most artful gardens in the world. Falls, lakes, mountains and woods are reproduced in miniature, as parts of palace grounds or temple complexes. Is a Japanese garden, because it expresses a love of nature, a natural environment? Only if one sees oneself as a part of nature. The survival of a Japanese garden depends on people's care, on wrapping the trees to protect them, on spreading mats over the moss to shield it from sun in summer or from cold in winter, on continually plucking out weeds, on ceaseless replanting, pruning and improving. Yet the Japanese garden does express a close observation of and real love for nature.

Whatever our attitude toward nature may be, it is clear that an environment unaffected by humans and the nature of humans cannot support many people, and even they would not be very comfortable. If people are to live in any comfort and to have the leisure for reflection and invention, they must modify a part of their environment as best they can. It is desirable that such modifications produce an environment that is healthful for people and for what else of nature they value. This need not include smallpox, malaria and mosquitoes. The environment should suit our taste, but the same taste is by no means common to all people. It seems desirable that some areas be preserved with little modification, both for those who like nature uninfluenced by people, as a sort of museum, and as a hedge against the future. However, preserving nature as it would be if uninfluenced by people is not easy. Thousands of acres of government land near Hanford, Washington, have been substantially modified simply by protection from and extinguishing of fires. The brush has thrived at the expense of the grasses.

Unless we consider humanity as a part of nature, the natural environment is something of an illusion. We must, and do, affect our environment. And yet our effect is far smaller than that of other forces.

WHAT CAN WE DO AND WHAT SHOULD WE DO?

What we can do depends on the power of technology and on our enterprise and malleability. What we feel we should do must depend on what we can do, but it depends also on our attitude toward humanity and surrounding environment.

What do we mean when we say that we can do a thing? We may mean that it has been done before and that the technology, materials, energy and skills to do it again are still available. Thus, a house, a dam, a new model of automobile can be ordered up, so to speak. We may, however, mean that the individual technologies needed have advanced far enough so that we believe there will be no insuperable obstacle in pushing them farther to accomplish some new thing. This was the case with President Kennedy's program to send a man to the moon and return him safely before the end of the decade. Nothing—not propulsion, guidance, life support, or re-entry—had been done on the scale or with the reliability required in order to accomplish the mission. But, to those most familiar with the technologies needed, it seemed that a straightforward effort could push the technologies far enough to accomplish the goal. This we were able to do, while the Russians failed.

Thus, when we say that we can do a thing, we mean either that we know we can, or that we believe that we can push technology far enough to accomplish the task. This second sort of ability to do a thing calls for more money and more time than the first. But, having in hand known technologies gives us some confidence that money and effort can push them farther.

Sometimes we *feel* that by gathering new knowledge and devising new technologies we will ultimately be able to do a thing. When this is the state of our knowledge, we cannot set a timetable, and high ability of the people who undertake the task is far more important than the total amount of money spent. Indeed, in this sort of endeavor it is not clear whether spending more money will speed progress toward the goal or slow it. I have used building a new house, or dam, or a new model of automobile as examples of things we *really* know we can do, granted the money. I have used the Apollo program as an example of something that we had good reason to believe we could do, granted a lot of money, because all the technologies needed had succeeded in a smaller and less demanding way. Deriving useful amounts of power economically by fusion is an example of something that informed people feel can be done by gathering new knowledge and devising new technologies. Money and effort cannot deliver fusion on a timetable. The central part of the technology needed has not yet succeeded on *any* scale. All we can do is to support the very best people in a degree that seems reasonable to them. In our present state of ignorance, spending a great deal more money or working on ancillary problems when we don't know what form fusion will take if it does succeed would be inexcusable folly.

In the field of energy, of which fusion may one day be a part, we *know* we can build safe, economical fission power plants. This has been done. We have every reason to believe that we can build safe, economical breeder reactors. In fact, breeders have been operated. We can only hope that fusion by *some means* may *some day* provide safe, economical power. But that is not something we can assert. We will know only when much more progress has been made. We don't know when that will be.

Because large amounts of money have sometimes produced startling results, some people have been misled into believing that money will buy anything. Indeed, ours has become the age of Mammon and Mammon worship. Money bought the atom bomb because the fundamental scientific knowledge and the beginnings of the required technology proved to be available. Making the atom bomb was, however, a chancy business, and we were lucky that there were no unforeseen and irremediable obstacles. Apollo was a better bet because the fundamental technologies had been demonstrated. When work on fusion was first started, some believed that a large enough effort would push things through. They were wrong.

In seeking fusion power, all sorts of problems turned up. Mammon worship was proved wrong; no amount of money would buy fusion in a hurry. Indeed, the big machines that people constructed in ignorance retarded progress—until people were brave enough to abandon them and seek knowledge patiently. Nonetheless, Mammon worshipers refuse to learn. They believe that enough money really will buy *anything*. Human weakness being what it is, Mammon worshipers can always find someone to spend money. Sometimes those who spend the money are deceived and corrupted by it and become Mammon worshipers themselves. Sometimes they try to do something they regard as good with a part of the money. Sometimes they merely enjoy spending the money.

Distinguishing among the things that it is clear we can do, the things that it seems likely that we can do, and the things that we have some reason to believe that we can do some day is not easy. Experts can be wrong. People who are not experts may be right, because chance may favor them. But nothing but luck favors the ignorant. Yet, knowing what we can do must be an important part of any consideration of engineering and the natural environment. It must take precedence over considerations of what we should do. If it does not, we may be tempted to undertake to do things that we cannot do, or to place great reliance on things we may (or may not) be able to do at some unknown time in the future. If we do not understand our real abilities, we will mislead ourselves and other people.

But consideration of what we should do, among the things that we can do, must be an essential part of any decent program or proposed program. Indeed, a long discussion of what we can do would be empty and misleading without some consideration of what we should do. Unhappily, *should* means very different things to different people because values differ fundamentally. Some regard all seemingly avoidable deaths as equally bad and wasteful. Others believe that some avoidable deaths, such as those resulting from political or legal action, are of great importance, and that others, such as those resulting from drunk drivers or inherent in the use of oil and coal as fuels, are of far less importance. Some believe that individuals should have a very wide choice of action, as long as this does not result in risk to others. Others believe that if a person can be protected, one should be protected, regardless of the constraint one may feel or the inability to gauge and take risks that may result. Some feel that the good life is knowable, and that all should lead it. Others believe that, while we may be able to judge some lives as bad, good lives can be as different as good books, and as hard to judge. Thus, while I feel that *should* as well as *can* must be a part of any discussion of technology and the environment, I cannot arrive at any clear *should*.

Neither can we very much alter the terrain we inhabit. We cannot exalt valleys or make mountains and hills low, except on a miniscule scale. Making the rough places plane is confined largely to highways and fields. In farming, we must cope with slopes by terracing, contour plowing, or perhaps better, by no-tillage farming. We can to some degree protect against floods and provide irrigation with dams, but these sometimes fail with disastrous results. Levees are even more prone to failure. To endeavor to make an uninhabitable or dangerous region habitable or safe, by means other than irrigation, may be asking for trouble. People who live behind levees or in other regions known to be subject to floods incur a very real risk. So do those who live in earthquake-prone regions. But at least buildings can be designed to withstand most earthquakes. Our compassion makes it incumbent upon us to try to relieve the sufferings of victims of natural disasters. If, however, the disasters recur, we must realize that we are paying out of general funds for the consequences of choices made by particular individuals.

The natural environment has features that we cannot alter for the better on a large scale. But we can move to other places. It is both common and natural for individuals to seek safer or more agreeable environments. Anyone who has pushed a spade into Iowa soil may well wonder why people ever tried to farm in Massachusetts. There are social reasons why people and businesses move from the Northeast to the South and Southwest, but there are reasons of climate and comfort also, and individual reasons of less expensive construction and less cost and expenditure of energy in heating. Wherever people exist, they should use their science and technology wisely in making life in the environment healthier, more productive and more agreeable. Sometimes, however, it is easier and wiser simply to move.

But in no environment can people live what we regard as a civilized life without housing, heating and sometimes cooling, transportation, and communication. All of these take materials and energy. Today we feel a good deal of concern about possible shortages of materials and energy, and we have recently seen the disastrous consequences of a shortage of natural gas. It seems that a shortage of materials would be more likely than a shortage of energy. After all, trees grow naturally and we can burn them. The sun shines down, the winds blow. It is, however, a shortage of energy that we suffer from. As various materials have become scarcer and more costly, we have found substitutes, often with superior qualities. Synthetic fibres are in many ways better than natural fibres. For many purposes, plastics are better than wood or metal. There are even plastic automobile bodies and composites stronger than steel. Glasses and ceramics have proved to be marvelously versatile substances. Indeed, it seems likely that transparent fibres will ultimately replace copper wires and tubes in communication. Some metals, such as aluminum and magnesium, are distributed very widely. Granted enough energy, we are scarcely likely ever to exhaust the supply.

It is energy that we are short of. And our rapid depletion of the world's oil reserves raises a specter of a very real materials shortage. For, through the petrochemical industry, oil is a source of all sorts of valuable products, including plastics and synthetic fibres. Because oil is such an exhaustible and seemingly irreplaceable resource (except perhaps, for the substitution of coal), some feel that it is far too valuable to burn. But, burn it we do. Although our reserves of coal are very large, we may well ask, Is not coal also too valuable to burn? Should we not reserve it largely for the material needs of generations to come, or for the production of synthetic hydrocarbons that can provide portable energy where we must have it?

The need for energy raises very real materials problems we should take into account. The production of energy raises other problems as well—of economy, of safety, of environmental damage and of storage and distribution. Oil is easily stored and easily distributed, by pipe, truck, rail or ship. Gas is less easily stored in quantity, but distribution by pipeline is so easy that production can be linked to use. Coal is less easily distributed than oil or gas, but it can be stored.

Hydroelectric energy can be distributed only as electricity, but it can be stored. Indeed, in pumped hydroelectric, water is actually pumped to a higher level so as to store energy for future use. Alas, there aren't many suitable locations in the United States. Nuclear energy is easily and copiously stored in the fuel elements of reactors. Like hydroelectric energy, nuclear energy must (for civilian purposes) be distributed as electricity. Except for pumped hydroelectric, large-scale storage of energy is very costly and requires large amounts of materials. Flywheels and superconducting electromagnets have been suggested, but improved storage batteries seem the nearest solution. We don't have them. We should work toward such batteries in a reasonable way.

The production, storage and distribution of hydrogen through pipes has been suggested as an alternative to the production, storage and distribution of electricity. Hydrogen is very light, and it is not easy to store large amounts of it. Hydrogen is an extremely dangerous gas. Unlike most other flammable gases, very small amounts of hydrogen mixed with air form an explosive mixture. Perhaps some day we will have a hydrogen economy. But at the moment a good many people would say that electricity will remain the common medium for energy exchange and that better means for storing electric energy will be developed. Ultimated we *may* have effective electric vehicles fueled from the electric system. Or vehicles may run on products derived from coal or vegetation.

More than anything else, the problems of energy production may have something in common in both developing and developed economies. Large-scale power production is more efficient of energy and materials than small-scale production. Electricity is a very convenient common medium of exchange of energy. Loads shared among many users are steadier than the energy demands of individual users, and this also makes for efficiency. Small power tools are a boon in any economy, and electric power tools are cheap, durable and effective. Electricity fits in well with decentralization, because expensive primary power plants need not be located everywhere. Thus, large-scale production of electricity may be a good feature for all nations and all social organizations. Or it may not.

Perhaps technology will provide cheap solar or wind power sources—cheap in the initial cost per kilowatt—which can be used for many purposes without storage. Perhaps technology will provide cheap means for storing energy—cheap in terms of initial cost. So far technology has provided neither. Or perhaps technology will provide small, cheap *and* efficient power sources that burn or use fossil fuels. Technology has not done so. Perhaps technology will. Until we have new or better technologies, it appears that solar energy will be best used for heating water, or for heating or cooling homes, and that it will be less wasteful to burn fossil fuels in large rather than in small power-generating stations.

In providing the power that will be needed in the near future in high-technology countries, and in some others as well, the alternatives (other than hydroelectric power) are coal and nuclear energy. We have had a good deal of experience with both. Of the two, the actual, demonstrable death rate per kilowatt hour, including mining, transportation and production, is clearly higher for coal. So is the disturbance to the environment, both in mining, transportation and operation. The waste-disposal problem in coal plants is formidable. In trying to cope with it, the Japanese find themselves saddled with large and uneconomic stocks of gympsum and ammonium sulfate.

There may be long-range reasons for preferring coal to nuclear energy. If we adopt coal, we should honestly face the cumulative loss of life, the environmental damage and the cutting into large but limited stocks of a very valuable material. People do make sacrifices, of life and of well-being, in a good cause. But if people are to make sacrifices, they should understand the goal of the sacrifice.

While materials and energy can be exhaustible resources, communication appears to be inexhaustible in amount and variety. In developing countries, communication is an essential means both for holding a society together and for changing it. The needs for communication can be met by rather simple means. Radio broadcast and transistor radios are cheap and very effective. Communication satellites have linked cities in all parts of the world to one another at a moderate cost. A few telephone lines or microwave or satellite circuits between principal points can provide essential two-way communication in a developing society. The society does not need nor can it afford a telephone in every house.

In a highly developed technological economy, communication appears to offer an alternative to much business travel, as well as a means for linking geographically distributed parts of large enterprises, private or public. In *The Telecommunications-Transportation Tradeoff*, Jack M. Nilles and his colleagues conclude that in a selected service industry, relocation from one to eighteen centers in Los Angeles County could reduce that one-way commuting distance from 10.7 miles to 3.9 miles. They conclude that the change would be cost-effective for the company. Hiring would be easier; it would no longer be necessary to pay premium salaries and to give fringe benefits to get employees to work in the downtown area, and the termination rate would be lower.

The automobile and adequate roads and freeways have had a wonderfully liberating effect. People have gained great freedom to seek economical and pleasant housing. They have gained freedom to go to the beach, to the mountains, or where you will. What seems unreasonable is that people should have to commute long distances to crowded areas where businesses have chosen to remain. Such commuting is wasteful of energy, and it is not enjoyable. But if work is decentralized in order to reduce the energy demands and discomfort of commuting, what will the future of the city be in a society of automobiles, roads and communication? Are cities to remain dangerous traps for poor people who cannot find rewarding jobs and yet cannot, or will not, or are induced not, to leave? Whatever the problems of the city may be, it is disheartening and it appears to defy solution. Either people know no remedy, or there is no remedy that anyone can apply or is willing to apply.

This seemingly intractable problem of the city exists in developing as well as in high-technology societies. In each we see jobless poor trapped in cities. In the high-technology societies, automobiles, good roads and an increased use of communication appear to allow a dispersal of work as well as of residence, with less unnecessary travel, less pollution and less energy consumption. In the developing societies, the problem is to make life on the land productive and more agreeable than a jobless existence in a huge city. An economical, small source of energy would help. One would hope that communication could be made to help rather than to hinder. The challenge is great, but the solution is not clear.

In contrasting the needs of a developing society with those of a high-technology society, it has been rightly pointed out that the developing society cannot afford a high capital investment per job. Except for the introduction of industries by outside companies, this points to simple mechanization and a modest use of scarce materials, including oil and fertilizers. I have pointed out earlier that if a country could so organize itself that 45 percent of its population was employed in the production of food and manufactured goods, in mining, in building and in supplying energy and communication, that country could have as much as we have even if the productivity was only a third as great per person. That country could have half as much physical goods and services as we have even if its labor was only a sixth as productive as ours.

Getting so large a fraction of the population to produce food and physical goods and services is probably impractical. It would mean that the young and old would have to work. Perhaps they would like to. It would mean that idle poor could not be allowed to accumulate in cities. It would mean a bureaucracy and an army of modest size. It would mean that school teachers, doctors and nurses and lawyers would constitute a small fraction of the population.

SOME WORDS IN CONCLUSION

The power of our technology is great in human terms but small in terms of our total environment. Apollo, the pyramids and other monuments are enduring reminders of that power. To my mind, the most striking measure of the power of our technology is the fact that about 15 percent of the U.S. population provides food, goods and material services for the nation, and that this percentage has been falling steadily. Yet volcanoes, earthquakes, changes in climate and geological epochs show us how small our power is.

In the minds of many people, humanity is a part of nature, though a rather special part. What we do cannot be unnatural; it can only be unpleasant. To whom? To ourselves. The power of technology can be realized through drastic changes in the way we live and work. Whatever the natural environment may be, the unaltered earth will not support many people very well. A look at Iowa or Southern California shows what we can do to a small part of a country's surface, and the look is not unpleasant. But for every acre we have changed, many acres of our land remain untouched.

Most of the forces and aspects of nature we cannot change; we can only protect ourselves against them. If we are realistic, we will try to do what we can do, not what we cannot do. If we are wise, we will do what will make us well and productive and, we hope, happy or at least cheerful. If we are to be realistic, if we are to have a chance to be wise, we must, as nearly as possible, see things as they are. We must neither overestimate nor underestimate our powers. We must take due account of the present, the near future and the far future. And we must take into account the needs and desires of people other than ourselves.

REFERENCES

A good deal of what I have written comes from the life I have led. I am not an expert figure-looker-upper. I have relied on a few sources for numbers and fewer for ideas. I have found helpful: *The Encyclopedia Britannica; The World Book, 1977; Statistical Abstracts;* James O'Toole (University of Southern California Center for Future Research), *Energy and Social Change* (Cambridge: MIT Press, 1976); Jack M. Nilles, F. Roy Carlson, Jr., Paul Gray, and Gerhard J. Hanneman, *The Telecommunications-Transportation Tradeoff* (New York: Wiley, 1976); Readings from the Scientific American, *Scientific Technology and Social Change* (San Francisco: W.H. Freeman and Company, 1974).

Chapter Two

Discussion of "Engineering and the Natural Environment," by J.R. Pierce

Harvey J. McMains

It is indeed a pleasure to have been asked to comment on Dr. Pierce's paper. It gives us much to think about and it is worth several readings. First, he reminds us that any concern with engineering and the natural environment stems from humanity's basic nature and from the power of our evolved technology. Dr. Pierce then states a most important fact: there exists a powerful technology, and because it exists we can, to some degree, influence our environment. This fact makes it possible for us to think and plan for all humanity's future. Next, Dr. Pierce divides his paper into three general subject areas: (1) The actual power of technology and the measure of that power; (2) what the natural environment is; and (3) what can we do and what should we do?

The measure of the power of technology that Pierce picks is the percentage of the population that provides us with all physical goods and services, including communications, electricity, gas, and water. He states that the percent of population is approximately 15 percent today, and that it was 21 percent in 1950. Whether this is the best measure is hardly worth debating. The important thing is that this has been a national focus for technological thought and innovation. Will it continue? Should it continue? Before we answer these questions, we need to study and research this trend in terms of its human consequences. Dr. Howard R. Bowen, in his introduction to the report of the National Commission on Technology, Automation, and Economic Progress, 1964, said, "Technology is not a vessel into which people are to be poured and to which they must be molded. It is something to be adapted to the needs of man and to the furtherance of human ends, including the enrichment of personality and environment." It does not seem quite right to me that our technology should be slowly eroding humanity's right to be a part of the production process for the physical goods and services it needs without our knowing that that is the way humanity wants it. It may not be important, but what if it is and we never bother to learn this until it is too late? We should keep in mind what Dr. Pierce reminds us: "Our technology changes profoundly those things that we deem important."

What is the natural environment? It is just about everything that exists on earth, including humans and what they do or do not do. People are, as Pierce points out, a part of the natural environment. Further, humans are creatures with a conception of change and the ability to plan for change even though they distrust and fear it. Without this ability, the world would be a rather dismal place considering the number of humans on the earth at this time, not to mention the number that will inhabit the earth a hundred years from now. Whatever is now on earth that will change, will happen either as a consequence of the power of nature or by humanity. It is worth noting that people are capable of recording facts and making analyses. They can determine what has happened and is happening and, with less certainty, what may happen. For example, how much of which materials are being used for the manufacture of certain products and services and how long will they last? They also think of alternative ways of doing things, including material substitution—people can determine who is doing what, and to some degree how well. They are able to dream beyond their capabilities or expectations and have a pretty good record of causing these dreams to come true.

A word of caution—as technology has continued to improve, it has become more complex. This has made it harder to determine what can be done and who should do it—if for no other reason than there is simply much more of it. Pierce suggests that the best we can do is pick good people and give them the resources they think they can use and hope they can do what they think may be possible. But somehow we must do better than this. We need to determine our priorities and which of these priorities offer the most, considering the risk of success. National planning and goal-setting in the past has not been done well, but maybe that is because we don't believe it is possible—and thus haven't ever given it a chance. People who could, may not be interested, because it does not advance their cause in science. The challenge is to make planning a point of focus for the capability for the best minds. Dr. Pierce asks the question, "What can we do and what should we do?" While it is true that we can really only do what we can do—what *are* the things we *can* do? Which are the important ones and what are they worth in these uncertain times?

Energy is probably the number one current problem for a country as industrialized as the United States. We presently use oil and gas as our principal source of energy and it is in short supply, but there are other sources of energy. Of those currently most promising, which are the best bets with existing technology, and how should we develop them? What should be the government role? What should be industry's role? And perhaps more importantly, what should be the role of the individual citizen? The private citizen needs to be informed with the facts as they exist. This is not a task to be taken lightly.

Planning has been left out of Dr. Pierce's paper, and yet it seems to me it is an important part of engineering and the natural environment. Planning and its implementation must be as creative as any applied technology—past or present. What is needed is to determine where we are, where we want to go, and establish the goals and objectives for our existing enterprise system to take us where we want to go. This sounds, of course, like a platitude, but determining the issues and setting about to solve them is what has been done so well by our enterprise system. Creative ingenuity is what has made our marketplace so effective. At the present time, too much of our talent is consumed by technology for technology's sake or in finding out what has been done wrong or what is being done wrong. We need to marshal a fair share of the superior talent to carry out the planning mission. We need the best talent available for determining, for example, what alternative sources of energy offer the best potential for development, what they will cost, and when and how they can be phased into our way of life. Effective planning should be a major goal of engineering and technology.

Technology has on balance surely been a great blessing to all of humanity, despite the fact that some of its benefits have been offset by costs. I would not propose slowing it down by diverting some of its talents to planning if I didn't think this would result in directing it more nearly to human concern and need and in the final analysis give us more of what is needed. We can no longer afford to squander our technical resources without good guidance. The questions engineering and technology should focus on in this critical period of natural resource evaluation and reevaluation is *what, when, who,* and *how.* Planning should guide the focus for effort, and not the means. The future need not be one of limits, but can be one of wise alternatives with an even higher quality of life.

Chapter Three

Discussion of "Engineering and the Natural Environment," by J.R. Pierce

Benjamin C. Dysart III

Eugene Odum (12) pointed out recently that "ecology" and"economics" come from the same Greek root, ecology translating as "the study of the house" and economics as "the management of the house." I believe that all of you share with me a strong desire to see our nation's, and our region's, substantial natural resources and environmental amenities handled in a manner that is both "manageable and managed" (6). I believe that is the task before us as natural resources engineers.

I am pleased to be able to discuss John Pierce's paper. It was refreshing, expansive, and stimulating, attributes all too frequently absent from typical "engineering" discourses. But refreshing and imaginative thinking alone will not suffice, I suppose, if we are to be responsive to the charter established for this symposium. Considering the challenges to society, and to our engineering profession in particular, we have little need to dwell on the more pedestrian aspects of technology, and less for bromides.

I find little in Pierce's paper with which to take strong exception. I will, however, from my very different background and vantage point, provide some alternative views and perspectives on some of his key assumptions, contentions, and conclusions.

Pierce begins by establishing some basic points of departure:

a. *Humanity* exists.
b. *Humanity* has a powerful technology.
c. *Humanity* can influence *its environment.*
d. *Humanity*'s concerns about *itself* and *its world* center on what it has done and what it may do.

27

To me, there seems to be a preoccupation with humanity, our environment, our world, and so on, before establishing, or speculating upon, what might be the appropriate or proper role for humanity. Then, Pierce might have even gone on to consider, at the outset, the responsibilities of engineering and engineers vis-à-vis all else but humanity.

Pierce elected to address three broad topics or questions:

a. What is the actual power of our technology, and can it be measured?
b. Just what is "the natural environment" anyway?
c. What can we do with our technology, and what should we do with it?

My discussion and comments will be organized under these same three major headings for convenience. My discussion will vary from the equivalent of footnotes to Pierce's paper to alternate or added arguments and conclusions.

THE POWER OF TECHNOLOGY

Pierce answered his questions about the power of technology. I wish to make some added points.

The Man-to-the-Moon Syndrome

When the matter of technology arises, our effort to land men on the moon and safely return them to earth usually follows closely. Pierce put this undertaking into perspective very well. Though a "triumph of high technology," Pierce feels that Apollo had "little significance for everyday human activities." There were the obvious beneficial spinoffs from the effort; but there was, at least in my mind, a substantial negative spinoff as well so far as natural resources management is concerned.

Since the touchdown of our first manned craft on the moon, many have felt that technology could therefore triumph over any and all mere earthbound problems. Many of the same firms that helped put men on the moon switched, or tried to switch, to environmental and natural resources work as America's space trip slowed down rapidly.

Too many, including not only the technology people but many in the general public, felt that the awesome technology that put men on the moon, and brought us "Tang," could surely clean up our rivers, unsnarl our transportation mess, improve health care, and so on. But regular people and their natural resources are, some learned, not totally amenable to control and optimization like a stainless steel, solid-state, computer-packed object commanded by a totally disciplined and highly conditioned crew of engineer/scientists, with a umbilical cord of sorts to ground control in Houston.

Another spinoff from Apollo, as I see it, was the idea that, if the nation throws enough dollars and technology at problems, they can be overwhelmed. (Pierce also speaks to this point later in his paper.) That has been tried with environmental and energy problems with mixed success.

In natural resources engineering, we also do a lot of "people engineering"; and we have to maintain a healthy respect for the differences between people and "things natural," as Leopold (8) would say, on the one hand, and objects, things, and problems that are completely described by and obey the immutable laws of thermodynamics and the like, on the other hand. The former are at least as complex as the latter, and our efforts as engineers are preordained to failure should we forget this.

The Practical as Great Monuments

I concur that our engineering feats pursuing practical ends are truly astonishing and rival the monuments humans have raised, and are raising today. Pierce alludes to the importance and magnitude of irrigation works in ancient times, as well as today in his home state of California. Since my principal interests are water resources and energy, I am also well acquainted with the great inland navigation, irrigation, flood control, and hydroelectric projects across our nation that have done, and will continue to do, so much for the nation's economic vitality. The U.S. Army Corps of Engineers and the Interior Department's Bureau of Reclamation have designed and erected many of the type of practical and astonishing works that indeed rival other human monuments per se.

Providing Material Goods

Pierce maintains that the power of our technology can be measured by the fact that only 15 percent of our people "supply the physical needs of the entire population." He points out further that our technology is well adapted to providing "material goods and services." "Our technology is very powerful indeed," Pierce states "in terms of producing what people need, or at least what Americans want."

The emphasis of this measurement and quantification of the power of human technology is clearly on the physical, the material. I would have little quarrel with this (since I have spent some years out in industry helping keep the wheels turning, producing physical goods) were I satisfied that we engineers in, or someone else, were giving appropriate attention to aspects in addition to the physical, the material, simply giving Americans what they "want."

I agree completely that being able to give our citizens the material things they want is truly indicative of a powerful technology. But are we, as engineers and in concert with others, discharging or sufficiently aware of our responsibilities to help define what our people—society in general—need? What is in their best long-run interest, and in the best long-run interest of our nation and our international posture?

Mine is not just a concern that we include the spiritual and esoteric in addition to the material in our plans and works. The attitude that may or could cause practitioners of our powerful technology to focus on the physical and the material goods has indeed massive implications for our natural resources and their wise use.

There is a growing interest in attempting to quantify, in some meaningful manner, the quality of the environment and the quality of life, both for comparison purposes and to describe trends. An example is the annual EQ Index (for environmental quality) compiled for eight years now by the National Wildlife Federation (11). It deals with the entire United States and rates resources separately—for example, water, wildlife, and minerals.

Ann Crittenden (5) recently reported the development of a physical quality of life index (PQLI) for nations. It is based on three factors: literacy, life expectancy, and infant mortality. (By the way, the United States scored 96 out of 100.)

It is to be hoped that we engineers are concerned about the total quality of life for the public, in addition to the fact that a shrinking percentage, now only 15 percent, is producing all our physical needs. We must be aware of the implications of our technology for the other 85 percent. And, when all the dimensions of the quality of life are considered, are the 85 percent, and the 15 percent, really better off because of our technology? I hope so.

Tomorrow's Different Problems

Pierce pointed out that, like pollution problems of the animal-power era early in this century, emissions from gasoline-powered vehicles, too, would vanish in the near future, if for no other reason than simply because we are running out of oil. I agree, for the most part, with Pierce that we must use technology to cope with current problems and that "present problems are problems left over from the past." He goes on to say that tomorrow and its problems will be "very different from the world of today and the problems of today."

With respect to energy, Charles Hitch (7) seemed to support, at least in part, this notion of great change for the future. Hitch stated that "we can expect that all kinds of unpredictable dynamic developments will occur during the next 25 years, let alone the next 1000." His editorial concluded with this sentence: "Our single clear criterion for the future is flexibility."

I am somewhat concerned, not so much with what Pierce is saying, but with what he could be construed as saying. One would be ignoring one's responsibilities if one were to interpret Pierce's message as: (a) problems that seem critical at some time fade into obscurity before too many years; and (b) since tomorrow's world and problems—and therefore the challenges to natural resources engineers—will be very different from today's, we will just take care of them then because we cannot anticipate them.

I do not believe that is what was meant at all. I believe the message is for us to cope successfully with natural resources and environmental problems on a current basis, so they will not become a heritage of dross to future generations. Since some natural resources and pollutant problems that are coming to the fore today are many orders of magnitude more complex, and persistent, than "horse dung" (nuclear wastes and persistent carcinogenic agents, for instance), the increasingly greater challenge to us to do a good job and stay ahead of the power curve is obvious.

Not too many years ago Kenneth Boulding (2) proposed, then rejected, this scenario:

> . . . The problems of the future can be left to the future. . . . The needs of the then present will determine the solutions of the then present, and there is no use giving ourselves ulcers by worrying about problems that we really do not have to solve.

In rejecting this attitude, Boulding argued convincingly that "tomorrow is not only very close, but in many respects it is already here."

It should be clear that we, as natural resources engineers, must do a better job of anticipating and predicting the impacts of our technology, the direct and the subtle effects, and feed this back into our decisionmaking processes. The most obvious and widespread opportunity to do this is the process of preparing meaningful environmental impact statements (EIS). As EIS frequently says much about the industry or the agency that prepares it. As stated well by the President's Council on Environmental Quality (4):

> The EIS itself is intended to be, and often is, the tip of an iceberg, the visible evidence of an underlying planning and decisionmaking process that is usually unnoticed by the public.

CEQ promotes, as I do, the "up-side" of environmental impact analysis (4): "Properly conceived and written, the EIS is an extremely useful management tool."

Humanity's Relatively Weak Technology

No one could possibly contest Pierce's contention that, in contrast to the power of nature, "our technology is puny indeed." He cites technology's biggest force, the hydrogen bomb, and compares it with a great earthquake or massive volcanic eruption. Human technology (in this case, a thermonuclear bomb) would indeed seem to release much less energy, inflict less direct physical damage, kill fewer persons at the time, and soon. But what about the longer-term effects? Are we, in reality, likely to be faced with a bomb and an earthquake, one-on-one? I submit that there are products of technology that, if utilized to their full capabilities, would have more impact, probably a longer-lasting impact, and certainly more trauma, than the forces of nature cited.

And, of course, there is another aspect of the comparison between the hydrogen bomb and, say, an earthquake. We could control our technology, whereas nature's hazards are beyond our control. Actually, though, we can probably design for, or otherwise minimize our risk from or exposure to, some natural hazards more readily than technological hazards. We can build earthquake-resistant structures, avoid certain types of development in flood-plains, for instance. But Pierce's conclusion that, though our technology is "weak compared with other natural forces, . . . it is powerful in altering human life," is inescapable.

Changes Made by Technology:
Are They Significant?
Pierce contends that the changes on the face of the earth that occurred before the advent of human beings render changes made by humanity "insignificant" by comparison. I agree, and would hasten to say that, for example, if glaciers should ever come through this immediate area, both human improvements and abuses to the land would surely pale into relative insignificance. But we as natural resources engineers or whatnot are, I believe, as powerless to deal with continental drift as we are to do anything about the changes to the earth before the era of humans. Our only concern should be with the present and the future, dealing with that which is within our control, within our control as individual citizens, within our control as competent and responsible professionals, or within the collective control of humanity and its institutions.

Our planning horizon, even when it is long, is infinitesimal compared to geologic time. But I believe we can and do make changes to "truly alter the face of the earth." Though I am sure they will not last forever, the changes to the face of the earth in the strip-mined areas of Appalachia will go beyond our usual planning horizons. And the "changes wrought by humanity" around Copper Hill, Tennessee are, in my opinion, extensive and, it would seem, rather persistent.

It is Pierce's contention that major human-caused changes to the planet have not yet occurred (I will concede to everyone the right to determine his or her own criteria as to just what constitutes a "major" human-induced change), and "it might be very difficult to make it happen." Quoting further: "Still, we should keep the possibility in mind." Again, I believe I know what Pierce is saying, and generally agree. If, however, someone were to misinterpret his message as: (a) this old world has taken a lot of licks and has not changed much; (b) it might be really difficult to cause a major change; (c) it could just possibly happen though; but (d) as a caveat, just to be on the safe side, watch out.

I believe such an interpretation could promote, or continue, natural resources brinkmanship. Somehow, we engineers have the idea that the processes we deal with are reversible. At least we hope so. If the environmental or natural resources analogy to "fatigue cracks" start to develop, we back off the load. Maybe we then slap on the equivalent of some super epoxy and see if we can go up to an even higher stress, before a new cracking point is reached. As Pierce says, in a way, no one has tested a world, or a "major" part of it, to failure yet. I hope, as the myriad pressures—old and new—being placed on our natural resources build up, we can and will "keep the possibility in mind" that, though nature is obviously resilient or in some cases malleable, failure is possible.

Although, as natural resources engineers, we have mastered much, we must maintain a healthy respect for failure, for discontinuities, especially as we sail into uncharted waters and encounter strange winds. This is to be expected, though, as we approach more closely the edge.

As my final comment on the power of our technology, I call to your attention another perceptive quote from Pierce, that "our technology changes profoundly those things that we deem important." So, in addition to the desired or wanted direct beneficial effects, the indirect, and perhaps the unanticipated, adverse effects will eventually be internalized. As Eugene Odum (12) said recently, "It is the secondary impacts that will get you if you do not consider the whole."

Of course, our technology also "changes profoundly" many things not "deemed important" by many, perhaps most, people. These may be some of the many small "cogs" and "wheels" that Leopold (8) spoke of. They may be important, even essential, but are not recognized as such. Today the responsible and perceptive natural resources engineer is going to recognize the true value of more "things" and "cogs" than his less well-informed, or perhaps even obsolete, peer.

WHAT IS THE NATURAL ENVIRONMENT?

Pierce effectively raised the vital, and normally overlooked, question: Just what is the "natural environment"? I do not believe he answered the philosophical question to my satisfaction. Nor, I freely admit, can I. But I shall add my perspectives in discussing several of Pierce's points.

Western Man and Genesis

In approaching the question of just what the "natural environment" is, or to deal with man-nature relationships, in general, perhaps the notion of Western man that he was given license to subdue nature, and all her parts, is a good place to start.

In policymaking circles today, people want to know where you are coming from. Perhaps we, as natural resources engineers and influential American citizens, should ask the same question. Roderick Nash (10) quotes from a pioneer settler's guidebook of 1849: "I vanquished this wilderness and made the chaos pregnant with order and civilization, alone I did it." John Wesley Powell and Gifford Pinchot were two prime movers in the development of this nation's land and water resources policy in the late nineteenth and early twentieth centuries. W. J. McGee, according to Nash (10) "a disciple of Powell and colleague of Pinchot," expressed an important attitude that prevailed near the turn of the century. Quoting Nash (10):

> The "Conquest of Water," W. J. McGee grandly declared, was as crucial to human progress as the "Conquest over Fire, Knife, Spring, and Wheel" and, indeed, "the single step remaining to be taken before Man becomes master over Nature."

And today our powers are, as pointed out by Pierce, "greater and more far-reaching" than those of "other animals." He points out that "no other animal has placed things on the surface of the moon or Mars, or has caused satellites to orbit the earth. No other animal has built works so complex as ours. . . ."

The conclusion is, I suppose, that our "technology" is superior to that of all the other species. I agree, but would add this thought: we are the only species that, in addition to being "intelligent" enough to do it, really cares whether things are put on Mars or not, or whether satellites orbit the earth or not. Such endeavors are of benefit to us.

As to whether water resources development projects, for example, are proportionately more "complex" than a beaver community's extensive water management program, I cannot say for sure. The latter's "technology" would appear to be entirely adequate to achieve the community's diverse needs. This "technology" of the beavers may have evolved over the centuries to the point where we might do well to study it, and emulate their example of optimizing resource utilization, their giving due regard to all the important and relevant constraints as well as the objective function, and their maintaining system stability in harmony with other systems.

Humanity as a Part of Nature

Pierce seems to argue that humanity and its works must be considered as a part of nature, instead of apart or aloof from nature. If his reasoning for this is to lead us to take what now exists and try to do the best job of managing it from here on out, I will not argue with him. It is frequently counterproductive to argue whether some section of a river or tract of land is (or is not) in a "natural" condition, and therefore suitable (or unsuitable) for preservation or some use. Too many parts of "nature" defy our attempts to ascertain their degrees of "naturalness," but responsible management decisions must be made.

In some notable instances, changes wrought by people give some areas greatly enhanced utility as "natural" areas, or at least areas possessing greatly increased values to humanity and other species. For example, many contend that the pools created to facilitate commercial navigation in the upper Mississippi River basin have produced a substantial net increase so far as fish and wildlife habitat is concerned.

Instead of dwelling on "nature," and whether man and his works are or are not a part thereof, I believe it would be much more useful to think in holistic terms of the total ecosystem. There can surely be no debate as to whether a person is or is not a part of an ecosystem, be it local, regional, national, or global.

Local and Transitory Changes

Pierce's position is most clearly articulated on the nature of humanity's effect on the environment. This effect, according to Pierce, "had been chiefly local and transitory . . . certainly so compared with those changes in the environment that have characterized geological history." For what it may add to this discussion, I quote Carl Sagan (13) on this topic:

> Science and, particularly, technology have not been pursued with sufficient attention to their ultimate humane objectives. For example, it has gradually dawned on us that human activities can have an adverse effect not only on the local but also on the global environment.

Sagan's views are echoed by Boulding (2), who stated that "fouling of the nest which has been typical of man's activity in the past on a local scale now seems to be extending to the whole world society." Ian McHarg (9) argues that major and long-lasting change to the landscape has taken place as a result of our activity. For instance, of the in-duced fire of the aboriginal hunter, McHarg says:

> Of the prairies there is hardly any trace and little more of the great beasts that once dominated them.

As previously stated, I believe there is room to differ as to how "local and transitory" some of humanity's effects have been. I must point out, though, that changes in the environment over geologic time allow for orderly adaptation or evolution of humans and all other life forms. Changes that take place according to the dictates of human in-stitutions and enterprises, within our relatively short planning horizons compared to geologic time, may not allow for such evolution.

Pierce seems to point up a conflict in our view of change. First, "Most of the environment untouched by humankind is hostile" and, further, "it is the nature of humanity . . . to change its environment." But also, "In the very process of changing our environment, we become distrustful and wish, somehow, that things were still as they had been before"; and further, "we are the only creature . . . with a fear and distrust of change."

Pierce points out correctly that the human is not the only life form that effects change in the environment. Though other animals create some measure of change, and some even use tools, humans are the only ones that create new technologies. Other animals, other life, seem to desire principally to get along with their environment, that is, stay at equilibrium (dynamic as it may be in the short term) with other forces in the ecosystem. Humans seem to be the only ones that can, with the help of their technology, effect widespread environmental change, on themselves and all other species, in a planned way. They are the only ones that attempt to gain control of the ecosystem and modify the "natural" equilibria, attempt to drive the total ecosystem to a dif-ferent final state, attempt to proceed there at a different rate. What are considered exogenous inputs to other species are, it would seem, but more knobs for people ("a part of nature," man the compulsive changer, man who fears change) to turn.

The fact that the great number of species that became extinct over geologic time prior to humanity dwarf the number since would seem to have little significance for the natural resources engineer of today. The fact that, for all I know, 10,000 species or subspecies or variants of, say, salamanders have gone by the board since time began is not, to me, a sufficiently compelling argument for letting another one or two go by. They may be wrongly viewed by us, perchance, as merely "uneconomic parts," when in reality they are necessary parts of Aldo Leopold's "biotic clock" (8).

I would reiterate that our responsibility, as professionals and deci-sionmakers, is to do the best we can with what we have, giving both the present and the future their due, as contrasted with dwelling on changes over geologic time. I cannot differentiate between a "bug" that produces an intestinal disorder and one that could produce a new miracle drug to alleviate suffering worldwide. But I do hope someone who can, or might, is in the loop as species of plants and animals become threatened, then endangered, and finally extinct.

The same applies to valuable lands that are being "con-sumed"—productive agricultural lands and our prime wetlands, for in-stance. For some reason I am, at this point, reminded of the engineer-ing executive who told me, not too long ago, "If you've seen one swamp, you've seen 'em all." To some, I suppose, pearls and pea gravel and purple-hull peas look about the same. But it is most unfortunate, in fact it is sad and even dangerous sometimes, when such persons are managing society's and the nation's natural resources.

WHAT CAN WE DO AND WHAT SHOULD WE DO?

Having addressed the questions of: (a) the power of our technology; and (b) just what the natural environment is or is not, Pierce proceeds to look to the future, the action phase. He poses two questions in one: What can we do and what should we do? I find these questions to be at least as difficult as did Pierce, who said he could not arrive at any clear notion of what we "should" do. I can only underscore a few of the several good points he made.

Reality and Expectations
Pierce does us all a great service by emphasizing the importance of knowing just what we, as natural resources engineers or others, can do. As he says: "If we do not understand our real abilities, we will mislead ourselves and other people." Considering our tremendous challenges in the environmental, natural resources, and energy areas, society can ill afford public disillusionment and a loss of credibility in those perceptive professionals who offer hope.

As a nation we could not "whip inflation now" by everyone's wear-ing a "WIN" button, or declaring that there was in effect a "project in-dependence" for energy did not help get us through the bitter winter of 1977. There are no quick fixes. Any who would promise quick fixes or propose slogans in lieu of hard, realistic, and implementable solutions is merely exacerbating already critical situations—critical not only to our future quality of life but literally critical to our very national sur-vival.

Throwing Money at Problems

Pierce emphasizes most effectively the fallacy of, as he calls it, "Mammon worship": throwing large amounts of money at problems to buy quick, and hopefully even easy, solution to hard problems. Unfortunately, too frequently the problem is that some agency has to obligate so many hundred million dollars by a certain date or lose it, or not have next year's budget increase. As Pierce points out, someone can always be found to spend the money. Too frequently there is, or appears to be, more concern with getting money and getting it spent and the related bookkeeping and endless "housekeeping chores" than with the quality of the product.

Energy Impacts on the Future

Pierce has much to say about energy, as well he should. It is unlikely that any major natural resources decisions in the foreseeable future will be independent of energy considerations. Many, perhaps most, will in fact be determined by energy dimensions.

The accelerating pace of energy-related change in the nation is illustrated by the following by Philip Abelson and Irene Tinker (1):

> What current U.S. technology would be useful to Third World countries for the long term? Much of the U.S. industrial and distribution system was designed to use abundant low-cost energy in the form of oil and natural gas. Now some of this technology is obsolete, and within a decade bulldozers will be knocking down facilities that were designed to use cheap fuels.

We as a nation have had tremendous faith in American science and technology. When something runs out or gets in short supply, a better substitute is always developed. The man on the street knows it is just this way. That may be a big part of our problem. Science and technology has always come through. With regard to energy and some other natural resources challenges looming large on the horizon, the ingenuity of American science and technology, and the will of our people, will in all likelihood be tested as never before.

Thinking of the Big Issues

I agree with Pierce that, whether we are talking about energy or any other really critical national natural resources issue, "high ability of the people who undertake the task is far more important than the total amount of money spent." He further suggests that we "support the very best people in a degree that seems reasonable to them." It is, unfortunately, sometimes difficult to do this in reality in the academic setting. When you identify high-priority research and development (or, for that matter, teaching) activities, then identify faculty (in-house or needs from external sources) capable of accomplishing such efforts in a scholarly manner, then concentrate enough resources there to get really substantial results, what have you got left? Too frequently you have a lot of nonsqueaky wheels also wanting to be greased. And the rusty wheels decry the notion of any priorities, preferring instead advocacy of the least common scholarly denominators, if anything. What excellence built is too often sacrificed to serve the endless needs of mediocrity.

Pierce is correct: there must be some, hopefully enough, individuals somewhere—in government, in the private sector, and in our universities with strong research capabilities—who are thinking and doing something innovative about the great and emerging problems of society and the nation. But it is hard to do this while burrowed down under endless minutiae or figuring out better ways to make left-handed wheelbarrows a little cheaper or out chasing Mammon's hubcaps.

Taylor Branch (3) speaks of "holy grail" agencies in the federal government as well as agencies whose mission is "delivering the mail." The same sort of distinction applies, of course, in industry and the academic community. Obviously, in the typical industrial, government, or university environment, more disciplines and departments and individuals will be figuratively "carrying the mail" than will be off searching for the "holy grail," that is, seeking innovative solutions to the really substantive questions of the time. Fortunately for the nation and its institutions, public and private, not everyone is off seeking the holy grail, else things would grind to a stop.

Perhaps the most difficult task, though, is for someone at a higher organizational level than the researchers—the "very best people" Pierce says need to be properly supported—to identify the areas to be pushed, and take the heat from those in nonpriority areas. These people topside, the upper layers of management, must frequently ask Peter Drucker's (6) basic question: What is our business, and what should it be?

CLOSURE

I wish to close with a final thought from Leopold (8):

> Man, while now captain of the adventuring ship, is hardly the sole object of its quest, and . . . his prior assumptions to this effect arose from the simple necessity of whistling in the dark.

We, as responsible natural resources engineers and decisionmakers, as managers and policymakers, as risk-makers and risk-takers, must become sufficiently aware of the current and, more importantly, the emerging resources challenges of our region and our nation, and what our options are. Better yet, we should take the lead in developing the options.

I believe we will be better able to discharge our responsibilities for having shared our thoughts at this symposium, better able to make the hard, but necessary, tradeoffs involving natural resources, tradeoffs that are intelligent and informed. I hope, also, that we find ourselves having to resort to "whistling in the dark" as infrequently as possible in the future.

REFERENCES

(1) Abelson, Philip H., and Irene Tinker. "Technology Transfer." Editorial in *Science*, 28 Jan. 1977.
(2) Boulding, Kenneth E. "The Economics of the Coming Spaceship Earth." In Environmental Quality in a Growing Economy, ed. Henry Jarrett. Baltimore: Johns Hopkins Press, 1966.
(3) Branch, Taylor. "We're All Working for the Penn Central." In *Inside the System*, ed. Charles Peters and James Fallows. 3rd ed. New York: Praeger, 1976.
(4) Council on Environmental Quality. *Environmental Quality: The Sixth Annual Report of the Council on Environmental Quality*. Washington: U.S. Government Printing Office, 1975.
(5) Crittenden, Ann. "A New Index on the Quality of Life." *New York Times*, 13 March 1977.
(6) Drucker, Peter F. *Management: Tasks, Responsibilities, Practices*. New York: Harper & Row, 1974.
(7) Hitch, Charles J. "Unfreezing the Future." Editorial in *Science*, 4 March 1977.
(8) Leopold, Aldo. *A Sand County Almanac*. Oxford University Press, 1966.
(9) McHarg, Ian L. *Design with Nature*. Garden City: Doubleday/Natural History Press, 1971.
(10) Nash, Roderick. "Rivers and Americans: A Century of Conflicting Priorities." In *Environmental Quality and Water Development*, ed. Charles R. Goodman, James McEvoy III, and Peter J. Richerson. W.H. Freeman, San Francisco: 1973.
(11) National Wildlife Federation. "EQ Index for 1977: The Year of the Invisible Crisis." *National Wildlife* (Feb.-March 1977).
(12) Odum, Eugene P. "The Emergence of Ecology as a New Integrative Discipline." *Science*, 25 March 1977.
(13) Sagan, Carl. "In Praise of Science and Technology." *New Republic*, 22 Jan. 1977.

Part II

Natural Resources

Chapter Four

Long-Term Availability of Natural Resources

Gordon J. MacDonald

Resources are conventionally classified as either renewable or nonrenewable. Renewable resources are generally taken to be of biological origin, that is, food and forest. The definition of nonrenewable resources is more difficult. Energy once used cannot be used again even though a small fraction of the used energy is chemically stored in the process of manufacturing or building. Phosphates and other components of fertilizers are similarly nonrenewable, though a portion of the constituent elements is stored in biologic matter. Metals are generally considered to belong to the nonrenewable class, although the potential for recycling blurs the definition. This paper deals with problems of what are conventionally called nonrenewable resources, that is, energy and materials derived from the earth's crust by extractive means.

In the current debate about the long-term availability of resources, there is a variety of views. The pessimist sees a future in which catastrophic exhaustion of resources is inevitable unless economic growth is brought to a stop by drastic measures. The optimist views the future as one in which nonrenewable resources are economically and physically infinite. There are, of course, gradations between these extreme points of view.

The simplest version of the pessimistic view is that growth is exponential in the consumption of metals and energy. Given a finite reserve of these materials, it is then a matter of simple arithmetic to show that exhaustion is inevitable. This thesis, explored in *The Limits to Growth*, has merit in dramatizing the qualitative implications of compound growth. Doubling of the resources does not double the time to exhaustion if there is exponential growth. For example, if the reserve in the ground is good for fifty years at current consumption rates, and if growth averages 7 percent per year (which is equivalent to a doubling time of ten years), then a doubling of the reserves extends the life of the reserve by only ten years. So, a doubling of reserves under the assumption of steady exponential growth increases the lifetime of the reserve by only 20 percent of its initially projected life.

Another less pessimistic view acknowledges that there are various economic feedback mechanisms that link consumption to scarcity. In this view the question is raised whether the efficiency of the marketplace can react quickly enough to impending shortages to avoid a disastrous situation. Actual or threatening scarcity of a particular resource will lead to price rises and consequent incentives to economize on scarce resources and substitute plentiful ones, but the question raised from this viewpoint is whether a society, consuming nonrenewable resources in all sectors, can react in time and in a way to prevent real economic dislocation?

A still milder form of pessimism assumes that the price mechanism will effectively ration scarce materials. However, the fraction of the society's total resources that must be allocated to the extraction and production sector grows. With this growth there will be fewer resources available for real income as relatively fewer goods and services are produced by the lowered resource base. This shift of economic resources toward the extractive and productive industry can result in major economic dislocations as the production of goods and services decreases, especially if the changes take place rapidly in relation to other time scales characterizing the economy.

Optimists are generally of one of two views, both of which rely on the efficiency of the market mechanism. Impending shortages generate rising prices. The rising prices act as a danger signal, discouraging the use of scarce minerals and stimulating technology and the use of alternative materials and energy sources. In this view there will always be enough materials and energy to satisfy demand, but at a price. The difficulty with this view is that the price may be great enough to impair the economic welfare, since capital and labor must be used to secure scarce raw materials and to develop the technology that efficiently employs these materials. In one form this view blends imperceptibly with the mildest form of pessimism discussed above.

The most optimistic view maintains that humanity through its inventiveness always will be able to counteract any possible effect of scarcity. New sources, substitution, recycling, and new technology, both in extraction and in the use of materials and energy, are conceived of as always being able to eliminate the evils of scarcity. The most optimistic optimist points out that the actual abundance of minerals, including energy resources, in the continental crust of the earth is many times—often millions of times—greater than known reserves. This observation is used to justify the position that the resources are essentially infinite.

Which view one adopts is very much a matter of judgment. However, some very basic considerations of the distribution of elements in the earth's crust and of the means of extracting metals rule out the most optimistic view with respect to the availability of many key metals. A critical examination of recoverable fuel resources suggests that the time scale for the exhaustion of fuel sources, hydrocarbon or nuclear, is indeed limited, though for how long is uncertain.

Of the resources for energy, the hydrocarbon fuels form a relatively straightforward case of the kind considered in *The Limits to Growth*. There are limited amounts of natural gas, oil, coal, peat, shale oil, and tar sands. Sedimentary rocks do contain in certain places trace amounts of hydrocarbons, but no one seriously would advocate that such traces could be enriched to form a fuel at any conceivable price. As hydrocarbon fuels become scarce, marginal resources will become reserves as the prices rise. New techniques for extraction and conversion of fuels to energy will become economical; but basically there is a finite limit to the resources. Once this limit is approached, then the price mechanism will favor the use of these resources for materials rather than for fuel.

The major question about hydrocarbon fuels is the extent of reserves and resources both proved and speculative. Most analysts would agree, however, that for oil and gas—assuming a continued world exponential growth for the next few decades—exhaustion will come within a few decades. A more precise estimate of the time to exhaustion will be explored in this paper. The situation with coal is somewhat more reassuring. Exhaustion comes, again with the assumption of exponential growth, in time measured in a century or so.

The situation for nuclear fuels, uranium and thorium, is less clear. Geochemically, uranium has certain properties that allow it to form separable minerals at low concentration. Further developments in the breeder reactor technology may make it possible to stretch existing reserves over a long time span. Fusion, if it becomes a reality, can also contribute to stretching uranium resources through a combined fusion-breeder reactor. Relatively little work has been carried out on determining the reserves of thorium, another potential nuclear fuel.

The present uncertainties in reserves and resources, particularly with regard to speculative resources, and the rapidly developing technical picture make it more difficult to assess the time scale for exhaustion of the nuclear fuels.

FUELS AND OTHER RAW MATERIALS

Fuels and other raw materials present very different problems of long-term availability. The workings of the law of conservation of mass ensures that metals once extracted from the earth can be used over and over again. Whether virgin or recycled metals are used depends on total demand and economics. If the demand for a particular metal exceeds that available from used materials, then economics dictate that new material will be extracted from the earth's crust. However, once extracted, the metal serves as a future source for reuse. The demand for new material is thus lessened by the availability of previously mined material.

Basically because of the second law of thermodynamics, energy cannot be recycled in the sense that metals can. Energy can be used more efficiently. Coal once burned to produce steam can generate only electricity, with the excess thermal energy dumped into the waterways or the atmosphere. Alternatively, the steam discharged from a turbine can be used in industrial processes so that the overall efficiency of the use of energy is increased. In the end, however, energy—once highly organized in the form of chemical energy in coal or oil or nuclear energy in the uranium ore—becomes dissipated as low-grade heat energy that is eventually radiated out into space.

Because of this fundamental difference between reusable materials and energy, primary attention is given in this paper to the availability of energy. In general, the problems of fuel availability, particularly fuels in a form that can be readily utilized by existing or developing technologies, seem more pressing than the problems of the availability of other raw materials. Data about reserves and resources of energy are in general more complete than those for most metals. Finally, for many if not all materials, substitutes can be found. There is no substitute for energy.

ENERGY SUPPLY AND DEMAND

An examination of the adequacy of fuels to support the economy of the United States and of the world requires some estimate of what future demands will be. Over the years many different estimates have been published. For example, the Ford Energy Study (5) outlines a number of scenarios for the United States. In the following, some limiting cases for future demand are briefly outlined.

Recently a number of surveys have been published of United States and world recoverable reserves and resources of hydrocarbon fuels and uranium (see, for example 1,6,7). These estimates and others have been used in developing the tables presented below, which provide one overview of the current resource picture. As in the case of estimate of demand, the estimates of recoverable reserves and resources remain most uncertain.

Data on reserves and resources together with estimates of demand can be combined to yield "index years" of availability. For the purposes of this paper, index years are an estimate of the time required to exhaust either the reserves or resources of a given fuel if that fuel is used to supply the total demand for energy for the world and the United States. The assessments of index years are made with differing assumptions about demand. Thus index years present a rough evaluation of the overall demand and supply picture for individual fuels.

Nonconventional sources of energy such as solar, geothermal, or fusion will not be considered. These sources may become important in the longer-term future but they are unlikely to make a major contribution to energy supplies during the critical transition period in which the world switches over from an economy based on liquid hydrocarbon fuels to one based on solid hydrocarbon or nuclear fuels.

Units to Measure Demand and Supply

The demand for energy differs greatly among developed and developing countries of the world. This demand is being met by a wide variety of fuels. Both the demand and fuel mixture are changing in response to changing industrial requirements, environmental constraints, patterns of transportation, and life-styles. In order to compare total energy demand with availability of various fuels, it is useful to discuss fuels in terms of a common unit rather than in terms of conventional bulk quantities such as barrels or tons in which fuels are measured. Since all energy can be converted into heat, the heating value of the fuels is a convenient common unit that allows for comparison across fuels.

The heating value of a fuel is the thermal energy that can be derived from a fixed quantity of the fuel. The derived thermal energy can then be converted by various means into more useful forms of energy to produce work. The conversion process will always involve some losses in energy. For example, hydrocarbon-burning electric-generating plants convert about one-third of the consumed thermal energy into electricity for an efficiency of about 0.33. Current methods of converting the

stored thermal energy of fuels into useful work are inherently inefficient, so a substantial portion of the available thermal energy of fuels
is directly dumped as waste heat into the environment.

Table 4-1 lists the conventional heating values of the major fuel
sources in terms of the quantities used to measure fuels in the United
States. The values listed are only approximations, since the precise
value will depend on the details of the physical and chemical nature of
the fuel. Government agencies have revised the conventional values
from time to time. Recently the U.S. Bureau of Mines (2,3) has shifted
the heating value of natural gas from 1,031 Btu per standard dry cubic
foot of natural gas to 1,024 Btu for consumption during 1974/75. The
value used by the United Nations in their compilations corresponds to
1,048 Btu/cubic foot.

The heating value of coal depends on its rank. In the United States
more subbituminous coal and lignite have been used by the electric
power industry in recent years so that the average heating value for
coal has decreased. On the world scene, the proportion of sub-
bituminous coal burned is greater than in the United States (4). The
heating value for coal of 20×10^6 Btu/short ton is an approximation,
probably high for many countries in the world and low for the United
States.

The heating value for uranium in burner reactors corresponds to the
amount of thermal energy to be derived by the burning of uranium in
conventional light-water reactors in use in the United States today.
The listed value approximates average current experience. The precise
value for any reactor and fuel will depend on the details of reactor

**Table 4-1. Heating Values Used in Converting from Conventional Quantities
to Units of Energy**

	Heating Value
Natural Gas	1031 Btu/cubic foot
Crude Oil	5.8×10^6 Btu/barrel
Syncrude from Shale Oil and Tar Sands	5.8×10^6 Btu/barrel
Natural Gas Liquids	4.1×10^6 Btu/barrel
Coal	20×10^6 Btu/short ton
Uranium Oxide U_3O_8 In burner reactors without plutonium recycle	400×10^9 Btu/short ton
In breeder reactors	30×10^{12} Btu/short ton
One metric ton of coal equivalent (tce)	27.778×10^6 Btu

Table 4-2. World Energy Use

	Energy Consumption (quads/year)	Population (millions)	Power per Capita (watts/capita)
1950	76.8	2,500	1,025
1960	124.0	2,990	1,386
1974	220.9	3,890	1,906
Average Annual Percent Change 1950-1974	4.50	1.85	2.62
Extrapolation to the Year 2000 at 1950-1974 Rate of Growth	693.8	6,265	3,734

design and on such factors as the degree of enrichment of U-235. The heating value for breeder reactors is far more speculative depending on the detailed nature of the fuel used in the breeder as well as on the reactor design.

Energy Use in the World and the United States

Since World War II world energy use has grown steadily, reaching a rate of about 221 quads (one quad equals 10^{15} Btu) per year in 1974 (see Table 4-2). The growth can be separated into two components: the growth in total population, and the growth in per capita use. In Table 4-2 the growth per capita is given in terms of watts, units of power (energy per unit time). Since World War II, the worldwide average yearly growth in energy use has been 4.5 percent. The larger part, 2.6 percent, comes from the increase in per capita consumption as industrialization and a general raising of the living standard has led to an intensive employment of energy. While the world average of per capita consumption in 1974 was about 1,900 watts per capita, there was a wide variation among nations. In the poorer nations of the world, energy use averaged less than 1,000 watts per capita, while the most energy-intensive country in the world, the United States, used energy at a rate corresponding to 11,400 watts per capita.

If the rates of growth of per capita energy use and of population for the years 1950-1974 were to persist until the year 2000, then the world would be consuming energy in the year 2000 at a rate of 694 quads per year, or about 3,700 watts per capita. With this rate of growth, the per capita consumption would still be a fraction, about a third, of the 1976 United States per capita consumption.

In developing estimates of the index years for world fuels, the rate of use in 1974, 220 quads/year, and the extrapolated value of 694 quads/year will be used. The 1974 value is certainly a "low" estimate of future energy use. Current trends indicate that there may be some slowing in rate of growth of world population, but there is no evidence of a decreasing rate of per capita use of energy. The industrialization of the developing countries, coupled with an increasing standard of living, will lead to a continued increase in the demand for energy for large parts of the world. The estimate of 694 quads/year for the world energy use will be taken as a representative extrapolation of what energy requirements will be in the year 2000.

The rate of growth of population and per capita energy use in the United States during the period 1950-1974 has been substantially less than for the world (see Table 4-3). The average yearly increase in per capita energy use in the United States was about 18 percent in the post-World War II years, corresponding to a total energy growth rate of 3.2 percent.

Energy use declined in 1974/75 as the effects of the Arab oil embargo came into full force, but energy use resumed its growth in 1976. Maintenance of the 1950-1974 rate of growth would yield an annual energy consumption in the United States of 164 quads in the year 2000, corresponding to a per capita consumption of 18,000 watts. While these figures are used later in constructing index year tables, these are very likely overestimates of the actual energy use in the year 2000. The rate of population growth has slowed in recent years so that

Table 4-3. Energy Use in the United States

	Energy Consumption (quads/year)	Population (millions)	Power per Capita (watts/capita)
1950	34.15	152.3	7,492
1960	44.82	180.7	8,283
1970	68.81	204.9	11,216
1974	72.58	212.2	11,424
1975	70.72	214.4	11,017
1976	73.0[a]	216.0[a]	11,288
Average Annual Percent Change 1950-1974	3.19	1.39	1.77
Extrapolation to the Year 2000 at 1950-1974 Rate of Growth	164	304[b]	18,000

[a]Estimate.

[b]This figure should be compared with Series I, Bureau of the Census projection of 287 million. The difference is due to the sharp drop in annual percent change in recent years to less than 0.7 percent.

the current high estimate of the Census Bureau for the year 2000 is 287 million, rather than the 304 million that would be expected from a continuation of the 1950-1974 trends. The Census Bureau estimates a more moderate rate of growth if current values of birth expectation are used, leading to a population of 262 million in 2000.

The per capita consumption of energy is also likely to slow in future years as the conversion of the economy from one heavily dependent on energy-intensive industries to one more dependent on light industries and services is very likely to contribute to a slowing of the rate of growth of per capita use. Conservation policies would further lower the rate of growth of per capita consumption. A rate of energy consumption of 164 quads/year for the year 2000 is almost certainly a substantial overestimate; the expected demand for the year 2000 is expected to be between the 1976 rate, 73 quads/year, and the extrapolated year 2000 rate.

The demand for energy in the United States has historically been met by a changing mixture of fuels. Table 4-4 lists the percentage contribution of the various fuels to total energy use from 1950 to 1975. Overall, as energy consumption increased, the percentage contribution from coal has halved, even though the yearly amount of coal burned has remained about constant. The percentage contribution of natural gas increased from 1950 to the late 1960s. By 1970 use of natural gas increased at a rate greater than the discovery of new reserves. By 1975, nuclear power contributed only a small fraction of the total energy requirements, somewhat over 2 percent of the total demand.

The expected demand for energy in the United States in future years will depend on both the rate of growth of population and the per capita consumption. Table 4-5 illustrates the dependence of total energy consumption on these variables. The Census Bureau periodically updates its projections of future population for the United States. In 1975 the estimates for the year 2000 varied between 287 million, under the assumption that the rate of growth is maintained at about 1.1 percent per year, to a population of 245 million if the assumption is made that

Table 4-4. Energy Sources in the United States, by Fuel (percent)

Year	Total Energy Use (quads)	Crude Oil	Natural Gas	Coal	Hydropower	Nuclear
1950	34.1	34.5	18.0	37.8	4.7	
1960	44.8	44.6	28.2	23.2	4.0	
1970	68.8	43.0	32.8	20.0	4.1	
1974	72.6	45.8	29.8	18.2	4.5	1.6
1975	70.7	46.0	28.4	18.9	4.4	2.3

Table 4-5.   United States Energy Demand at Current Power Consumption (11,300 watts/capita) and at an Annual One Percent per Capita Growth Rate

Year	Population (Series I)	Energy (quads/year)		Population (Series II)	Energy (quads/year)		Population (Series III)	Energy (quads/year)	
		Current per capita use	1 percent annual growth		Current per capita use	1 percent annual growth		Current per capita use	1 percent annual growth
1980	226	76.4	79.5	223	75.4	78.4	220	74.4	77.4
1990	258	87.2	100.2	245	82.8	95.2	236	79.8	91.7
2000	287	97.0	123.2	262	88.6	112.4	245	82.8	105.1
2020	362	122.3	189.6	294	99.4	153.9	252	85.2	132.0

Series I assumes annual percent increase of about 1.1.
Series II uses current data of birth expectation.
Series III assumes a gradual decline in annual percent change to zero in the years 2015-2020.

the rate of growth declines steadily and reaches zero sometime between 2015 and 2020. The intermediate projection of 262 million is based on current data about birth expectations of American women.

Depending on population projections, estimates of energy use in the year 2000 range from 83 quads to 97 quads per year if the current per capita rate of energy use is maintained. If the per capita energy use increases at an average rate of 1 percent per year, the range of energy use lies between 105 and 123 quads/year, depending on assumptions about population growth. An intermediate rate of population increase, coupled with an assumption of a 1 percent per year growth, yields an energy consumption of 112 quads per year, a value within the range of 73 and 164 quads/year discussed above.

Reserves and Resources

Estimates of fuels in the ground are usually categorized as either reserves or resources. The difficulty with this separation is one of definition. Definitions differ across fuels and among institutions responsible for the assignment of deposits to the categories of reserves or resources. As far as oil and natural gas are concerned, reserves refer to material in the ground that can be produced and sold with currently available technology at prevailing prices. Reserves of coal are defined by their physical characteristics such as depth of the deposit and thickness of the seam. The definition of uranium reserves involves the cost of recovery; in general detailed economic consideration does not enter into the definition of reserves of fuels other than uranium.

The concept of a reserve is further complicated by the existence of environmental regulations. Materials that could have been classed as reserves a few years ago now are questionable as limits on sulfur content or other regulations have been set. Reserves of coal may be appreciably affected as new mining methods are developed in response to new regulations governing surface mining.

The definitions of a resource are even less precise than those of reserves. In the view of some, everything in the earth's crust of a particular substance would be considered a resource, despite overwhelming technical difficulties and resulting high costs of ultimate recovery. For example, oil may be found in small deposits in isolated locations. It is difficult to conceive of conditions under which such a deposit could be economically developed.

In the United States Geological Survey (USGS) has had primary responsibility for estimating resources of hydrocarbon fuels. In its resource estimates, use is made of qualifying adjectives such as hypothetical and speculative. Resource estimates on a world basis differ greatly among the countries; the net effect is to make world estimates even more uncertain than those for the United States.

The Energy Research and Development Administration (ERDA) has inherited from the Atomic Energy Commission primary responsibility for estimates of the uranium resources of the United States. As in the case of the USGS for estimates of reserves and resources of fuels such as coal and oil, ERDA relies heavily on the industry for resource estimates. This reliance can lead to a distortion of the estimates as industry's view can be conditioned by market prospects. Further, resource estimates—like reserve estimates—may be affected, often in uncertain ways by changing environmental requirements.

The accuracy of resource estimates depends to a substantial extent on the availability of geological information. Coal deposits are found in layered strata that are more or less continuous. As a result, surface outcrops of coal seams can lead to a relatively accurate inference of the extent of the resources at depth and over an extended geographic area, particularly when test drilling is used to determine thickness and depth. Oil shale and tar sands deposits are similar to coal in that they occur in layered deposits. In contrast, oil and natural gas are found in relatively discrete deposits. Sophisticated geophysical methods generally used only by industry are required for resource estimation. In the United States most uranium deposits are found in discrete locations and thus also pose difficult problems in estimation.

Crude Oil

Reserves of crude oil in the United States are estimated on a regular basis by a number of organizations. The estimate listed in Table 4-6 represents the joint effort of the American Gas Association, American Petroleum Institute, and the Canadian Petroleum Association published in 1976 (1,11). Other estimates vary by a few billion barrels, with the difference due primarily to the interpretation of the definition of reserve rather than on a disagreement as to the amount of oil actually in the ground.

The principal published sources of worldwide oil reserves are the *Oil and Gas Journal* and *World Oil* (1,2,13). Both journals try to obtain reserve data for each producing country. The data in these publications refer to proven reserves, though a comparison with other sources suggests that the appropriate adjective may be probable (1). In any case, in areas undergoing rapid development, such as the North Sea, changes in the reserve category may take place rapidly.

Estimation of petroleum resources is much more difficult than that of proved reserves where information obtained from drilling provides a degree of precision. Geological and geophysical data are useful in locating potential sites, but such sites may not meet the conditions required for the formation of petroleum. The amount of oil accumulated in any one site will depend on many variables, including the character

Table 4-6. Crude Oil Reserves, Resources, and Production

	Recoverable Reserves		Recoverable Resources		Production-1975	
	Billion bbl	*Energy in quads*	*Billion bbl*	*Energy in quads*	*Billion bbl*	*Energy in quads*
United States	33	190	160-370	930-2100	3.0	17.4
World Excluding U.S.	510-610	3,000-3,500	1,100-1,700	6,500-10,000	16	95
World	530-640	3,200-3,700	1,500-1,900	8,700-11,000	19	110

of the reservoir rock and the nature of the adjoining geologic structure. As a result the amount of oil may vary greatly from site to site. The location of large accumulations are very unevenly distributed geographically, leading to further uncertainties in resource estimation; giant fields are the principal source of today's world oil.

A further uncertainty is the recoverability of oil. The recoverability in a particular site will depend on the physical parameters of both the reservoir rock and the oil. In the United States the current recovery factor in producing regions averages about 30 percent. This can be increased somewhat by the use of secondary and tertiary recovery techniques. Discussions in the literature suggest that over the next twenty years the recovery factor may increase to 40 percent. Higher figures would require the development of wholly new technologies.

A variety of models have been constructed over the years to obtain estimates of the world oil resources. Some models have been based primarily on geological information, while others have used historical data on such factors as the relationship of discovery to drilling rate. For the world, estimates of recoverable oil range from 1.5 to 2 trillion barrels. For example, the National Academy of Sciences (7) on the basis of a review of various estimates, concludes that undiscovered recoverable oil amounts to 1.1 trillion barrels. Moody and Geiger (14) estimate a value of 2 trillion barrels for the ultimate recovery, with 900 billion barrels as yet undiscovered.

Similar uncertainties surround estimates of recoverable resources in the United States. Past estimates of the U.S. Geological Survey and of the National Petroleum Council have tended toward the higher values. More recent estimates, including those of the Geological Survey, have favored values about half those previously published.

Table 4-6 also lists the production figures for petroleum in 1975. For the United States the ratio of imported petroleum to domestic production has increased markedly since 1950 (see Table 4-7). In the years prior to World War II, the United States had been a net exporter of petroleum. The discovery of large reservoirs in Venezuela and the Middle East in the 1930s changed this picture as these resources became available on the world market at low cost.

Despite the Voluntary Oil Import Program initiated in 1957 to stem the flow of imports, imports of petroleum grew during the 1959-1967 period at an average annual rate of 4 percent. From 1968 through 1973 U.S. production fell increasingly short of demand, with the result that imports increased at a rate of 16 percent annually. Much of this increase came from Canada, Saudi Arabia, which has a large production capacity, and Nigeria, whose crude oil is especially adaptable to the U.S. market. The economic and political interest in the U.S.

Table 4-7. United States Dependence on Petroleum Imports (average annual growth rate of domestic demand: 4 percent for 1950-1974)

	Domestic Demand		Imports		Ratio of
Year	*Thousands bbl/day*	*Quads/year*	*Thousands bbl/day*	*Quads/year*	*Imports to Domestic Demand*
1950	6,507	13.8	850	1.8	13.1
1960	9,661	20.4	1,911	4.0	19.8
1970	14,697	31.1	3,419	7.2	23.3
1972	16,367	34.6	4,741	10.0	29.0
1973	17,308	36.6	6,256	13.2	36.1
1974	16,629	35.2	6,112	12.9	36.8
1975	16,288	34.5	5,993	12.7	36.8
1976[a]	17,185	36.4	7,217	15.3	42.0
1977[a]	18,039	38.2	8,324	17.6	46.1

[a]Forecast.

dependence on foreign imports came into sharp focus during the 1973/74 oil embargo. During 1974 and 1975 U.S. imports of petroleum products were at a slightly reduced level, initially because of the embargo. Reduced economic activity, higher prices, and conservation practices contributed to the reduced demand. However, imports rose significantly during 1976 as the economy picked up. The contribution of imported oil to demand is expected to increase further in 1977 in response to severe weather and continued improvements in the economic situation.

The recoverable reserves of the United States listed in Table 4-6, together with the historical pattern of events illustrated in Table 4-7, strongly suggest that regardless of energy policies that may be adopted over the short term, the United States will continue to depend heavily on imported oil. A decrease on the reliance of foreign oil can result only from a shift away from the historical dependence of the United States on crude oil as the major source of energy in meeting overall energy demands (see Table 4-4).

Natural Gas

The difficulties in estimating recoverable reserves and resources of natural gas parallel those of estimating these quantities of oil. Oil and natural gas are frequently found together and the geological and geophysical methods of resource estimation are similar. However, the differences among individually published estimates are greater for natural gas than for oil. For example, recent estimates of the worldwide remaining natural gas range from 7,000 to 16,000 trillion cubic feet.

Table 4-8 lists estimates of recoverable resources and reserves. The lower number represents evaluation by the National Academy of Sciences (7), while the higher values are derived from publications of the Institute of Gas Technology and the USGS (1). Special problems are associated with data on natural gas production since a distinction must be made between total production and marketed production. In 1975 U.S. gross production amounted to 21.1 trillion cubic feet, of which 20.1 trillion cubic feet were marketed (see Table 4-8), while the rest was used for re-injection in order to maintain pressure in oil reservoirs and a small part was flared. On a world basis, a far higher fraction of the natural gas produced is either vented or flared. Oil and natural gas together furnished 75 percent of the total energy for the United States in 1975 (see Table 4-4). While the fraction due to natural gas has begun to decline, these two fuels will continue to provide a major if not the largest source of energy through the end of the century.

Coal

Coal is a complex mixture of organic and inorganic compounds. Each coal bed differs from others in both physical and chemical properties. The variations in heat content, ash, and sulfur compounds complicate the use of coal to provide thermal energy for electricity and process steam or the use as a source of liquid or gaseous synthetic fuels.

In the United States the coal industry has passed through a variety of phases. Until well into the twentieth century, coal was a primary domestic source of energy for both stationary and mobile power. As early as 1885 the United States was producing over 100 million tons annually. The production continued to increase steadily, reaching 600 million tons in the early 1920s. In the years following, coal production declined as a result of cheap oil and the Depression. In the 1950s and

Table 4-8.   Natural Gas Reserves, Resources, and Consumption

	Recoverable Reserves		Recoverable Resources		Consumption in 1975	
	Tcf^a	Energy in quads	Tcf^a	Energy in quads	Tcf^a	Energy in quads
United States	230	240	530-1,300	540-1,300	20.1	20.6
World Excluding U.S.	1,500-2,300	1,500-2,300	7,600-9,100	7,800-9,300	28	29
World	1,700-2,600	1,700-2,600	8,900-9,600	9,100-9,800	48	49

[a]Tcf = Trillion cubic feet.

1960s production averaged between 500 and 550 million tons annually, increasing in the 1970s to 650 million tons by 1975 (see Table 4-9). In terms of percent contribution to the total energy use, coal declined from 50 percent in the mid-1940s to less than 20 percent in the 1970s (see Table 4-4).

The U.S. Bureau of Mines (2) has published data on the coal reserve base. The bureau estimates that the coal in place at depths less than 1,000 feet with bituminous seams at least 28 inches thick and sub-bituminous at least 5 feet thick amounts to 434 billion tons. Of this amount, 137 billion tons are in beds so near the surface as to be unsuitable for underground mining but suitable for surface mining.

The Bureau of Mines estimates recoverability of the coal in place to vary between 40 and 90 percent, with an average of about 50 percent. If the recoverability of the underground deposits is taken as 50 percent and that of surface deposits as 90 percent, then the total recoverable reserve for the United States amounts to 273 billion tons (see Table 4-9).

Table 4-10 gives estimates of the demonstrated reserve base and recoverable coal by geographic area and potential method of mining. About 54 percent of the total reserve base is found west of the

Table 4-9. Coal Reserves, Resources, and Production

	Recoverable Reserves		*Recoverable Resources*		*Production in 1975*	
	Billion short tons	*Energy in quads*	*Billion short tons*	*Energy in quads*	*Billion short tons*	*Energy in quads*
United States	273	6,000	1,000-1,800	22,000-40,000	0.65	12.6
World Excluding U.S.	452	9,000	2,400-6,800	64,000-120,000	2.85	57
World	725	15,000	4,200-7,800	86,000-160,000	3.5	70

Table 4-10. Demonstrated Coal Reserve Base in the United States

Location	*Reserve Base (millions short tons)*	*Recoverable Coal (millions short tons)*	*Recoverable Energy (quads)*
East of Mississippi			
Underground	169,000	84,500	1,853
Surface	34,000	30,600	673
West of Mississippi			
Underground	131,000	65,500	1,441
Surface	103,000	92,700	2,039
Total	437,000	273,300	6,006

Mississippi. About half of the western coals can be strip mined, while only 17 percent of the eastern coals can be recovered by surface mining. The western coals have lower sulfur content: nearly 85 percent of the coal with 1 percent sulfur or less is found west of the Mississippi.

Estimates of the world's coal reserves have been developed by the World Energy Conference (6). Estimates of recoverable reserves are thought to be reasonably accurate for industrialized countries that have had a long history of mining coal. Geologic exploration in these countries has been extensive, and it is unlikely that new large coal deposits will be found. The estimates for the Peoples Republic of China are most uncertain, but the consensus is that the potential for coal resources is high. Table 4-9 lists estimates of the world coal reserves assuming a 50 percent recoverability.

In the United States coal resources as estimated by their geologic occurrence are large, much larger than the resources of oil and natural gas. Coal-bearing rocks are known in at least 37 states. Since coal occurs in the form of continuous beds, geologists can estimate the areal extent. Test drill holes provide data about thickness and continuity. Table 4-9 indicates the range of values for U.S. recoverable resources. A part of the uncertainty is caused by assumptions about the thickness of seams that can be economically recovered. Averitt (15) for example, would exclude thin beds—14-28 inches for bituminous and 2-5 feet for lignite—and this assumption yields a lower value for recoverable resources.

The world resource picture is much more uncertain. In addition to the question concerning the Peoples Republic of China, little exploration has been carried out in Central and South America and in much of Africa, South Asia, and Oceania. Because of this the values listed in Table 4-9 represent a substantial underestimate of world coal resources.

Oil Shale and Tar Sands

Tar sands are rocks in which the hydrocarbon is present as a highly viscous material approaching the consistency of a solid. Oil shale differs from normal oil deposits and tar sands in that the "oil" is a waxy solid material known as a kerogen. Oil can be recovered from oil shale by the application of heat, which causes distillation of the lighter fractions.

Deposits of tar sands and oil shales are rated according to the oil content. It is conventional to regard a content of 25 gallons per ton as minimal for economic recovery. Uncertainties in seam thickness, reservoir size, and depth of overburden all complicate the estimation of recoverable resources. The USGS and the National Petroleum Council

(16) both estimated U.S. recoverable resources in the range of 1 to 2 trillion barrels (see Table 4-11).

U.S. tar sands deposits are small in comparison to those of Canada and the world. However, the United States has about three quarters of the world's recoverable oil shale, according to the World Energy Conference. As the values given in Table 4-11 indicate, large uncertainties exist in estimates of the world hydrocarbon resources tied up in oil shale and tar sands.

Hydrocarbon Fuels in the United States

Table 4-12 summarizes the energy content of the recoverable reserves and resources of hydrocarbon fuels in the United States. The dominance of coal as an energy source is apparent even when consideration is given to the large uncertainties in estimates of oil shale and tar sands.

In looking toward the future, it is essential to recognize that 75 percent of the total U.S. energy requirement is derived from oil and natural gas. These fuels are convenient for many energy uses, and with our current technology, indispensable for some. Natural gas provides a convenient and environmentally acceptable fuel for residential use, while derivatives of crude oil are almost the sole source of energy for transportation. Since the economy is so largely based on oil and natural gas, there is a large stock of existing equipment that is dependent on these fuels and cannot be replaced for many years.

Table 4-11. Recoverable Resources from Oil Shale and Tar Sands

	Recoverable Resources	
	Billions of barrels	*Energy in quads*
United States	1,000-2,000	5,800-11,000
World	2,400-17,000	14,000-99,000

Table 4-12. Summary of U.S. Hydrocarbon Fuel Recoverable Resources and Reserves (units-quads)

	Recoverable Reserve	*Recoverable Resource*
Crude Oil	190	930-2,100
Natural Gas	240	540-1,300
Coal	6,000	22,000-40,000
Oil Shale and Tar Sands	⎯	5,800-11,000
Total	6,430	29,270-54,400

Oil and gas can be produced from coal. Coal gasification is a relatively old technology developed before cheap natural gas became plentiful. Coal gasification plants are in production today in countries where natural gas is unavailable. Industrial coal liquefaction plants were developed in Germany during World War II.

For the United States the principal barriers to the development of a synthetic fuels industry have been cost and environmental and resource considerations. The existing price structures for both natural gas and oil make synthetics uncompetitive. Current estimates of the cost of synthetic oil run at about $20 per barrel with natural gas at $4 per thousand cubic feet. Synthetics will become price competitive only as the scarcity of natural gas and oil drives the price up. Environmental regulations, either existing or proposed, coupled with uncertainties in the supply of water in the western states, provide additional constraints on private investment in the synthetic fuel industry.

The danger of a dependence, over the longer term, on synthetic fuels lies in the appreciable time—at least a decade—required for the development of such an industry. The need for synthetics as natural supplies of gas and oil dwindle must be anticipated on a timely basis if major disruptions in the energy economy are to be avoided.

Uranium

In considering sources for nuclear power, only uranium will be discussed. Uranium is the only nuclear fuel in commercial use today, and current plans indicate that it is likely to be the sole source in the next few decades. Thorium can be used as a nuclear fuel source and may be in the future, but little is known about thorium reserves and resources.

Uranium is found in a variety of compounds widely distributed in the earth's crust, but at low concentrations. Large deposits have been identified in the United States, Canada, South Africa, and Australia. In addition, deposits are known to exist in the Soviet Union, the Peoples Republic of China, and the Democratic Republic of Germany. Because of the importance of uranium to nuclear weapons programs, up-to-date data about reserves and resources in Communist countries are incomplete. Tables 4-15 and 4-16 list world resources, and refer only to non-Communist countries.

While all estimates of reserves and resources are uncertain, uranium presents special problems. Originally, in the non-Communist world, the U.S. government was the single buyer for noncommercial purposes: weapon-making. Prior to the development of a commercial market, the U.S. government set a "fair" price, and entrepreneurs developed deposits to meet the buyer's terms. Uranium was originally bought for about \$8 per pound of U_3O_8, and it was not until the late sixties that higher-cost U_3O_8 reserves were considered. Current U.S. surveys estimate reserves that could be available at various costs up to \$30 per pound.

The use of cost in defining reserves can be misleading, since for historic reasons the cost is not the actual cost of production or the selling price. The cost used in the surveys refers to the operating and capital cost not yet incurred at the time the estimate is made. The use of cost is further complicated by changes over time as inflation and the cost of labor and materials change. The use of cost associated with reserves can give the impression that these reserves are much better defined than for fuels for which cost data are not used. In fact, the geologic character of uranium deposits leads to large uncertainty in reserve estimation. Actual prices of U_3O_8 declined in the early 1970s but rose sharply in 1974, as did the price of other energy sources, and contract prices for future delivery have risen dramatically. The higher prices led to increased exploration and mining activity in 1975/76.

Table 4-13 lists the 1976 ERDA estimates of reserves and potential for the United States. The cost group into which a uranium deposit falls depends in a general way on the grade and geologic setting. For example, the bulk of the reserves in the up to \$15 group ranges between 0.1 and 0.15 percent in grade, lies at a depth less than 700 feet below the surface, and is found almost exclusively in sandstone; the \$30 ore averages 0.08 percent in grade. It should be noted that the estimate for \$30 uranium includes tonnages available at lower costs.

ERDA has classified potential deposits in three categories of declining levels of confidence: probable, possible, and speculative. The defini-

Table 4-13.   U.S. Uranium Resources (thousands of short tons of U_3O_8)

		Potential			
\$/lb U_3O_8 Cutoff Cost[a]	*Reserves*	*Probable*	*Possible*	*Speculative*	*Total*
10	270	440	420	145	1,275
15	430	655	675	290	2,050
30	640	1,060	1,270	590	3,560
50	–	–	–	–	8,400[b]
100	–	–	–	–	17,400[b]

[a]Each class includes material in lower class or classes.

[b]A. Weinberg, *Report of the Cornell Workshop on the Major Issues of a National Energy Research and Development Program* (Cornell University, College of Engineering, 1973).

Source: Energy Research and Development Administration, *Statistical Data of the Uranium Industry* (Grand Junction, Colorado, 1976).

tions are based on the geologic setting, in particular whether the rock of interest lies within areas that have previously proved productive.

Most of the exploration for uranium in the United States has been conducted in the western states, the Colorado plateau, the Wyoming basin, and the Texas coastal plains. Other areas in the country have not received as much attention, and as a result the values listed in Table 4-15 may be low.

Early U.S. uranium discoveries were made in sandstone. As a result, less attention has been given to other host rock environments. However, uranium has been found in a number of rock formations other than sandstone (see Table 4-14). These discoveries parallel experiences in other countries. Canada's uranium is found in veins and conglomerates, Australia's in veins and calcrete, Sweden's in shale, and Brazil's in granite. New ERDA programs are designed to explore geologic environments other than those found in the western states.

Estimates of world reserves and resources have been prepared by a number of agencies, the Nuclear Energy Agency of the Organization for Economic Cooperation and Development, the International Atomic Energy Agency, and the World Energy Conference. Table 4-15 lists representative estimates.

Current U.S. production accounts for about 45 percent of the world's 1975 production of 26,000 tons of U_3O_8. Canada contributes about 25 percent, South Africa 15 percent, and France and Nigeria the bulk of the remaining balance.

The energy obtainable from uranium depends greatly on the manner of usage. Table 4-16, listing the thermal energy content of uranium deposits, is based on a conventional value of 400 billion Btu per short ton of U_3O_8, assuming a burner reactor without plutonium recycle and 30 trillion Btu per short ton of U_3O_8 if a breeder reactor is employed.

Table 4-14. Distribution by Host-Rock of $30/lb U_3O_8 in the United States (thousand tons U_3O_8)

Host Rock	Probable	Percent	Possible	Percent	Speculative	Percent
Sandstone	847	80%	820	64%	358	61%
Conglomerate	56	5	76	6	53	9
Veins	100	9	202	16	162	27
Limestone	16	2	5	21	13	2
Lignite	15	1	2	21	4	41
Volcanic Rocks	26	3	165	13	0	0
Total	1,060	100%	1,270	100%	590	100%

Source: Energy Research and Development Administration, *Statistical Data of the Uranium Industry* (Grand Junction, Colorado, 1976).

Table 4-15. World Uranium Resources and Production (thousands of short tons)

	Recoverable Reserves at up to $30/lb	Total Recoverable at up to $30/lb	Production 1974	1975
World Excluding U.S. and Communist Countries	1,100-1,800	3,000-8,100	12.6	14.8
World Excluding Communist Countries	1,740-2,440	6,600-11,000	24.1	26.5

Future Fuel Availability

The considerable variation in published estimates of recoverable reserves and resources has made it necessary to give range of values in most of the tables discussed above rather than a single most probable value. The numbers given should not be regarded as fixed, since future production, exploration, and development can cause changes. Indeed, changes—for the most part upward—are to be expected for estimates of the world resources and reserves, since major geographical areas, South America for example, have not been well explored and may prove to have more fuel resources than now known.

The values assigned to the estimates depend on a variety of institutional, technological, and economic considerations outside the physical definition of the deposits. For example, changes in U.S. regulatory practices toward natural gas may bring about rapid increases in the discovery rate.

U.S. recoverable reserves of hydrocarbon fuels are sufficient to provide for the total energy demand of the country for a period of between 40 and 90 years, depending on the assumptions made about the average rate of annual energy consumption (see Table 4-17). These estimates are based on the consumption of no net imports. The striking feature of Table 4-17 is that recoverable reserves of oil and natural gas can supply only three to six years of the total energy demand for the United States, even though these fuels—domestic and imported—are currently providing 75 percent of the total domestic energy demand.

Worldwide recoverable reserves of hydrocarbon fuels are sufficient to supply world needs for comparable times, 30 to 90 years (see Table 4-18). As in the case of the United States, coal is the dominant source, although oil reserves would have a greater potential than those of the United States.

If recoverable resources in the United States are considered, then the time scale of availability is lengthened from decades to hundreds of years, though uncertainties in these estimates are far greater than in the case of reserves, both because of the unknown nature of demand

Table 4-16.   Energy Content of Uranium Reserves and Resources (in quads)

	Recoverable Reserves at up to $30 per Pound		Recoverable Resources at up to $30 per Pound	
	Burner Reactors without Pu Recycle	*Breeder Reactors*	*Burner Reactors without Pu Recycle*	*Breeder Reactors*
United States	260	19,000	1,400	110,000
World Excluding Communist Countries	700–1,000	52,000–73,000	2,700–4,400	200,000–330,000

Table 4-17. Index Years for Total Energy Production for the United States

Fuel	Use at 1976 Rate (73 quads per year)		Use at Extrapolated Year 2000 Rate (164 quads per year)	
	Reserves	*Resources*	*Reserves*	*Resources*
Crude Oil	2.6	12.7-28.8	1.2	5.7-13
Natural Gas	3.3	7.4-17.8	1.5	3.3-7.9
Coal	82	300-550	36	130-240
Oil Shale and Tar Sands	–	80-150	–	35-67
Total Hydro-carbon Fuels	88	400-740	39	170-330
Uranium (burner reactor)	3.6	19	1.6	8.5
Uranium (breeder reactor)	260	1,500	120	670

Table 4-18. Index Years for Total Energy Production for the World

Fuel	Use at 1975 Rate (221 quads per year)		Use at Extrapolated Year 2000 Rate (694 quads per year)	
	Reserves	*Resources*	*Reserves*	*Resources*
Crude Oil	14-16	39-50	4.6-5.3	12-16
Natural Gas	7.7-12	41-44	2.4-3.7	13-14
Coal	68	390-720	22	120-230
Oil Shale and Tar Sands	–	63-450	–	20-140
Total Hydro-carbon Fuels	90-96	530-1300	29-31	160-400
Uranium (Burner Reactor, Excl. Communist Countries)	3.2-4.5	12-20	1.0-1.4	3.9-6.3
Uranium (Breeder Reactor, Excl. Communist Countries)	230-330	900-1500	75-100	290-470

over the longer period of time and the larger uncertainty in the estimate of resources. As in the case of reserves, coal is the dominant fuel source, though oil shale and tar sands can significantly aid in meeting future needs. On the world scene, hydrocarbon resources are sufficient to supply demand for a time measured in centuries.

The principal problem with depending on hydrocarbon resources for future energy is that the present economy is based on liquid hydrocarbon fuels, while the reserves and resources for the future are either solid hydrocarbon in coal and oil shale or highly viscous hydrocarbon in tar sands. There appear to be no insurmountable technical problems in shifting to the solid fuels of the future, but the institutional and economic barriers are real and have not been subjected to detailed analysis.

The values in Table 4-17 illustrate the vulnerable position the United States is in with respect to liquid hydrocarbon fuel supplies. Domestic reserves and resources are only sufficient for a very few decades if liquid hydrocarbons are to be correct, then domestic supplies are sufficient for only ten to fifteen years.

The addition of uranium to the potential fuel supplies for the United States does not alter the projections of energy availability in any major way if uranium is used in burner reactors without plutonium recycling. The same conclusion holds for the world energy supply.

The introduction of breeder reactors on a large scale would significantly lengthen the time over which reserves and resources of uranium could supply U.S. and world energy demand. The future dependence of the energy economy on breeder reactors raises a host of institutional and economic questions as well as the environmental and safety issues. Present and projected reactors are designed to generate electricity. Currently, in the United States only about a quarter of the total energy consumed is used in generating electricity. The shift to an electric energy economy based on breeder reactors, would require major adjustments in the transportation, residential, and industrial sectors of the economy. The character and time scale of such adjustments have not been subjected to detailed analyses.

Summary of Fuel Availability

If the total energy demand in the United States grows at an annual rate of 3.2 percent, representative of the years 1950 to 1974, domestic coal reserves can supply this demand for about fifty years, while domestic oil and natural gas reserves can only make a minor contribution. Nuclear power in the form of conventional light water reactors is capable of adding only a few years' supply to the total energy demand. If domestic coal resources can be converted to reserves, then the energy supply measured in thermal units is sufficient for at least one to two centuries. Similarly, the use of uranium in breeder reactors can make this fuel sufficient for times measured in hundreds of years.

The use of either coal or uranium poses difficult environmental problems in mining and in the control of effluents. In the case of coal, its use would be enhanced by the further development of technologies for more efficient and cleaner burning, such as fluidized bed combustion; technologies for transforming coal to gas and oil; and technologies for the more efficient transportation of energy. The further development of the breeder reactor hinges on the solution of a host of problems dealing with the handling of, and prevention of diversion of, plutonium; and the development of acceptable methods of dealing with the waste products of the operation of the nuclear fuel cycle.

The shift toward either a coal- or breeder-based energy economy will require the shift of substantial economic resources from other sectors of the economy to support the development of the extraction of new energy sources and the production of energy. At present in the United States, energy extraction and production represents about 5 percent of GNP. The development of new resources could conceivably double the energy part of GNP. Such a doubling could have disruptive effects on the economy if the change takes place over a short period of time—on the order of a decade. Adjustments over considerably longer periods could likely take place without major alterations in the functioning of the economy.

AVAILABILITY OF NONENERGY RAW MATERIAL

While the effects of the 1973/74 oil embargo have highlighted the impending shortages in certain energy sources, relatively less attention has been focused on the longer-term availability of metals and other raw materials. Because of their importance to society, it is necessary to discuss their geologic occurrence and means of extraction in order to place gross limits on their future availability.

With some exceptions—such as gold and platinum—metals do not occur as elements in the earth's crust. They are present as compounds of two or more elements; the compounds are called minerals. In recovering metals from the mineral, the least expensive option is to extract and process only the minerals that contain the desired metal. In practice this means choosing those minerals that require the least expenditure of energy to bring about chemical disintegration and release of the metal. Sulfides, oxides, hydroxides, and carbonates all require less energy for their disintegration than the highly refractive silicates that make up the bulk of the rocks in the earth's crust.

The production of metals from ores and rocks requires two separate and quite different steps. The first involves mining the desired mineral from the ground and separating it from valueless and unwanted minerals with which it occurs. In the concentration process the material is crushed to a fine grain and then the minerals are separated on the basis of differences in physical properties of the desired mineral and the waste products. While the crushing and concentration of desired minerals are not very energy-intensive processes, the next step in separating the metal, the smelting and refining process, is. During smelting the concentrated mineral is broken down chemically and the desired metal is separated from the unwanted elements. Because of the energy requirements of smelting, less refractory minerals are selected as the principal sources of the desired metal.

The upper tens of kilometers of the earth form the earth's crust and contain minerals that are accessible with current or projected technologies. The crust under the continents has the average chemical composition given in Table 4-19, although individual rock types vary greatly in composition. Several of the most abundant elements are those that are in common use today: aluminum, iron, magnesium, titanium, manganese, and phosphorous. Minerals containing these elements, present in abundance, can, in principle, be mechanically separated and then refined and smelted. For these elements the entire crust can be considered a potential resource. The parent minerals occur in high enough abundance in the earth's crust that usual techniques of concentration can be employed. Given the total mass of the earth's crust, there is virtually an infinite source of these abundant elements to be recovered by conventional methods, although at a relatively high energy cost because of difficulties in refining and smelting refractory silicate minerals.

Table 4-19. Concentration of Major Chemical Elements in the Continental Crust

Element	Concentration (weight percent)
Oxygen	45.20
Silicon	27.20
Aluminum	8.00
Iron	5.80
Calcium	5.06
Magnesium	2.77
Sodium	2.32
Potassium	1.68
Titanium	.86
Hydrogen	.14
Manganese	.10
Phophorous	.10
Total	99.23

The geochemically scarce metals—those present in concentrations much lower than the abundant elements listed in Table 4-19—present an entirely different situation. Rarely do the scarce elements form separate minerals that can be separated and concentrated by usual mechanical methods. Instead, these scarce elements form a dilute solution with the more abundant elements in common rock-forming minerals. For example, lead is found in concentrations of about 10 parts per million in common rocks, contrasting with much higher concentrations, 10-15 percent, in rare ore deposits. Lead does not occur as a separate mineral in common rock, but appears in a chemical solid solution with potassium in the mineral feldspar. Concentration of the mineral feldspar by conventional means will lead to a concentrate with a proportion of lead of no more than about 100 parts per million. In order to release the lead from the silicate cage in which it is chemically bound, the entire mineral must be broken down and the small concentrations of lead separated chemically or by some other means from the other much more abundant constituents such as potassium. This is a complicated and very energy-intensive process. The extremely low concentration of lead and the high energy requirements for separation make lead in common rocks a highly uneconomical resource. This implies that when ores having a high concentration of lead in minerals in which lead is a major component are exhausted, lead will no longer be available except at an exceedingly high cost in energy.

Lead and other geochemically scarce metals are mined today from ores containing minerals with a high concentration of these metals. Ore bodies are the result of unusual geological processes that have naturally brought the metal to a concentration of a few percent in the rock rather than a few parts per million found in abundant crustal materials. Of the total amount of scarce metals in the crust, only a small fraction is found in rich ores; by far the larger fraction is found in very small concentrations in ordinary rock. A consequence of this bimodal distribution of metals in ores and rocks is that there exists a concentration of the metal in the rock below which the metal does not appear in a mineral of its own. Instead it appears in a solid solution with other elements in common rock-forming silicates. There is thus a mineralogical barrier or limit to concentration below which the metal appears only in common rock-forming minerals, and at very low concentrations in these minerals. The limit, with a few exceptions such as gold and uranium, appears to lie at concentrations between 0.1 to 0.01 percent. At concentrations of less than 0.1 to 0.01 percent, the scarce metal occurs only as a minor solid solution substitute for the more common elements and not as a separate mineral that can be concentrated mechanically in the usual way. Gold and uranium form separate minerals at concentrations of less than 0.01 percent, but they are the exceptions to the rule.

The total amount or mass of metal in concentrated ores, rocks in which scarce metals occur in minerals of their own, can be estimated if the assumption is made that the total amount of the element in rich ore deposits is proportional to the concentration of the metal in the crust. This assumption is suggested by the fact that the discovered reserves of various metals are roughly proportional to the crustal concentration. With this assumption all that is needed to calculate total available ore is an estimate of the total amount of one metal. The National Academy of Sciences' Committee on Mineral Resources and the Environment (COMRATE)(7) has carried out the calculation leading to an estimate of the abundance of one such metal, copper. The committee estimates that the barrier at which copper no longer forms a separate mineral occurs at a concentration of 0.1 percent. It also estimates that no more than 0.01 percent of the total amount of copper in the continental crust will be found in ore bodies with a copper concentration of 0.1 percent or greater. The committee's reasoning was based on the volume percentage of mineralized rock in the most intensely mineralized region so far discovered and on the frequency of copper deposits in the crust. The committee's figure of 0.01 percent must be taken as a maximum possible yield. The maximum amounts of scarce metals concentrated in ore deposits, calculated relative to copper, are given in Table 4-20. These values are intended to indicate the

Table 4-20. Estimate of Maximum Quantities of Metals in Ore Deposits in Continental Crust

Metal	Abundance in Continental Crust (percent)	Maximum Tonnage in Ore Deposits (millions of metric tons)
Copper	0.0058	1,000
Gold	.0000002	0.034
Lead	.0010	170
Mercury	.0000002	0.34
Molybdenum	.00012	20
Nickel	.0072	1,200
Niobium	.0020	340
Platinum	.0000005	0.084
Silver	.000008	1.3
Tantalum	.00058	100
Tin	.00015	25
Tungsten	.00010	17
Uranium	.00016	27

maximum amount of metal that can be recovered from ores; the remainder of the metals are in exceedingly low concentration in common rocks.

Using the above kind of reasoning, COMRATE estimated that present reserves plus past production of copper already amount to 3 percent of the world's ultimate yield from ore deposits. The equivalent figure for the United States is estimated to be 16 percent. With such large depletions the time scale for exhaustion, assuming exponentially increasing consumption, cannot be more than a few decades.

For the geochemically scarce metals found in high concentrations only in rare ore deposits, the concept of a finite resource is appropriate. Like hydrocarbon fuels, there is a finite reservoir of materials available in a mode that can be exploited. The scarce metals are thus different from the abundant metals for which the entire crust can be considered a resource. Copper is definitely a limited resource, while iron and aluminum are essentially unlimited. At present rates of usage, combined with an exponential rate of increase, it will take only a few decades to exhaust the readily available ore resources of copper. On the other hand, aluminum—present in a variety of common rock-forming minerals—can be expected to be available in substantial quantities for the indefinite future. Once bauxite or other rich reserves of aluminum are depleted, alternate deposits of aluminum in such minerals as anorthite or nepheline would become abundant sources of the metal. In summary, geochemically abundant metals such as iron, aluminum, titanium, and manganese will be plentiful in the indefinite future, while the supply of scarce metals such as copper, lead, and zinc will be exhausted in a matter of decades.

These observations on abundant versus scarce materials suggest the priorities for future research. Studies should be undertaken to identify how the geochemically abundant metals can substitute for the geochemically scarce metals. For example, steps have already been taken with aluminum replacing copper in a variety of uses. A further research priority should be in the area of the metallurgical treatment of the abundant elements. The means of smelting and refining silicate minerals will differ from the classical metallurgy of simpler compounds. Finally, there should be continued emphasis on reuse, particularly of the scarce metals.

ECONOMIC GROWTH AND RESOURCE AVAILABILITY

The issues of the availability of nonrenewable resources and of economic growth are closely linked. Growth has depended on, and indeed demanded, abundant natural resources, particularly energy. The relationship between economic growth and natural resources is well illustrated by the pattern of events in the United States between 1900 and 1970:

1. Population climbed from 76 million to over 200 million, or by an increase of less than a factor of three.
2. Gross National Product expanded from around $100 billion to about $1 trillion (1967 dollars), or by a factor of ten.
3. Natural resource consumption (excluding food) increased from $7 billion to $35 billion, or by a factor of five.
4. Energy utilization alone increased from $2 billion to more than $20 billion a year, or by a factor of ten.

Gross National Product and energy utilization have had parallel rates of growth, leading to the often-quoted observation that an abundant supply of cheap energy is essential to economic growth. Total demand on all natural resources went up at half the rate of GNP, or energy increase, but at almost twice the rate of population increase. The proportion of GNP devoted to energy resources is relatively small, in absolute terms. The extraction, preparation, and consumption of energy amounts to about 5 percent of GNP. What makes energy nevertheless a subject of great concern is that, unlike any other resource except labor, energy enters into every sector of the economy. It is input that is small but critical. At the same time it follows that the key factor in the energy equation is not the cost of energy but its availability. On the average, a doubling of energy cost over five years would only preempt an extra 1 percent of economic product each year. This increase could be accommodated without reducing real income. However, a reduction of energy availability by 50 percent over 5 years would virtually paralyze large sectors of the economy and substantially change the life-style of a modern industrial society.

In simplified terms, growth in a modern economy includes the following items. Individuals wish to acquire goods. Producers increase output to meet demand. This means more jobs and probably greater earnings for the worker. The newly employed, together with employees who are earning more, have additional money to spend or save. In either case, more production is necessary. As the economy grows, more nonrenewable resources are used. As fossil fuels and metals become scarce, a greater fraction of income and savings goes into securing natural resources. This, then, implies fewer dollars for other goods and services and a slowing of the overall increase in real income. Until the 1973/74 oil embargo, the U.S. government and industry operated largely on the assumption of an unlimited supply of energy and of all natural resources. The dependence of economic growth on an abundant energy supply was assumed and the availability of that supply not seriously questioned.

Since economic growth both in the United States and abroad was a major goal, government planning and implementation were concerned largely with stimulating demand. To implement a policy of increased demand, the U.S. government used government spending, taxing, borrowing, and movements in the bank rate. To stimulate a lagging economy, government prods demand by stepping up its own spending, thereby placing more money in the hands of individuals or corporations, or both. For example, in the early 1970s government stimulation caused demand to outrun supply. During that period there was a worldwide boom; in the United States the Federal Reserve Board, the Administration, and the Congress each took turns trying to forestall a downturn. As a result, demand continued to increase at a rate greater than could be met by scarce natural resources—for example, natural gas. In virtually all countries, national policy toward the use of natural resources has resulted from a heritage of an era of abundance and low prices. These policies have called for economic growth based on the lavish use of irreplaceable or difficult-to-replace nonrenewable resources.

In view of the limited nature of many of the natural resources, assumptions of the past need serious reconsideration. The goals of a fuel and materials policy for the United States should include a reduction in the rate of growth of demand as well as an increase in supply, taking into account recoverable quantities and time intervals needed for major readjustments in the materials and technology employed. This will require a comprehensive natural resources policy that includes the following:

1 . Reduction of demand by conservation, substitution, and new technology.
2 . Increase supply by exploration, investment, and new technology.
3 . Prepare for emergency shortfalls, including stockpiling of materials vulnerable to foreign actions.
4 . Determine the management method, private or government, or a combination of both.

In all of this it is very important to consider the issue of lead times. The problems of time and money dominate any discussion of materials and fuel scarcity. It takes at least five years to locate and bring offshore oil into production. It takes ten years or more to put a nuclear plant into operation, and at least as long to open up a new coal mine.

The more exotic sources of energy or materials are decades away.

Demand virgin materials can be reduced by conservation. The demand for geochemically scarce metals will be lowered by the substitution of geochemically abundant metals. This substitution will require the development of improvements in technology that will permit the smelting and refining of refractory silicate minerals.

In the short term, major efforts should be mounted to extend the supply of oil and natural gas reserves and resources. These are limited and will be depleted in a few decades. Because of this, new investment will be required to bring into production coal and the coal-based synthetic fuels. Since nuclear fuels are certain to make some contribution to the overall fuel economy, uranium reserves and resources need to be better defined and expanded if possible. Since uranium, coal, and oil are all finite resources, the development of new technologies to use less limited resources, such as fusion and solar power, needs attention.

As long as their energy programs are primarily based on oil and gas, the Western nations will continue to be dependent on foreign sources, particularly the OPEC countries. To guard against future embargoes, the Western nations need a standby capacity to carry them through any emergency. In the longer term a synthetic fuel capability is badly needed by the United States to counteract any threat of an embargo.

Government is heavily involved in the fuel and raw materials industries through such mechanisms as tax policies, leasing, and the various permit programs. Government also plays a major role through budgetary and monetary means in determining whether and to what extent the economy is a demand economy. A further role of government is that of financing key research and development activities that will encourage new technology, conservation, and the capability for substitution. The future degree of government involvement remains a matter for debate. There is general agreement that government should take the lead in providing for an emergency stockpile of key materials. Less clear is the extent of government financing of new developmental activities, particularly of synthetic fuels. Even less certain is whether government should participate in the marketplace by placing a floor under the price of synthetic fuels.

In sum, fossil and nuclear fuels are finite resources with a lifetime of a few decades for oil and a century for coal. Solar and fusion sources have the potential for supplying energy for long periods of time, but the technology remains to be developed. Scarce metals, in the geochemical sense, are also finite resources. While the geochemically abundant elements are in principle nearly infinite, the time scale for depletion depends heavily on the nature of the economy. If government policies foster a demand economy, where increased demand drives growth, then the time scale for depletion is diminished. If, on the other hand, the economy emphasizes a reduction of demand by conservation, substitution, and new technology, the time scale for depletion is increased. Because of the nature of the economic dislocations that are bound to arise in any shift from one energy or material source to another, the lengthening of the time scale is desirable in that this allows time for adjustment.

REFERENCES

(1) Parent, J.D., and Linden, H. *A Survey of United States and Total World Production Proved Reserves and Remaining Recoverable Resources of Fossil Fuels and Uranium as of December 31, 1975.* Institute of Gas Technology, 1977.
(2) U.S. Department of the Interior. Bureau of Mines Industry Surveys. *Weekly Coal Report.* No. 3058. Washington, D.C.: U.S. Government Printing Office, April 1976.
(3) U.S. Department of the Interior. Bureau of Mines. *Mineral Industry Surveys, Petroleum Statement, December 1975.* Washington, D.C.: U.S. Government Printing Office, April 1976.
(4) Organization for Economic Cooperation and Development. *Statistics of Energy, 1959-1973.* Paris, 1974.
(5) Ford Foundation Energy Policy Project. *A Time to Choose.* Cambridge: Ballinger, 1974.
(6) U.S. National Committee of the World Energy Conference. *Survey of Energy Resources, 1974.* New York, 1974.
(7) National Academy of Sciences. *Mineral Resources and the Environment.* Washington, D.C. 1975.
(8) Schurr, S., ed. *Energy, Economic Growth and the Environment.* Baltimore: Johns Hopkins Press, 1972.
(9) United Nations. Department of Economics and Social Affairs. Statistical Office. *World Energy Suplies 1950-1974.* New York, 1976.
(10) U.S. Bureau of the Census. *Projections of the Population of the United States, 1975-2050.* Series P-25, No. 601. Washington, D.C.: 1975. U.S. Government Printing Office, 1975.
(11) American Gas Association; American Petroleum Institute; and Canadian Petroleum Institute. *Reserves of Crude Oil, Natural Gas Liquid and Natural Gas in the United States and Canada and the United States Productive Capcity as of December 31, 1975.* Vol. 30, 1976.
(12) "Worldwide Oil at a Glance," *Oil and Gas Journal* 73 (1975):86.
(13) "Productive Capacity Grows as World Demand Falters," *World Oil* (1975):181.
(14) Moody, J., and Geiger, R. "Petroleum Resources: How Much Oil and Where?" *Technology Review* 39 (1975).
(15) Averitt, P. *Coal Resources of the United States, January 1, 1974.* U.S. Geological Survey Bulletin No. 1412, 1975.

(16) National Petroleum Council Committee on U.S. Energy Outlook. *U.S. Energy Outlook.* Washington, 1972.

(17) Energy Research and Development Administration. *Statistical Data of the Uranium Industry.* Grand Junction, Colorado, 1976.

(18) Weinberg, A. *Report of the Cornell Workshop on the Major Issues of a National Energy Research and Development Program.* College of Engineering, Cornell University, 1973.

(19) Organization for Economic Cooperation and Development. *Uranium: Resources, Production, and Demand.* A Joint Report by the OECD Nuclear Energy Agency and the International Atomic Energy Agency. Paris, 1975.

(20) Skinner, B. *Earth Resources.* 2nd ed. Englewood Cliffs, N.J.: Prentice-Hall, 1976.

(21) Skinner, B. "A Second Iron Age Ahead?" *American Scientist* 64 (1976):258.

Chapter Five

Discussion of "Long-Term Availability of Natural Resources," by Gordon MacDonald

John R. Meyer

Professor MacDonald's paper on the "Long-Term Availability of Natural Resources" represents a very useful point of departure for analyzing that always difficult question of the extent to which future economic development is likely to be seriously constrained by shortages of energy and raw materials. It is an impressive tour de force. He summarizes and organizes a remarkable range of statistics relevant to assessing the relationship between supply and demand for natural resources, energy in particular. Above all, his paper is replete with suggestions for further analysis and research.

My remarks, in fact, will be primarily focused on these very possibilities. As an economist, of course, I find discussions of demand and supply inherently interesting, if not intriguing. However, as I read Professor MacDonald's paper, I also find his approach to these concepts at least somewhat different from those to which I have become professionally accustomed or attuned. Specifically, price as a rationing mechanism plays a somewhat minor role in Professor MacDonald's narrative.

A particular charm of the market mechanism for economists is that it induces specialization, and thereby efficiency, in the use of factors of production. Even noneconomists are probably familiar with Adam Smith's famous Pin Factory as an illustration of these principles. In general, economists look to the market mechanism to allocate resources and consumption so as to maximize economic well-being. For an economist there are many, many benefits derivable from a well-operating market mechanism, but almost surely the most important is that it helps insure—or at least substantially increases the probability—that various resources will be used efficiently and consumption will pursue logical and rational patterns that maximize society's satisfactions.

I was therefore struck by Professor MacDonald's central metric for relating supply and demand, his "Index Years of Availability." Index years as he defines them are "an estimate of the time required to exhaust either the reserves or resources of a given fuel if that fuel is used to supply the *total* demand for energy for the world and the United States" (emphasis added). The striking thing to an economist in this definition is the use of the world total. Specifically, there is only a very limited meaning in such a construct for an economist since, as Professor MacDonald points out, many raw materials and sources of energy are rather specialized in their adaptability to different functions. A more useful construct, therefore, might be years of availability of a resource or its reserves, taking into account necessary, probable, or optimal specialization of resources by use. This line of inquiry led me to speculate to what extent Professor MacDonald's major conclusions might be altered by shifting from his generalized metric to one that was more specialized. Specifically, what would be the adequacy of various energy reserves if only used in their most productive applications?

To perform such an exercise, an identification must first be made of the major functional uses of energy. I must admit that I am not enough of a specialist in these matters to be able to specify this distribution with any precision. However, by manipulating some of the numbers in Professor MacDonald's paper and by calling on some of my own knowledge of at least one major application, transportation, I did manage to construct some figures that I think are at least suggestive. Specifically, it would seem that about 25 percent of U.S. energy is consumed by transportation, 35 percent for electrical generation, 30 percent for space heating (exclusive of electrical), and 10 percent for a variety of miscellaneous uses, the most important of which are direct inputs to industry. I would stress that these numbers are tendered as only rough approximations to facilitate discussion. I do believe, though, that they are within some rough order of accuracy. Perhaps, too, greater precision would be impossible without more detailed information than is now available on energy use in the United States.

This crude functional breakdown does, in turn, permit one to make some inferences about how energy resources might be deployed more sensibly in a world, say, in which the market mechanism had not been too inhibited and prices had been permitted to allocate fuels to their most logical or economically efficient use. Technological limitations also play a role, of course. Thus, transportation under current technological conditions is heavily dependent on the use of oil derivatives as an energy source. For the generation of electricity, by contrast, the technology is not so limiting; for this application one would expect that in a more rational world natural gas would not be used and the major reliance would be on coal and uranium, as augmented by hydroelectric power.

Development of recent concerns about air pollution would only fortify this conclusion, since cleaning up air pollution is apparently characterized by considerable economies of scale. Accordingly, in a rational allocation, one would expect clean fuels, such as natural gas, to be used primarily or almost exclusively in small-scale applications such as space heating; cleaning up air pollution at a relatively few electrical generation plants should be, by comparison, relatively inexpensive. In sum, in a world in which markets were permitted to achieve a rational allocation of resources one would expect that: (1) transportation energy requirements would be mainly, although not exclusively, satisfied by oil derivatives; (2) space heating would be primarily done by natural gas and electricity; and (3) electrical generation would be primarily performed by the burning of coal or the development of nuclear energy, augmented wherever possible by hydroelectric power.

With such specialization, the consumption of various major energy sources (at current or 1976 economic activity levels) might be as reported in column 1 of Table 5-1. I would emphasize that I am *not* asserting that these consumption levels represent a sensible target for

Table 5-1. U.S. Energy Reserves at Current Use Levels with Specialization by Sources and Uses

	Annual Consumption (quads/yr)	Recoverable Reserves	Recoverable Resources
		(years)	
Crude Oil (exclusive of tar sands and oil shale)	18	10	50-115
Crude Oil (inclusive of tar sands and oil shale)	—	—	370-725
Natural Gas	15	16	36-87
Coal	23	260	950-1,740
Uranium	13	24-1,500	100-8,000
Hydroelectric	4	N.A.	N.A.
	73		

U.S. energy policy. For example, it is not at all clear to me that total self-reliance or independence in energy resources is a sensible policy for the United States; if petroleum can be imported from abroad for a reasonable price—with reasonableness being defined as being cheaper than alternative and equivalent sources—then it is not apparent to me that we should eschew all imports. With the continuation of imports, of course, 18 quads per year of crude oil consumption may well be an impractically low goal. Similarly, it is obvious that one could not move quickly from the present U.S. production of approximately 12 to 13 quads of coal per year to 23 or so. I have also finessed the coal versus nuclear debate for electrical generation; in constructing Table 5-1, I simply assumed that these two fuels would share equally in filling any void created by withdrawing liquid hydrocarbons from electrical generation.

Though counterfactual in construct, the numbers in column 1 of Table 5-1 do indicate some directions in which American energy consumption might sensibly move. The figures in columns 2 and 3 also indicate that with specialization in use, and reliance on U.S. domestic reserves and resources only, we have *slightly* more time to adjust our economic patterns than would be suggested by the numbers in Professor MacDonald's Table 4-17, a table that would seem most directly comparable to my Table 5-1.

The numbers in my table do *not*, however, indicate anything more than a minor qualification to Professor MacDonald's major conclusion; namely, that if the U.S. is determined to be more self-sufficient in energy, we must make a major shift from oil and gas to coal and nuclear energy. We may have three or four decades to do this rather than one or two, but the inevitability of making some such shift seems well established.

These extra decades, though, can be important. As Professor MacDonald notes, a gradual evolution is the only sensible way for such a transition. For an economist, moreover, it is also obvious that the simplest and most effective way to bring about this gradual transition is to unleash the pricing mechanism in energy markets. Without much question, much of what we now consider to be a natural gas shortage is one that is artificially created by government action—specifically, regulation of natural gas prices to levels that dissuade seeking of new supplies or through exploitation of existing sources and proper conservation of that output we now have. Much the same applies, with only slightly less vigor, to government intervention in crude oil and uranium prices. In a certain sense, present energy crises are not so much functions of a *lack* of government policy as perhaps a consequence of too much policy—although in deference to government it has *not* created all the cartel arrangements in the energy industries by any means. I should also quickly add that a more coherent government policy toward developmental research, stockpiling, and other such possibilities still has much to recommend it.

I was tempted at times, reading through Professor MacDonald's paper, to wonder whether the whole exercise of attempting to estimate resource availability really has much meaning in a world of cartels and government controls. My skepticism surfaced whenever Professor MacDonald indicated the extent to which availability was, as an economist would have guessed right from the start, dependent on relative factor prices. In essence, the characteristics that determine availability are also a function of availability. In a market economy, the feedback between supply shortages and demand excesses would be pronounced and reasonably prompt; these feedbacks, moreover, should provide a bit more advance warning of where demand excesses or shortages are likely to develop next, and thereby provide investment incentives to forestall the worst of such developments in the future.

This does not mean, of course, that there wouldn't be transition difficulties in moving from where we are now to a less regulated environment. Nevertheless, these difficulties may be easily exaggerated. Oil, after all, is used to heat many homes and its price has shot up about as much as gas might if deregulated; society has been buffeted by this oil price change, but does seem to have survived. In general, the maldistribution of wealth in today's regulated structure may be as great as under deregulation. Furthermore, in an economy such as ours with well-developed fiscal mechanisms, equity issues are almost surely better treated by tax policy or direct government transfers than by market distortions.

I would conclude by observing that I have long been struck by the sharply different intellectual approaches that economists, on the one hand, and physical scientists, on the other, bring to these considerations of identifying resource availability and needs. Engineers, I might add, seem to fall somewhere in between the two. At any rate, most (though certainly not all) physical scientists, particularly biologists and ecologists, when pursuing these problems seem to have an affinity for unstable or degenerative models. (I would immediately remind everyone that Professor MacDonald is a geophysicist.) Economists, by contrast, are clearly much more comfortable with relatively stable and equilibrium-oriented systems; that is, economists seemingly prefer models that, when disturbed by an outside shock, return to some acceptable equilibrium value. Many biological or ecological models, by contrast, degenerate or move inexorably toward what can be construed as intolerable or highly unfavorable asymptotic values. As a consequence, it is easy enough to divide the different disciplines into Professor MacDonald's optimists and pessimists. For those of us coming from the "dismal science," it is rather heady stuff to be known as optimists!

Clearly a certain pessimism or alarm is to be found in many physical science analyses of these problems that is not widely shared by economists. Indeed, the natural instinct of an economist when encountering unstable or degenerative systems is to seek devices to make them automatically stable or to presume that human behavior almost invariably has a large corrective component built into it. The pricing mechanism, as I have pointed out (perhaps ad nauseum), is surely one of the more potent of these corrective possibilities. I suspect that we economists overemphasize its potential, but on the other hand, I also suspect that many others vastly underestimate its possibilities.

Chapter Six

Discussion of "Long-Term Availability of Natural Resources" by Gordon MacDonald

Bruce Yandle, Jr.

Gordon MacDonald's paper has three components: a discussion of nonrenewable resources and how their scarcity may be viewed; an identification of scarcity with respect to presently defined energy resources and other minerals; and a discussion of economic growth and the attendant policy for dealing with scarcity. My comments follow the same outline.

PESSIMISTS AND OPTIMISTS

The first part of the MacDonald paper develops an interesting psychological interpretation of resource scarcity. Depending on one's belief in or interpretation of data, one is either classified as a pessimistic pessimist, an optimistic pessimist, a pessimistic optimist, or an optimistic optimist.

At one extreme are individuals who do not accept the idea that particular physical resources matter, at least in the long run. For example, the optimistic optimist would not have become distraught in the 1800s when the world appeared to running out of whale oil, a principal source of energy at the time.[1] It would not have been technical knowledge about whales or other energy sources that would have made the double optimist less concerned. That viewpoint, as suggested by MacDonald, may have been this: Whale oil is not the question, energy or utility is. And given the incentive structure of a market system, if there is to be a specific solution, it will be developed.[2] If there is no specific energy solution, the price system will allocate whatever resources available in a way superior to any other system. That is, the optimistic optimist's concern is how to draw on human *resourcefulness* when faced with scarce natural resources.

At the other extreme, using the same example, were the pessimistic pessimists. These people perhaps believed that they knew all that would ever be known. In other words, they were convinced that the world's store of knowledge had reached its zenith just at the time when whale oil hit its nadir. Thus, in their book, rising prices would not produce whales. Facing the exhaustion of whale oil, the double pessimist must have: (1) moved to the tropics or the land of the midnight sun; (2) tried to cartelize the whale industry and ration the oil; or (3) called for repentance, for the end of the world was at hand.

On the other hand, those between the extreme optimists and pessimists probably cursed the rising price of whale oil, which made them seem poor, and in the meantime tried to modify their lifestyles in order to economize on energy. Other greedy souls saw an opportunity to get rich and got busy looking for substitute fuels. The high price of whale oil prodded them along and made the search potentially profitable. Those fortunate ones who found new energy sources—flaxseed oil and ultimately kerosene—got rich by increasing the supply of energy, which led to even lower prices. They no doubt joined the ranks of the double optimists. Those entrepreneurs who went broke in their search for new energy sources were called pessimistic optimists. They had the right idea but the wrong solution. That is, the price system worked, but not as they intended.

Thus, in the first part of his paper, MacDonald reminds us that how one views any problem of scarcity—particularly that of nonrenewable resources—depends on one's acceptance of the price system as a means of communication.[3] I would put greater emphasis on the ability of efficient markets to minimize the problems of scarcity, to maximize human welfare no matter how scarce a given resource in the short run, and, if a future substitute for a nonrenewable resource is to be found, to identify it and bring it forward at the optimal time. Of course, my emphasis generally reflects the economist's view.

THE DIMENSIONS OF SCARCITY

The dimensions of scarcity are important, no matter what view one takes of the problem. And the second and third parts of MacDonald's paper give some important insights into some of these dimensions. As an addition to the data he has presented, I would suggest that further emphasis be given to the *economic* nature of reserves and man's historic success in dealing with lower quality ores.

The recent report of the National Commission on Materials and

Shortages contains the kind of evidence I have in mind.[4] For example, the question of "known reserves" is discussed in some detail. We are reminded that such reserves are a function of price:

> Resources are more properly measured in economic terms. Additional productive land can be "created" by swamp drainage, irrigation, forest clearing, etc., and yields per acre can be increased. New mineral resources can be "discovered" by investments in exploration and by technological change which allows the mining of ores previously not amendable. In other words, advancing technology can add to supplies of "fixed" resources.[5]

While the statement is based on economic theory it is buttressed with empirical evidence. Consider the percentage increases in known reserves calculated for the period 1950 to 1970, shown in Table 6-1. Bear in mind that these are increases in known reserves after twenty years of production. As reported in Table 6-1, tungsten is the only metal listed where reserves declined. Such evidence suggests that the market or price system has communicated scarcity and has in the past been reliable in providing an incentive to listen for the market signal.

MacDonald's paper suggests that the approaching age of scarcity may raise serious questions about the ability of the market to maximize humanity's social well being. In other words, this new age of scarcity comes at a time when the old rules may not work. Of course history is a pageant of scarcity. Not only do we encounter new scarce

Table 6-1. Increases in Known Reserves: 1950 to 1970

Ore	Percentage Increases in Known Reserves
Iron	1,221
Manganese	27
Chromite	675
Tungsten	−30
Copper	179
Lead	115
Zinc	61
Tin	10
Bauxite	279
Potash	2,360
Phosphates	4,430
Oil	507

Source: National Commission on Materials and Shortages, *Government and the Nation's Resources* (Washington: Government Printing Office, 1976), p. 16.

resources but we are often confounded by our scarce knowledge. Both scarcities appear to have been dealt with historically. But let us focus on a very brief period—current history in a sense—to see how economic forces have driven technology to reduce the cost of minerals.

Table 6-2 shows a measure of real cost for five important minerals: copper, iron, zinc, aluminum, and crude petroleum. The index numbers in the table were developed by William Nordhaus for the years 1900 to 1970 and are the ratios of the nominal U.S. price of the commodity to the average wage of American workers.[6] I have extended the series to include 1974, 1975, and 1976 data.

As may be noted these rough indexes shows dramatically lower costs for all five commodities when compared to 1900. The 1976 index-es, when compared with 1970, are lower for copper and aluminum. The index for zinc is 50 percent higher today than it was in 1970. Iron ore is 3 percent more costly. And crude petroleum is more than twice as cost-ly. However, even with its higher cost, crude oil is just slightly more costly in real terms than it was in 1950.

Results similar to these have been reported by Richard Erb in his re-cent survey of international raw materials.[7] In Erb's analysis of world prices of petroleum, copper, tin, lead, zinc, and aluminum, he notes that "Inflation-adjusted prices began to rise for lead and zinc in late 1971, for tin and copper in late 1972, and for aluminum in mid-1973."[8] This noted increase reached its peak in 1974 and was pressured by two actions by the U.S. government. First, Erb notes that "U.S. zinc refinery capacity was reduced by 17 percent during 1971, to a large ex-tent because of pollution controls."[9] Second, the United States impos-ed embargoes on soybeans in 1973, which caused Japan particularly to begin stockpiling commodities, including metals, as a protection against future shortages.[10]

After the 1974 peak, metal prices began to fall on international

Table 6-2.   Price of Minerals Relative to Average Cost of Labor (1970 = 100)

	1900	1920	1940	1950	1960	1970	1974	1975	1976
Copper	785	226	121	99	82	100	101	76	74
Iron	620	287	144	112	120	100	98	93	103
Zinc	794	400	272	256	126	100	111	100	152
Aluminum	3,150	859	287	166	134	100	92	97	81
Crude Petroleum	1,034	726	198	213	135	100	160	224	234

Source: 1920-1970: W.D. Nordhaus, "Resources as a Constraint on Growth," *American Economic Review* (May 1974), p. 24, as reported in National Commission on Supplies and Shortages, *Government and the Nation's Resources* (Washington: U.S. Government Printing Office, December 1976), p. 19; 1974-1976 calculated from U.S. Department of Commerce data. Crude Oil price based on refiner acquisition cost for composite crude.

markets, eventually reaching or going below the 1967 price. Again, however, zinc was the exception. The point is this: significant technological change has occurred across the years and, as a result, output has increased from lower grade ores and deeper wells and at a lower cost.

Over the last 26 years, mining's share of total investment in new plant and equipment in the United States has fallen, not increased.[11] That is, our national experience still indicates that many stubborn scarcities have been dealt with at a diminishing cost to society. Since market forces were able to function rather freely during much of the period, the result described might increase the ranks of the optimists. However, governments around the world now have a heavy hand in the control of basic metals and petroleum.

In the last part of his paper, MacDonald describes the economic process and suggests that "as fossil fuels and metals become scarce, a greater fraction of income and savings goes into securing natural resources." Since we are not given a time period for the development, one might conclude that the time of scarcity has not yet arrived. However, some people might debate that conclusion. By examining data on personal consumption in the United States for the period 1960 to 1976 one can see if there have been any apparent changes in the share of consumption expenditures going to commodities related to nonrenewable resources. Table 6-3 reports the consumption data.

It may be surprising to see that the proportion of expenditures out of consumption for all durable goods was almost constant across the 16-year period. Furthermore, the proportion of all consumption expenditures spent for gasoline and oil was the same for 1976 as for 1970, and relatively constant. The same result is seen for fuel oil and coal. Simply put, there appears to have been no disruption of consumer expenditure patterns among the broad and narrow categories reported. In other words, consumers have found substitutes for the higher priced commodities. Perhaps even the optimists would be surprised. But the story is not complete.

POLICY IMPLICATIONS AND CONSTRAINTS

On the basis of his presentation of data and knowledge of the social environment, MacDonald recommends certain goals regarding national policy for dealing with energy and mineral resources. They include a reduction in the rate of growth of demand; an increase in supply; stockpiling of vulnerable materials; and a determined management policy.

The double optimist would quickly suggest that the policymakers

Table 6-3. Proportion of Personal Consumption Expenditures by Major Category (current dollars 1960, 1965, 1970-1975) (percent)[a]

Expenditures	1960	1965	1970	1971	1972	1973	1974	1975	(est.) 1976
Durable Goods	13.3	14.6	13.7	14.5	15.2	15.3	13.7	13.5	14.6
Motor Vehicle & Parts	6.1	6.9	5.6	6.5	6.9	6.8	5.4	5.4	6.6
Furniture & Household Equipment	5.4	5.7	5.9	5.9	6.1	6.3	6.2	5.9	5.9
Other Durables	1.8	1.9	2.1	2.1	2.3	2.2	2.2	2.2	2.1
Nondurable Goods	46.5	43.6	42.8	41.6	40.8	41.2	42.4	42.0	40.8
Total Food	21.7	19.9	19.2	18.3	17.8	18.1	18.8	19.0	18.5
Nondurables Less Food	24.8	23.9	23.6	23.3	23.0	23.1	23.6	23.0	22.3
Clothing & Shoes	8.2	7.8	7.5	7.6	7.5	7.6	7.4	7.2	6.9
Gasoline & Oil	3.7	3.4	3.6	3.5	3.5	3.4	4.1	4.0	3.8
Fuel Oil & Coal	1.2	1.0	.9	.8	.9	1.0	1.1	1.0	1.0
Other Nondurables	8.5	8.6	8.8	8.6	8.5	8.5	8.5	8.3)	10.6
Alcoholic Beverages	3.3	3.1	2.9	2.8	2.7	2.6	2.6	2.5)	
Services	40.2	41.6	43.5	43.9	44.0	43.6	43.9	44.4	44.6
Housing	14.8	15.2	15.2	15.4	15.3	15.2	15.4	15.4	15.4
Household Operation	6.2	6.1	6.2	6.2	6.3	6.2	6.3	6.6	6.5
Transportation	3.3	3.2	3.4	3.6	3.5	3.4	3.5	3.5	3.5
Personal Care	1.8	1.7	1.4	1.3	1.2	1.1	1.1	1.0)	
Recreation	2.0	2.0	2.1	2.0	2.0	2.0	2.0	1.9)	
Personal Business	4.4	4.6	5.1	5.1	5.1	5.0	5.0	5.2)	
Medical Care	4.7	5.6	6.7	6.9	7.1	7.2	7.4	7.7)	19.2
Private Education	1.2	1.3	1.6	1.6	1.6	1.6	1.5	1.5)	
Religious & Welfare	1.5	1.4	1.4	1.4	1.4	1.3	1.3	1.2)	
Foreign Travel	.4	.4	.5	.5	.5	.5	.4	.4)	

[a]Totals may not add due to rounding.

Source: Computed from U.S. Department of Commerce, Bureau of Economic Analysis data, reported in J. Dawson Ahalt, "Trends in Food Consumption, Prices and Expenditures," paper presented at the American Enterprise Institute Conference on Food and Agricultural Policy, Washington, D.C., March 10-11, 1977, Table 9, p. 29.

accept the recommendation, pointing out that MacDonald has described the normal operation of efficient markets. That is, when a resource becomes more scarce, its relative price goes up. The rising relative price reduces the quantity demanded and increases the quantity supplied. Furthermore, the rising price signals the start of exploration and the development of new technologies and substitutes. As to stockpiles, if investors predict that embargoes or other interruptions in supply are to occur, they will likely speculate and stockpile, causing scarce resources to be allocated efficiently between present and future consumption. The optimistic optimist sees no need for government concern. The private market can handle the problem. In my opinion, the double optimist is correct. However, many laws will have to be repealed to clear the way—and that is why the optimistic optimist is getting slightly pessimistic.

While the market system *could* handle the problem, policymakers have chosen to take a different approach. Instead of allowing the price of scarce petroleum products to rise, prices have been controlled and shortages are now added to scarcity. Natural gas, gasoline, old oil, new oil, entitlements—all are a part of our policy. The quantity demanded wants to increase instead of decrease. Of course, the control of price drives down the incentive to increase supply. We have the opposite result to that recommended by MacDonald.

Since there is so much concern over profits, speculators are now fearful to invest in a stockpile that might become more valuable. Windfall profits are to be avoided. Thus the speculator cannot cover his "windfall losses." What was a normal operation of the market has now been removed. In its place is the Energy Policy and Conservation Act of 1975 (P.L. 94-163), which requires a government stockpile of 150 million barrels of oil by December 1978 and 500 million barrels by 1982.[12] The estimated taxpayers' cost of storage, transportation, and purchase of this oil is $8 billion. We are in the stockpiling business. The price system has been moved away.

One can find other indications of the movement away from the price system. For example, government policies have moved the economy to a system of barter, where economic studies of government programs require that impact be measured in the number of barrels of crude oil which may be used. In some cases, measurements are made in oil, not dollars.[13] Government-mandated fuel-economy measures are also based on saving oil, not dollars or energy in all forms.[14] It is possible that auto producers may use more energy-intensive materials and more oil in order to show increased miles per gallon. Even the pessimistic pessimist could become more pessimistic.

In terms of other minerals, air pollution regulations have effectively cut off the expansion of copper production until 1983. A recent study for EPA indicates that the enforcement of the Clean Air Act will cause a copper shortfall of as much as 28.6 percent over baseline production in 1985; employment in the industry could be reduced by as much as 20,300 jobs by 1985.[15] In short, the supply of copper has been reduced significantly as efforts are made to reduce the amount of emission from the industry. The real cost of marginal improvements in air quality could be rather high in this case.

The problems related to scarce minerals discussed by MacDonald are made graphic when the effect of environmental regulation on mining is considered.[16] The U.S. mining industry expects to invest $2.5 billion in new facilities between 1975 and 1983. Of the $2.5 billion, $862 million or about 35 percent of total investment will go for water-treatment equipment. In barter terms, the equipment will require 1.4 million barrels of oil annually to operate. Approximately 50 percent of the additional investment will go to reduce effluents by another 5 percent. The tradeoff here is very clear.

When we consider MacDonald's recommended policy for expanding the supply of energy resources we might be aware of the environmental constraints faced by the U.S petroleum industry. A study prepared by Battelle Columbus Laboratories for the American Petroleum Institute reports that the p etroleum industry can expect to invest $28.9 billion in environmental control equipment by 1985.[17] Annual operating costs for the equipment could reach as high as $17 billion, which translates into a price increase of $2.05 per barrel of crude oil or 20 percent of total cost.[18] The values here represent Battelle's most restrictive analysis. Eighty percent of the cost derives from reaching for another 3 to 5 percent reduction in emissions or effluent discharge. In terms of energy impact, by 1985 it will take 322.7 million barrels of oil annually in equivalent energy to operate the pollution control equipment in the petroleum industry.[19] That is equal to 14 days supply of oil for the entire nation.

A recent Commerce Department report explained the petroleum industry's problem in yet another way.[20] The investment requirements mentioned above would construct plants capable of producing 1 million barrels a day of shale oil, or 4 million barrels a day in additional refining capacity.

The regulatory constraints imposed on the mining and petroleum industry in the pursuit of environmental quality indicate that humanity may have added significantly to the problem of resource availability. In some cases, nature's bounty has been hidden in a maze of regulatory red tape. To remedy the problem of environmental degradation, standards have been promulgated which, because of their inherent inefficiency, foster unnecessary consumption of valuable energy and other resources.

The experience with the National Environmental Act of 1969 (NEPA), and its requirement of environmental impact statements for actions by federal departments and agencies, provides a final straw for the optimists who hope that market forces may break through the problem of scarcity.[21] Due partly to NEPA and other safety constraints, the Nuclear Regulatory Commission now takes approximately seven and one-half years to review and approve an application for a new nuclear facility.[22] This estimate does not include litigation delays that arise in many cases. In other words, if a group of investors was ready today to go forward with complete engineering plans and all the attendant documentation required for a proposed nuclear generating plant, they would consider themselves fortunate to have the plant on line by 1985. They could anticipate that much delay in their planning. Litigation and other regulatory problems might bring unanticipated delays, which generate unplanned costs. Along these lines it has been estimated that by 1980 the *daily* cost of delaying a nuclear generating facility will be $6.7 million.[23]

CONCLUSION

This brief discussion of some of the more onerous regulatory constraints faced by the energy and mining sectors may help to explain the dichotomy between pessimists and optimists presented early in MacDonald's paper. Those who argue that the free market cannot be relied on to assure a long-run supply of energy and other resources may have unwittingly based their judgment on markets that have not been allowed to function. They are pessimistic, but may have pointed to the wrong culprit in placing the blame for "market failure." Those who see market forces as beneficial but question the ability of the market to respond quickly to new scarcities may know about the complex of government mandates that muffle, delay, and sometime even make illegal the legitimate operation of markets. They are pessimistic optimists for logical reasons. Finally, those who survey the situation described by MacDonald, understand the regulatory dilemma, and still think that market forces will prevail, are truly optimistic optimists. And let us hope that they are correct.

In the long run, costs will be paid no matter how we seek to assure supply. And nonmarket institutions that attempt to outperform free market forces will likely fail and be pushed ultimately to one side. James Schlesinger, now chief energy advisor to the President, described ultimate institutional change in this way: "Perhaps only dramatic, interest-arousing events are sufficient to persuade the public that the productive period of an institution's life is near its end."[24]

Perhaps we are now witnessing such a conflict, one which will bring a more rational time when free markets will be aided, not eroded, in performing their function of minimizing social cost, that is, maximizing happiness in a world of scarce resources. As has been suggested before, scarcity can be the prelude to plenty. It is the potential of humanity that we question. The free spirit of all people when released can perform a Titan's task in dealing with scarcity.[25] Perhaps there is something to learn from the optimistic optimists.

NOTES

1. For an interesting discussion of this early energy crisis see Paul H. Giddens, "The Shortages that Yielded Oil," *Petroleum Today* 16 (1975):1-5; and Walter B. Wriston, "Whale Oil, Baby Chicks and Energy," *National Review*, June 7, 1974, pp. 643-46.

2. After the whale oil crisis, the nation faced its first natural gas shortage in the mid 1900s. Just as in the current situation, doomsday prophets saw no solution and attempted to regulate. However, national regulation had not developed. Thus prices went up, allocations of natural gas changed, and in five years new technology provided new supplies. For a complete discussion of this and other related points, see Edmund W. Kitch, "Regulation of the Field Market for Natural Gas by the Federal Power Commission," *Journal of Law and Economics* 11 (October 1968): 243-80.

3. For a discussion of this function of the price system in the same context, see H. H. Macaulay and Bruce Yandle, *Environmental Use and the Market* (Lexington, Mass.: Lexington Books, D. C. Heath, 1977).

4. National Commission on Supplies and Shortages, *Government and the Nation's Resources* (Washington: U.S. Government Printing Office 1976).

5. Ibid., p. 15

6. The original table and this discussion is drawn from the report of the National Commission on Supplies and Shortages, op. cit., pp. 18-19.

7. "International Raw Materials Developments: Oil and Metals," in William Fellner, ed., *Contemporary Economic Problems* (Washington: American Enterprise Institute, 1976), pp. 323-69.

8. Ibid., p. 349.

9. Ibid.

10. Ibid., p. 352.

11. See *Economic Report of the President, 1977* (Washington: U.S. Government Printing Office, January 1977), p. 237.

12. See Federal Energy Administration, *Strategic Petroleum Reserve Plan* (Washington: U.S. Government Printing Office, December 15, 1976).

13. For example, OMB Circular 107, which implemented Executive Orders 11821 and 11949, required the executive regulatory agencies to perform economic impact analyses of all "major" regulator agencies. The agencies were allowed to define "major" subject to OMB approval. Most agencies include in their major criteria any action which increases the demand or reduces the supply of crude oil by 0.1 percent of annual crude oil usage (approximately 25,000 barrels daily). I will give some of this data later in the paper.

14. See Council on Wage and Price Stability, "Passenger Automobile Average Fuel Economy Standards," a filing before the National Highway Traffic Safety Administration, Docket No. FE 76-2 (January 3, 1977).

15. See Arthur D. Little, Inc., *Economic Impact of Environmental Regula-*

tions on the U.S. Copper Industry (draft report) (October 1976). Appreciation for permission to quote is expressed to the U.S. Environmental Protection Agency.

16. This discussion is drawn from American Mining Congress, *Study of Cost of Compliance with Federal Water Pollution Control Act* (Washington, D.C., 1976).

17. Battelle Columbus Laboratories, *The Economic Impact of Environmental Regulations on the Petroleum Industry—Phase II Study*, A Report to The American Petroleum Institute (Washington: American Petroleum Institute, June 1976), p. I-3.

18. Ibid.

19. Ibid., p. I-19.

20. U.S. Department of Commerce, *Toward Regulatory Reasonableness*, (Washington: U.S. Government Printing Office, January 13, 1977), p. 105.

21. For a discussion of NEPA and environmental impact statements, see: Council on Environmental Quality, *Environmental Impact Statements: An Analysis of Six Years' Experience by Seventy Federal Agencies* (March 1976).

22. Based on private conversations with Mr. Jim Fitzgerald, General Counsel's Office, Nuclear Regulatory Commission, March 3, 1977.

23. This estimate was given by Mr. J.L. Leporati, Vice President of EBASCO Services in a speech, "The Expanding Role of the States in Power Regulation," Hilton Head, S.C., October 1976. Appreciation is expressed to Mike Maloney, Department of Economics, Clemson University, for providing this item.

24. James R. Schlesinger, "Systems Analysis and the Political Process," - *Journal of Law and Economics* 11 (October 1968): 293. Current efforts to bring about regulatory reform may indicate that we have reached the "Schlesinger Point" with some institutions. In this sense, it appears that the most stringent regulations offer the greatest prospect for revision. For example, among environmental regulations, the Clean Air Act of 1970 sets the most stringent regulatory framework. That law resulted in the identification of "nondegradation" and "nonattainment" areas. The first were "very clean" while the latter did not meet national ambient air quality standards. Industrial expansion was cut off in both situations. Recent pressures for industrial growth have reached the point where revision is being made in both the interpretation of the Clean Air Act and perhaps in the Act itself. See Council on Wage and Price Stability, "Air Quality Standards: Interpretative Ruling," a filing before the U.S. Environmental Protection Agency (March 3, 1977).

25. For an excellent expansion on this theme and the source of the idea, see Wilfred Malenbaum, "Scarcity: Prerequisite to Abundance," *Annals of the American Academy of Political and Social Science* 420 (July 1975): 72-85.

REFERENCES

Ahalt, J. Dawson, "Trends in Food Consumption, Prices and Expenditures."
A paper presented at the Conference on Food and Agricultural Policy,

American Enterprise Institute, Washington, D.C., March 10-11, 1977.

American Mining Congress. *Study of Cost of Compliance with Federal Water Pollution Control Act.* Washington: American Mining Congress, 1976.

Battelle Columbus Laboratories. *The Economic Impact of Environmental Regulations on the Petroleum Industry—Phase II Study.* A report to the American Petroleum Institute. Washington: American Petroleum Institute, June 1976.

Council on Environmental Quality. *Environmental Impact Statements: An Analysis of Six Years' Experience by Seventy Federal Agencies.* Washington: U.S. Government Printing Office, March 1976.

Council on Wage and Price Stability. "Air Quality Standards: Interpretative Ruling." A filing before the U.S. Environmental Protection Agency, March 3, 1977.

Council on Wage and Price Stability. "Passenger Automobile Average Fuel Economy Standards." A filing before the National Highway Traffic and Safety Administration, Docket No. FE 76-2, January 3, 1977.

Econoic Report of the President, 1977. Washington: U.S. Government Printing Office, January 1977.

Erb, Richard. "International Raw Materials Developments: Oil and Metals." In *Contemporary Economic Problems*, William Felner, ed. Washington: American Enterprise Institute, 1976, pp. 232-69.

Federal Energy Administration. *Strategic Petroleum Reserve Plan.* Washington: U.S. Government Printing Office, December 15, 1976.

Giddens, Paul H. "The Shortages that Yielded Oil." *Petroleum Today* 16 (1975): 1-5.

Kitch, Edmund W. "Regulation of the Field Market for Natural Gas by the Federal Power Commission." *Journal of Law and Economics* 11 (October 1968): 243-80.

Leporati, J.L. "The Expanding Role of the States in Power Regulation." A speech delivered at Hilton Head, S.C., October 1976.

Little, Arthur D. *Economic Impact of Environmental Regulations on the U.S. Copper Industry* (draft report). October 1976.

Macaulay, H. H. and Bruce Yandle. *Environmental Use and the Market.* Lexington, Mass: Lexington Books, D.C. Heath, 1977.

Malenbaum, Wilfred. "Scarcity: Prerequisite to Abundance." *Annals of the American Academy of Political and Social Science* (July 1975): 72-85.

National Commission on Supplies and Shortages. *Government and the Nation's Resources.* Washington: U.S. Government Printing Office, December 1976.

Nordhaus, W. D.. "Resources as a Constraint on Growth."*American Economic Review* 64 (May 1974): 22-32.

Schlesinger, James R. "Systems Analysis and the Political Process." *Journal of Law and Economics* 11 (October 1968): 281-98.

U.S. Department of Commerce. *Toward Regulatory Reasonableness.* Washington: U.S. Government Printing Office, January 13, 1977.

Wriston, Walter B. "Whale Oil, Baby Chicks and Energy." *National Review*, June 7, 1974, pp. 643-46.

Part III

Food Production

Chapter Seven

The Natural Environment and Food Production

Pieter Buringh

Studies on Food Production

In a speech in 1898 the president of the British Association
for the Advancement of Science, Sir William Crooks, stated
that the area of virgin land that could be reclaimed for growing crops
was very small. He predicted a worldwide famine for the year 1930
unless chemical nitrogen fertilizers could be made by using nitrogen
from the air. (Russel, 1954; Baade, 1960). During World War I
chemical nitrogen fertilizers were manufactured, and plant genetics
and plant breeding had produced new crop varieties. There was no
worldwide famine in 1930, and now it is known that the acreage of land
suitable to be reclaimed is even larger than the acreage of land
cultivated.

In 1923 Baker published an article on land utilization in the United
States. He believed that within a few years more agricultural products
would have to be imported than could be exported, because of the increasing population, and he anticipated that food from tropical countries would come to American markets in increasing quantities.

These two examples demonstrate that it is difficult to predict the
future. It is wiser not to predict but instead to study the problem of
food production and find out how national and international policies
could be changed to prevent famine. This is what has been done in recent years by some groups of scientists. It is well known that hunger
and malnutrition in the poor countries of the world is one of the most
important problems of today. The food problem is caused not only by
the exponential growth of the world population, but also by the simple
fact that not enough food is produced in the countries where it is need-

ed. Moreover the food problem is not a problem of the poor society alone, it is also the problem of the rich societies, and it is our problem, too, as we shall elaborate on later.

Without mentioning various authors who have tried to study the possibilities of food production for specific countries or for the whole world, attention will be given to recent studies and their results. An important report was made by the President's Science Advisory Committee (PSAC) for the President of the United States in 1967 (PSAC, 1967). Based on knowledge of soil conditions and climate, an assessment was made of land suitable for cultivation. PSAC stated that the cultivable area is 1,406 million hectares (Mha) and the potential cultivable area is 3,190 Mha (respectively 11 percent and 24 percent of the total non-ice-covered land area of the world). Part of this land can be cropped twice or three times annually. Some 400 Mha can be irrigated; 200 Mha are already irrigated. The conclusion is that much more food can be produced than is done at present. Revelle (1976), a member of the PSAC, and Meadows (1975) estimate that some 50 billion people could live on the earth.

Since the modern computer and a new scientific method—systems analysis—became new tools for dealing with a complex system and a large amount of information, world models dealing with the food problem have been developed. The first model by Meadows et al. (1972), described in the famous book *The Limits to Growth* (the first report for the Club of Rome), did not give hopeful results. With an increasing population, more land is needed for nonagricultural purposes, and on all land available more food has to be produced. It was expected that by the year 2000 no new land for reclamation would be available if trends continue as they did during the last decades. And if the productivity of the land would be quadrupled, this situation would be reached before the year 2050.

The second study for the Club of Rome by Mesarovic and Pestel (1974) was not too optimistic either. It has many mistakes on the points of land suitability and possible crop production. The third study, *A Latin American World Model: Catastrophe or New Society?* (Herrara et al., 1976), had radically different and much more optimistic results. It was argued that the major problems are not biological and physical but sociopolitical. The work was performed at the Fundation Bariloche in Buenos Aires.

The fourth world model, *Model of International Relation in Agriculture* (MOIRA), made by a Dutch team guided by Professor Linnemann, will be published shortly. The main parts are already available (de Hoogh, 1976; Linnemann, 1977). As a member of this group, I studied, together with some other specialists, the potentialities of all land, as well as the theoretical maximum food production on this land, in order to have some idea of the ultimate possibilities of the world food production (Buringh et al., 1975).

The results of this investigation indicate that the area of potential land suitable for cultivation is 3,419 Mha (26.3 percent of the land surface). This is almost the same as the result of the PSAC, although we have used much more up-to-date information on soils, as the new soil map of the world (FAO/Unesco, 1971/77) became available. Taking into account various physical limitations (soil conditions, climate, photosynthesis, and so on), we found a theoretical upper limit of food production of 40 times the present production, when this production is expressed as grain equivalent. Approximately 65 percent of the cultivated land is used for cereal crops; some 30 times the present grain production could be produced on that land.

These results, like those mentioned here, should not be used without studying in detail the original publications, because various assumptions have been made and limitations are indicated. Moreover it is necessary to introduce various reduction factors to get realistic data. The economists of the MOIRA group have used the data on available land and productivity for other model studies to find out, for various policies, if the world food problem can be solved by the time the population has doubled, approximately the year 2010. The conclusion is that this is hardly possible; food aid will still be necessary, poor countries will have to try very hard to produce food for their respective populations, and the rich countries will have to change policies drastically.

The general conclusion of the PSAC, the Bariloche, and the MOIRA studies is that economic, social, and particularly political conditions in the world are limiting the production of food and not the availability of cultivable land or the productivity of this land. It is not agriculture or the present knowledge of agricultural technology that sets the limit now and for a long time ahead. Reference is made to a series of interesting articles in *Scientific American*, September 1976, in which, for example, Wortman (1976), Revelle (1976), and Loomis (1976) state that the situation about the world food problem is hopeful.

Clark and Cole (1976) have made a comparison of the four major world models mentioned previously. From the point of view of food production, an important difference in these studies is that Meadows studied the world as one region, Mesarovic and Pestel divided the world into 10 regions, the Bariloche group into 4 regions, and the MOIRA group into 222 regions (for the economic studies in 116 regions). In the MOIRA study (Buringh et al., 1975), maps of all continents showing these 222 regions are presented, and all formulas, data, and assumptions are given.

From these investigations it is easy to see that studying the world food problem based on extensive information has just started. Much more detailed work has to be done, methods have to be improved, and more reliable information is badly needed. The reliability of global and national data, at least of most countries, is rather weak. The reasons for this have been published by Farmer in Hutchinson's *Population and Food Supply* (1969). In the meantime some of the groups already mentioned, as well as groups in Austria and Japan, are working on new and improved world models in relation to the food problem.

Food Production Compared with Food Needed

The main food is grain (wheat, rice, and corn). The world grain crop was 1,220 million metric tons in 1975 (U.S. Department of Agriculture) and 1,270 million metric tons was the average for 1972-1975. If this could be equally distributed over the world population, nobody would be hungry. But, because of the unequal production and distribution of these cereals, millions of people are undernourished or hungry, and thousands of them die each year. According to the United Nations, 400 to 500 million people of the total world population of 4 billion are hungry or undernourished. Poverty is the reason that the hungry people cannot buy food. It is a problem of 10 million villages with 2 billion inhabitants and of the people living in slums around big cities.

In 1985 some 700 or 800 million people will be hungry. In the year 2010 the world population will be double, 8 billion. Some specialists believe that, from the year 2125 on, the world population will be constant, with 12 billion persons, who will need five times the quantity of food we produce at present (Koppejan, 1976).

Although some specialists state that the number of hungry people estimated by the United Nations is too high (400 million—it should be 70 million), it is generally agreed that the world population will double in 35 years' time. This means that at least two to three times more food has to be produced by the year 2015.

In calculations, food has to be expressed in a comparable unit; for example, in kilocalories per day per person, in kilograms protein per day per person, in kilograms grain per year per person or in hectares per person, or the acreage needed to produce food for a person. In the last case a person's need for space to live and for the infrastructure has to be calculated as well. As there is no consensus on the figures for these units, the results of various calculations often are rather different, particularly when they are used on a global scale.

The production of food depends greatly on soil conditions, climate, types and varieties of crops, and, in particular, on farm management.

Consequently there are not only important differences among the various countries, but also—and even more important—regional differences in food production. This is the reason that computations are made for 222 regions in the MOIRA study, although even this study is still rather crude.

Some countries produce much more grain than they need for their own population. The United States, Canada, and Australia are the main grain-exporting countries (exporting 96, 12, and 7 million tons respectively in 1975/76). In the tropics, Thailand is the only country exporting rice and corn. The total world trade in grain averages 115 million tons a year. The main importing countries are the USSR, Western Europe, and Japan. The need of all importing countries is expected to increase annually by 30 million tons of cereal-grain (Brown, 1974). In 1968 there was a grain stock of 128 million tons. Because of several reasons to be mentioned later, this stock was only 24 million tons at the end of 1974.

For those countries where people are poor, only a small amount of food can be bought; and, if there is a shortage in the rich countries or in the centrally planned countries, cereal prices will increase rapidly and the poor countries cannot buy. According to a 1974 United Nations' report, the poor countries will need 85 million tons of grain annually during the next eight years. Wortman (1976) estimates the deficit of grain in 1985/86 at 100 million tons if trends of the last 15 years do not change. These figures indicate the problem of today as well as tomorrow.

The cultivated grain (mainly wheat, rice, and corn) provide 75 percent of the energy and protein needs of man. These cereal crops are grown on 65 percent of the cultivated land of the world. Not all land that is cultivated provides a yield every year, because part of it is fallow or is temporarily used for grazing. The cropping intensity of the cultivated land in the world therefore is approximately 60 percent (figures vary from 50 to 65 percent). The remaining part of the cultivated land (35 percent) is used for growing root and tuber crops, vegetables, fruits, and the like, and for nonfood crops.

Besides the 1,406 million hectares of cultivated land, there are currently 4,000 million hectares of grazing land. The animal production on this grazing land contributes a very low portion (2 percent) of total food production; consequently it is hardly necessary to take this into account in global models. Livestock today is mainly raised on good pasture land (part of cultivable land), or is fed with products of cultivated land. The PSAC (1967) concludes that, in addition to the 3,200 million hectares of cultivated land, some 3,600 million hectares could serve for grazing livestock. However, this grazing land can provide only a few grams of animal protein per person per day for the estimated world population in the year 2000.

Food production of the sea can also be neglected in calculation on a global scale, because it is only 1 percent of all food. Marine organisms will never produce considerable amounts of food when compared with production of food on land. Fresh water fishing is 12 percent of the total world catch, and the total protein from fish is less than 2 percent of the world protein production, even when the fish catch is considered to be very high (Korringa, 1972).

Synthetic food is no solution for the world food problem (Wortman, 1976), nor is industrial food made from nonedible farm products. So on a global scale food products from grazing land, oceans, fresh water, and synthetic food can be overlooked in calculation. These products, however, can be important for specific regions.

The conclusion is that cereal grains (65 percent of the cultivated land, 75 percent of the food energy) are most important for mankind; consequently more attention should be given to cereal crops.

Cereal-Grain Crops

The annual yield of a cereal crop may vary from 600 to over 20,000 kilograms per hectare. The low yield reflects the traditional farm technology of almost two-thirds of the world's agriculture that is characterized as subsistence farming, with simple farm management, absence of chemical fertilizers, and therefore small energy subsidy and low output.

The yields are mainly limited by the amount of nitrogen supplied by nature. Such traditional farming has existed in Western Europe since the Middle Ages, when the yield of cereals was an average 800 kilograms per hectare. From this the farmer needed 200 kilograms for seed for the next year, 300 kilograms for beer and food for animals, and the remaining 300 kilograms for food for the farmer's family (de Wit, 1973).

Later on the yields were increased by using a somewhat improved traditional farming system (crop rotation, introduction of legumes, fodder crops, and consequently production of more and better stable manure). Yields of 1,500 and sometimes 2,000 kilograms per hectare were obtained. The next step was a farming system improved still further (better tools, some machines, some fertilizers, and so on), which grdually became a rather modern and finally a modern system of farming based on scientific technology.

Now the average yield of wheat crops in a modern system of farming, as in the Netherlands, is over 5,000 kilograms per hectare, the U.S. average being 2,200 kilograms per hectare (1972). With a very modern system of farming, yields of 7,000 kilograms per hectare and more can be obtained. The biological maximum yield (the photosynthetic potential) of a wheat crop in the Netherlands is over 10,000 kilograms per hectare. This is an absolute maximum since it is assumed that there are no limitations in nutrients and water supply, no pests and disease, and no weeds; therefore, the solar radiation, and consequently the photosynthesis of the crop, is the final limiting factor (de Wit, 1973).

The biological maximum depends on climatic conditions, which are more favorable in the tropics than in more temperate zones. A rice crop, for example, may produce almost 10 tons of padi; and when three crops can be grown in one year, the yield per hectare increases to 26,000 kilograms (de Vries et al., 1976; van Ittersum, 1971). However, as the average yield of rice in the tropics is only approximately 2,000 kilograms per hectare padi, this indicates that a traditional system of farming (including some irrigation) is the general farm practice. Irrigated rice fields have a more natural supply of nitrogen, because of blue algae, than nonirrigated fields.

For corn the average yield in traditional subsistence farming in the tropics is 1,000 kilograms per hectare. When advanced farm technology is applied in the tropics, an average yield of 7,000 kilograms per hectare is obtained (Young, 1976), whereas the maximum yield on an experimental field has been 20,000 kilograms per hectare. The average corn yield in the world is approximately 2,100 kilograms per hectare, the average of the U.S. Midwest is over 6,000 kilograms per hectare, and the highest yield has been 17,000 kilograms per hectare.

Similar examples can be given for many other crops. They simply demonstrate the fact that in general most farming in the world is still done in a very simple way based on traditional technology. Farming techniques have remained almost unchanged for centuries. Farming is mainly subsistence farming on small areas; 80 percent of the world's farmers till an area smaller than 5 hectare! Modern farming is practiced on a rather small scale. Agriculture in industrialized countries has made great progress during the last decade. In the United States, where farm technology recently is changing from semimodern to modern, however, it is still of intermediate intensity (Loomis, 1976). Although agriculture in the United States is highly mechanized, much can be improved. The average yield of wheat and corn is respectively 2,200 and 4,000 kilograms per hectare. Examples of high yields on some farms indicate that much higher averages are possible. The biological maximum for a cereal crop is calculated at 11 to 18 tons per hectare for the central part of the United States (Buringh, et al., 1975).

Sometimes individual farmers may get very high yields under favorable conditions. On experimental fields yields may be one and a half or two times the average farm yields. Ittersum (1971), who has made calculations on rice yields, states that farmers who apply modern farm technology will obtain 65 to 75 percent of the photosynthetic maximum.

It is concluded, and this is not new, that most farmers in the world can produce much more food on the land that is currently cultivated if they apply better agricultural technology. It is unrealistic to compute the world cereal-grain production for all cultivated or for all potentially cultivable land on a basis of modern farm management applied by all farmers or on a basis of the photosynthetic maximum production, because the modernization of farming cannot be obtained in a few years. Improvements in farming are made step by step.

Statistical data collected by FAO give an idea of food production per hectare in the various countries. These data, however, are not very accurate, at least for most countries. To get an idea of the present performance of the world's farmers, as far as cereal-grain production is concerned, an approximation has been made of the present production classes and the acreage involved, taking care that the total production is 1,270 million tons—the average 1972-1975 cereal production of the world. This quantity is produced on 65 percent of all cultivated land (1,406 million hectares). Consequently 914 million hectares are cereal crops.

The world average maximum photosynthetic production on such an area is 13,400 kilograms per hectare (Buringh et al., 1975). If it is assumed that 0.1 percent of the harvested land is yielding 50 percent of the maximum yield (6,700 kilograms per hectare), the total production of this land would be 67 million tons of cereal grains, which is 0.5 percent of the world total. This and a similar calculation for five more groups is given in Table 7-1. If the world's agricultural technology is somewhat improved so that half of the area in each group could go one class up, the results would be a total production of 138 percent (see Table 7-2). Both tables, although they are rough approximations, indicate what the world production of cereal crops can be if agricultural technology is somewhat improved all over the world for half the area of each group.

Another possibility to increase the amount of food available in the world is better storage. Specialists estimate storage losses of 10 to 40 percent. In the United States post-harvest losses are 10 percent (Wortman, 1976), whereas in most tropical countries they are 40 percent or more. If these losses are limited to 20 percent, approximately 150 million tons more grain is made available for human consumption.

Table 7-1. Estimated Production Classes and Their Average of Cereal-Crop Production in the World (present situation)

Area			Yield		
Percent	*Mill. Hectare*	*Percent of Biol. Max.*	*Kg/Ha*	*Million Tons*	*Percent of Total*
0.1	1	50	6,700	6.7	0.5
.4	4	40	5,400	21.6	1.7
2.5	23	30	4,000	92.0	7.3
17.5	160	20	2,700	432.0	34.4
35.7	326	10	1,300	423.8	33.7
43.8	400	5	700	280.0	22.4
100.0	914			1,256.1	100.0

Table 7-2. Estimated Production Classes and Their Average of Cereal-Crop Production in the World (somewhat improved situation)

Area			Yield		
Percent	*Million Hectare*	*Percent of Biol. Max.*	*Kg/Ha*	*Million Tons*	*Percent of Total*
0.1	3	50	6,700	20.1	1.2
.4	14	40	5,400	75.6	4.4
2.5	91	30	4,000	364.0	21.0
17.5	243 .	20	2,700	656.1	38.0
35.7	363	10	1,300	471.9	27.3
43.8	200	5	700	140.0	8.1
100.0	914			1,727.7	100.0

The number of horses and mules in the United States was 25 million in 1916 and 3 million in 1959 (Baker, 1960). This demonstrates how much land that formerly was needed to feed these animals (in general the yield of one hectare for one horse), has become available for human food production because of mechanization. There are 350 million farmers in the world, and there are only 10 million tractors. Maybe here, too, is a key to increased food production, although not all land producing food for animals is suitable for growing cereal or other crops.

It is well known that much more fossil energy is needed for modern agriculture than for traditional or improved agriculture. During recent years various investigations have been carried out. Most traditional farmers only use human labor or human labor and animal traction, and have simple tools. From the viewpoint of fossil-energy consumption, traditional subsistence farming has a high overall efficiency because of very small energy subsidy. In highly mechanized farms much fossil energy is needed for chemical fertilizers (1 kilogram nitrogen fertilizer is produced with 1.5 kilograms fossil energy) for fuel and for manufacturing the farm machinery. In modern agriculture in industrialized countries, about 5 to 7 percent of the total fossil-energy consumption is used in agriculture. A similar percentage or more is needed for all activities outside the farm until the bread or other food reaches the consumer's table.

Solutions of the World Food Problem

Most agronomists and economists agree that more food can be produced by reclaiming more land, by intensifying farming, or by both. Various proposals are based on: applying fertilizers; introduction of high-yielding crop varieties; controlling weeds, diseases, and pests; mechanization; more efficient irrigation; improvement of credit facilities and infrastructure; education of farmers; and so on. In addition, more agricultural research and enlargement of the agricultural extension services are necessary. It is also proposed that large-scale plantation farming for food crops in poor countries be introduced. Others prefer large-scale land reform or nationalization of land.

The food problem of the world is a complicated problem of production, transportation, processing, marketing, and the like, a problem with many agronomic, economic, social, and political aspects that are difficult to solve. It would be, and sometimes is, considered a rather simple problem, because it seems not so difficult and complicated to produce more food, although conditions of climate, soils, and farm technology are not favorable in some regions.

The main point is to improve the conditions of poor farmers, who have to adapt their farm technology to make better use of the land-production potentialities. This cannot, for example, be reached simply by increasing prices of farm products, but it needs a completely new approach in the fields of economy, sociology, and, in particular, politics. It is easier to propose simple solutions than to take appropriate measures. In this connection reference is made to interesting articles by Mellor (1976), dealing with the situation in India, and by Wellhausen (1976) on agriculture in Mexico. In both countries the so-called green revolution has improved the situation of landowners and commercial farmers.

But production revolution has hardly improved the situation of the small and poor farmers; the reverse has often been true. Many of them even became landless farmers as a result of the green revolution. In the developing countries 78 percent of the farmers have less than 5 hectares. Together they cultivate only 21 percent of the land. It is more difficult to increase food production on this land than on that of the larger holdings because small farmers cannot take risks.

Until a few years ago many influential persons believed that the agronomists could not solve the food problem, because not enough food could be produced and because the exponential growth of the world population was the most important problem that had to be solved, particularly in the poor countries. Since the results of some recent studies on potential cultivable land and on their productive capacity are known, most people are convinced that the food problem is mainly a social-economic-political one.

Even if people were to agree on methods, techniques, organization, and finance to increase food production, and the work could be carried out, it would take at least 25 years or more to reach the final goal of all countries producing all the food they need. Building up larger food reserves and increasing foreign aid for agricultural development in the poor countries will be needed for many years to come.

LAND USE AND PRESERVATION OF NATURAL ENVIRONMENT

Present Land Use

The total non-ice-covered land surface of the world is 13 billion hectares, of which 1,406 million hectares (11 percent) is cultivated, 3,000 to 4,000 million hectares is grazing land, and 4,000 million hectares is forest. The remainder is desert, tundra, mountainous, or rocky. At present about 200 million (or 14 percent) of the cultivated land is irrigated. It has already been mentioned that 65 percent of the cultivated land is used to grow cereal crops that provide 75 percent of the energy and protein needs of humanity. In addition 8 percent of the energy needs is provided by root and tuber crops, 9 percent by sugar crops, and 5 percent by peas, beans, nuts and oil seeds (Loomis, 1976).

Grazing land has an average carrying capacity of one animal unit per 20 hectares (PSAC, 1967); the production is less than 5 kilogrms of meat per hectare per year. Of the forested area, some 2,500 million hectares is natural tropical forest. Less than 1 percent of the forest in the tropics is plantation forest. The overall average wood production is estimated at 4 m^3 hectares per year. It is somewhat higher in the tropical rainforest. Of all the timber cut in the world, 50 percent is used for firewood. In the tropics even 80 percent of the annual cut is firewood, because 90 percent of the population in the tropics relies on firewood for domestic needs (IDRC, 1976).

The area used for cultivating crops is increasing because grazing and forest land is being reclaimed. These reclamations contribute more to the annual growth of food production (2.5 percent) than intensification of the cropping system. An estimated 0.5 to 1.0 percent of the cultivated land is lost annually to nonagricultural land use (housing, industry, transport, recreation, mining), that is increasing rapidly. Approximately 5 percent of the former cultivated land is already occupied for nonagricultural purposes. The loss of rather good land to new housing schemes and roads is rapidly increasing in densely populated regions. One has to bear in mind that within the last 30 years the population has doubled. On West Java, whose land surface of 4.6 million hectares makes it one of the most densely populated regions of the world, already 18 percent of its once cultivated land is now used for nonagricultural purposes.

In most all countries of the world and in particular those in the tropics and subtropics, large areas of cultivated land are damaged by wind and water erosion, by salinization and sodication, and by desertification. This misuse of land is approximately 500,000 hectares annually, which is 10 hectares every minute (5 hectares erosion, 3 hectares salinization, and 2 hectares desertification and degradation). Some estimations made recently are higher and are probably exaggerated; for example, Dumont (1973) supposed that the loss of land because of misuse is 38 hectares per minute, and Kovda (1973) found 100 hectares per minute. FAO is now undertaking an assessment of soil degradation in the world.

Reference must be made to the effective loss of soil nutrients in exported agricultural products. Ferwerda (1970) mentioned, for example, a loss of 4.6 million kilograms of K_2O annually in Ecuador by export of bananas, 2 million kilograms in Hawaii by export of pineapples, and 2 to 3 million kilograms by export of tea in Sri Lanka. The conclusion is that the world in general is not taking good care of its land, which is caused partly by too low prices for agricultural products. Techniques to stop the misuse of various types of cultivated land are well known.

Land-use Potentials

Although it was already known from rough estimations that approximately as much land as is now cultivated is available for reclamation, the first more profound study was made by the PSAC (1967) and the second by the MOIRA group (Buringh et al., 1975). The studies were carried out in different ways, but the results are similar. The MOIRA group has used recent and more detailed information on soils and climate of the world, and therefore a differentiation in 222 regions has been made. It is now known, at least roughly, where the various areas of potentially cultivable land are situated and what is the potential productivity. An example of one of the continents (South America) is given in Figure 7-1; the classes are explained in Table 7-3.

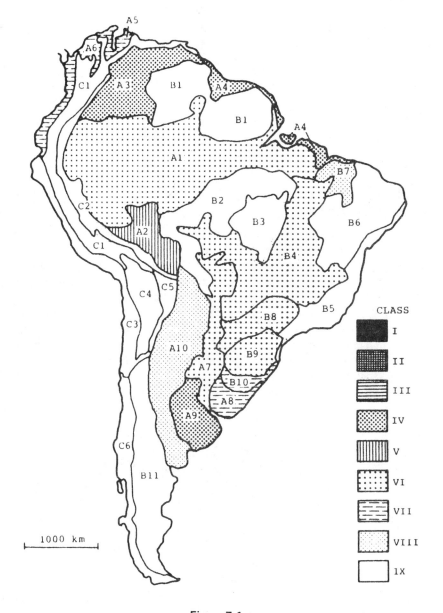

Figure 7-1.

Table 7-3. Classification of the Relative Importance of Potential Agricultural Land in the Broad Soil Regions of South America

Class	Importance	
I	Extremely high	> 50
II	Very high	> 45 - 50
III	High	> 40 - 45
IV	Moderately high	> 35 - 40
V	Medium	> 30 - 35
VI	Moderately low	> 25 - 30
VII	Low	> 20 - 25
VIII	Very low	> 15 - 20
IX	Extremely low	≤ 15

Classes I up to IX indicate (in percentages of the areas concerned) the land area potentially suitable for cultivation, expressed in equivalent land with potential production, including irrigation.

The outcome of the studies is that the potential cultivable land surface is 3,200 million and 3,400 million hectares, respectively (24 or 26 percent of the total land surface), which is approximately three times the actual harvested area. Of the potentially cultivable land, some 400 million and 470 million hectares, respectively, are potentially irrigable.

The PSAC (1967) states that, in addition, there are 3,600 million hectares available for grazing livestock. In various publications summaries of the PSAC study are given; for example, Simonson (1967) Kellog and Orvedal (1969), and Revelle (1973 and 1976). In the FAO Indicative World Plan (1969), the reclamation of 97 million hectares for the period 1970-1985 was foreseen. It seems that the annual increase in food production (2.5 percent) is a bit more than the annual increase of the population (1.9 percent), and is mainly the result of cultivating land that was not cultivated before. A much smaller increase is the result of improving farm technology.

The potential for increasing the cultivated land surface are largest in Africa and Latin America and not in Australia, as suggested by Mesarovic and Pestel (1974). Recent studies also have revealed that there are still enormous potentials in Southeast Asia that contradict what was generally believed earlier. Van Liere (1977) refers to development studies of the MeKong River basin, which has a food-production potential comparable to the present food production of North America. It is my impression that more detailed regional studies, already made in some countries, will reveal that even more potentially cultivable land is available than indicated before.

Very often it is said that large areas in the tropics—in particular those characterized by old, deeply weathered soils—are not suitable for cultivation. Fortunately specialists of tropical agriculture and tropical soil science have a different opinion, which is supported by results of recent experiments and research.

There are almost 80 small countries with a population of less than 5 million people; 30 of these have even less than 1 million people. Some economists believe that it will be difficult for those countries to extend the area of cultivated land. This is not true, in general, because it depends mainly on how much land is potentially cultivable in each country. Surinam for example (350,000 people) has the potential for several million people as far as food production is concerned (Buringh, 1977).

During recent years the potentials of some countries have been studied, particularly of Australia (Gifford et al., 1975; Nix, 1976) and of Canada (Nowland, 1975a and b) in order to have a basis for immigration policies. Such studies are important from the viewpoint of results and also for the methodology used. In Australia the area of potentially cultivable land seems to be much smaller than was expected in the American and Dutch studies. It is interesting to learn that Gifford et al. (1975) conclude that, on a low level of existence, Australia can support a population of 200 million people, whereas it can support only 22 million people if Australia wants to continue to export 65 percent of its food production and the population wants a high standard of living (present population in Australia: 13 million). Such an example is instructive, because several kinds of calculations are made to get a rough indication of how many people could live on the earth. Sometimes this number is stated as 40, 50, or even 80 billion people. Such calculations are confusing and unrealistic, not only because they are based on poor information, but also, even more, because it should indicate which standard of living will be provided. There is, moreover, no need for such predictions.

Land Reclamation

It seems that in most countries reclamation projects, and therefore an increase of the cultivated area, often are preferred to improvement and intensified use of present agricultural land. Unfortunately many reclamation projects in poor countries have not had the good results that were calculated or predicted. Some projects are complete failures, although often this fact is not published. One such exception is the Dejaila project in Iraq (El Hakim, 1973). Irregular and often unofficial settlement of private farmers along newly constructed roads in tropical forest areas sometimes are a success; however, a failure is often experienced mostly because of poor soil conditions or insufficient financial means.

Large-scale projects carried out during the last decades in Central Asia by the Soviet Union (Breznev, 1974) also have failed to a great extent, because of the great climatological risks. The consequences of low wheat yields in 1972 and again in 1975 are well known, not only in the United States but also all over the world, particularly in the poor countries, which did not have enough money to pay the high wheat prices as a consequence of the Soviet Union's import of American wheat. In the United States this has led to higher food prices, followed by a sharply increased value of land, intensification of cropping, cultivation of former pasture and forest, and to large reclamation projects in the Amazon basin in Brazil, mainly by private American persons and firms (Eckholm, 1976; *Time*, 15 November 1976). Gruhl (1975) reports that in the Amazon region 36 million hectares of natural forest is to be cut down. A few years ago it became clear that food—particularly wheat and corn—might become a major political weapon considered more important than oil.

A food war has already been going on since 1972, and earth satellites of NASA and CIA are the most important tools. Food intelligence has become a new field of research. It studies actual land use, monitors all changes in land use, and provides monthly predictions of food production of all major countries in the world (MacDonald, 1976).

Protection of the Natural Environment
The natural ecosystem in many parts of the world is destroyed because of human activities. Since the population grows so rapidly, it is possible that the remaining natural regions in the world will be destroyed in the near future. This can be a catastrophe for various reasons. Some ecologists are not content with publications that indicate a large available land surface of potentially cultivable land, because they are afraid all this land will be cultivated soon. This fear, however, is no reason why people should not know facts. In the MOIRA study not all cultivable land of the regions is used in the computation; some 10 to 20 percent, sometimes even 50 percent (Amazon basin) of it not used for agriculture is assumed being used for wildlife, recreation, and so on.

The expanding agricultural and nonagricultural land use and the misuse of land are real problems. All means to prevent misuse of land are available; they only have to be put into effect. But this costs money. It would be wise to locate new housing and industrial schemes on poor or nonagricultural land. Moreover, the policy of most countries can be changed to intensifying agriculture on the currently cultivated land in order to produce more food. The possibilities for this will be discussed in more detail in the following section.

In addition, the grazing land can be considerably improved. Grass production of two to five and even more times the present production is possible. In the forests, particularly in the tropics, much more timber can be produced if wood collection and timber robbery of the natural tropical forests is stopped and if plantation forestry is practiced. In doing this, reclamation of new land can be limited, the area of grazing land can be much smaller than it is at present, and very large areas of natural forest can be reserved. If this is done, then there are regions large enough to conserve flora and fauna species. No doubt there is a real solution; however, better care must be taken of all types of land. All these activities will cost research, personnel, practical political solution, management, and investments, and therefore a greater part of the consumable income of people in the rich countries must be spent on food and nature care.

If there could be an agreement on future main types of land use, as proposed tentatively in Table 7-4, agriculture (including some 500 million hectares of plantation forest for timber and firewood production) would need only 3 billion hectares; whereas 5 billion hectares are available as nature reserve, not counting the 4 billion hectares of land with a very cold or very dry climate.

It is supposed that pollution of the environment is under control and misuse of land has stopped. If the world population will increase to some 12 billion people in about 150 years, and from then on remain almost constant, the population will be three times larger than the present population. The food requirement is estimated at five times more than at present. Psomopoulos (1976) states that 22 billion people can live on the globe in a "high quality environment."

Although it seems rather unrealistic to make this kind of far-ahead global view, we know that the situation is not hopeless. There is still

Table 7-4. A Rough Scheme of Land Use (millions of hectares)

Land-Use Type	*Present Use*	*Future Use*	*Future Reservation*
Cultivated land	1,400	1,500	—
Grazing land	3,000	1,000	2,000
Forest	4,000	500	3,000
Nonagriculture	600	1,000	—
Too cold, too dry	+ 4,000	+	+ 4,000
	13,000	4,000	9,000
		+	
		13,000	

enough land for food production, and the environment can be protected. However, on a regional basis physical limitations can be serious and pollution and stress on the environment do occur, because population is concentrated in specific areas. It therefore is necessary that ecologists join groups of specialists who study land-use problems. If intensified cropping on the existing cultivated land is given priority over reclaiming noncultivated land, the problems of nature protection probably could be solved in most countries. It is concluded that present land use can be considerably improved. Reclamation of new land must be limited, and much more attention be given to nature reserves to keep good conditions for present use.

FOOD PRODUCTION POTENTIALS

As stated before, it is possible to increase crop production by intensifying the cropping system. References have already been made to the very low level of food production in many countries, especially in the poor ones. It is not new to mention that crop production could be three, five, or even tenfold the present production, because this has been shown by many agronomists.

On a global scale a rather detailed computation has been made for the MOIRA study. For each of the 222 regions of the world indicated on small-scale maps of the continents, a computation has been made of what is called "the absolute maximum production" expressed in grain equivalents (tons of cereal grain). Maybe the term "maximum photosynthetic production of grain" is better.

In each region soil and climate conditions and possibilities for irrigation are studied in relation to land use, natural vegetation, and topography. It is supposed that shortage of nutrients is corrected by adding fertilizers. Then for each region a soil-reduction factor is determined, because most soils do not have such properties to get optimal yields. The various data on climate indicate the length of the growing season, the energy available, the quantity of water available for plant growth, and so on. If soil-water conditions are not optimal, a reduction factor for water deficiency is calculated. The various climatic data also assist in calculating the production of crop dry matter. In Figure 7-2 an example of one of the continents (Latin America) is given. The classes are explained in Table 7-5. In addition the data of the various regions are indicated in Table 7-6. Table 7-7 gives the total for seven continents.

The final result is that the maximum photosynthetic production of cereal grain (on 65 percent of the potential cultivable land) is 32.4 billion tons, or approximately 30 times the present world cereal-grain

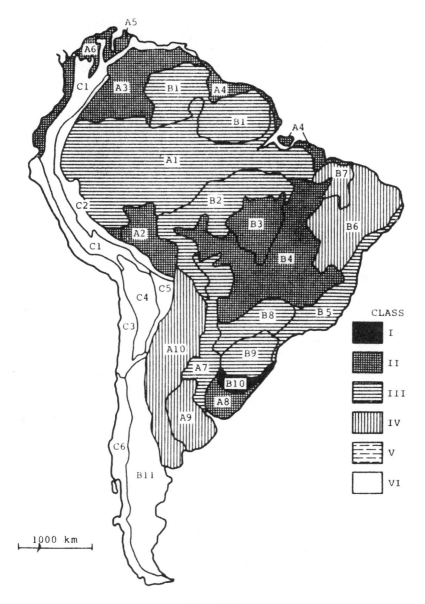

Figure 7-2.

production. The computations of the MOIRA group are made on the basis of cereal grains. If they had been made for root and tuber crops, the photosynthetic maximum production is even higher.

A possible world production of 11.4 billion tons of food grain was calculated by the PSAC study (Revelle, 1976), assuming yields as oc-

Table 7-5. Land Productivity Classes for the Potential Agricultural Land

Class	Land Productivity	
I	Extremely high	> 25
II	Very high	> 20 - 25
III	High	> 15 - 20
IV	Medium	> 10 - 15
V	Low	> 5 - 10
VI	Very low	⩽ 5

Classes I up to VI indicate the computed maximum photosynthetic production of grain equivalents in 1,000 kilograms per hectare.

cur in U.S. Midwest, and for lower quality soils, half of such a yield. This is nine times the present food production. In soil-survey and land-classification reports of parts of various countries, figures on possible crop productions are given. In those reports the present production is compared with yields obtained on experimental farms, which often are two or three times higher. The conclusion of all these studies is that almost everywhere, but in particular in countries in the tropics and subtropics, food production can be trebled or quadrupled.

In Thailand (van Liere, 1977) the average one-crop rice (padi) yield is almost 2,000 kilograms per hectare, whereas the yield on experimental farms is 6,000 kilograms per hectare. For corn it is 2,200 and 8,500 kilograms per hectare, respectively; and for soya 1,000 and 3,500 kilograms per hectare. In Indonesia (Ismunadji, 1973), where the average one-crop rice yields slightly more than 1,000 kilograms per hectare, the yield can be increased to 3,000 to 4,500 kilograms per hectare without fertilizers, and to 5,000 to 8,500 kilograms per hectare with fertilizers on the major soil types of Java. Hopper (1976) describes stages in development of farm management in Japan where average rice yields increased from 1,000 to 2,500 to 4,000 and now to 6,000 kilograms per hectare, and a yield of 8,000 kilograms per hectare is expected in the near future. Breadfield (1972) has given interesting examples on maximizing food production through multiple cropping systems in the tropics. A system of intercropping yielding 5,000 U.S. dollars per hectare was obtained on a two-hectare farm.

The yield of Cassava, actually less than 10 tons per hectare, can be increased up to 50 tons (Jennings, 1976); on modern farms 20 to 40 tons per hectare is a normal yield. In Western Europe the average wheat yield is 2,500 kilograms per hectare, whereas the production on experimental farms is 8,000 kilograms and the photosynthetic maximum is at least 10,000 kilograms per hectare.

In the USSR the average wheat yield is 1,540 kilograms per hectare, improved farming yields 4,000 to 5,000 kilograms per hectare, and the maximum on experimental fields is 10,030 kilograms per hectare. Hedrick Smith, in his *The Russians*, revealed that 27 percent of the total value of Soviet farm output comes from small private plots that occupy less than 1 percent of all agricultural land in the USSR.

In the tropics and subtropics, fields around villages produce much more than other fields, because these fields get much more organic manure and compost. In Mexico (Wellhausen, 1976) the average yield of wheat increased from 700 (1950) to 3,200 (1970) to 3,600 (1975) kilograms per hectare. Some farmers already produce 6,000 kilograms per hectare, and at experimental stations yields are as high as 10,000 kilograms per hectare. Reference is also made to the well-known achievements of the farmers in Israel, where farm output has risen some eightfold in the past 25 years (Hopper, 1976). Intensive farming also can be observed in the Nile delta in Egypt.

More examples are given on world crop productions in literature and in reports of agricultural experimental stations. It turns out that most yields obtained at a traditional level of farm management are 10 to 20 percent of yields obtained when advanced technology is applied. The best farmers can get 65 to 75 percent of the maximum photosynthetic production.

To get a better general idea of crop yields under various management practices, a crop-performance index (CPI) is introduced. It refers to the fraction of maximum photosynthetic production that is obtained under prevailing conditions and farm management. It is a fraction of the yield and is not related to cost, labor, and other economic factors. Table 7-8 indicates the crop-performance indexes. Each figure is the center of a class; for example, a 0.3 index reflects the class between 0.25 to 0.34. This index is independent from soil conditions, because each soil will have its specific photosynthetic maximum yield, when a reduction factor for soil and water deficiencies is introduced in the theoretical photosynthetic potential for a specific crop in a region with a well-defined climate. The CPI are applied in some general calculations on a global basis in order to get at least an idea of possible food production.

If 65 percent of all potentially cultivable land (3,419 million hectares) is used for cereal-crop production, with a cropping intensity of 70 percent, some 1,500 million hectares could be harvested. If half of this area has a CPI equal to 0.1 and the other half a CPI equal to 0.2, which means a low-level farming using no fertilizers and applying human labor and some animal traction, the world cereal-grain production would be 3,110 million tons, which is 2.5 times the present world production.

Table 7-6.   South America

1	2 A	3 A%	4 PDM	5 FPAL	6 PAL	7 DCC	8 FSC	9 FWD	10 IPAL	11 MPDM	12 PIAL	13 IPALI	14 MPDMI	15 MPGE
A1	297.8	16.7	74	0.5	148.9	5	0.6	0.8	89.3	6611	0.0	89.3	6611	2856
A2	40.9	2.3	80	.5	20.5	4	.6	.7	12.3	982	.0	12.3	982	424
A3	81.8	4.6	80	.5	40.9	2	.7	.7	28.6	2290	.4	28.7	2294	991
A4	24.9	1.4	80	.5	12.5	3	.7	.8	8.7	697	1.2	8.8	707	305
A5	10.7	.6	80	.4	4.3	4	.6	.4	1.7	137	2.2	2.6	208	90
A6	24.9	1.4	80	.3	7.5	3	.7	.7	5.2	418	1.1	5.3	427	185
A7	53.4	3.0	78	.6	32.0	4	.5	.7	16.0	1250	.0	16.0	1250	540
A8	16.0	.9	72	.3	4.8	3	.8	.8	3.8	276	.0	3.8	276	119
A9	37.4	2.1	56	.6	22.4	2	.9	.6	13.5	754	.0	13.5	754	326
A10	112.2	6.3	64	.4	44.8	1	.8	.4	18.0	1149	1.5	18.5	1185	512
B1	108.6	6.1	78	.2	21.7	5	.5	.8	10.9	847	.4	11.1	856	370
B2	97.9	5.5	80	.3	29.4	5	.5	.6	14.7	1175	.0	14.7	1175	508
B3	46.3	2.6	78	.2	9.3	4	.7	.7	6.5	506	.0	6.5	506	218
B4	170.8	9.6	80	.5	85.4	3	.6	.6	51.2	4090	.0	51.2	4099	1771
B5	56.9	3.2	76	.3	17.1	4	.5	.8	8.5	649	.0	8.5	649	280
B6	97.9	5.5	84	.3	29.4	3	.7	.3	8.8	740	2.7	10.2	854	369
B7	23.2	1.3	82	.5	11.6	3	.4	.5	4.6	380	.0	4.6	380	164
B8	40.9	2.3	76	.5	20.5	4	.6	.7	12.3	933	.0	12.3	933	403
B9	35.6	2.0	74	.5	17.8	4	.6	1.0	10.7	790	.0	10.7	790	341
B10	10.7	.6	72	.3	3.2	4	.8	.9	2.6	185	.7	2.6	190	82
B11	121.1	6.8	48	.1	12.1	3	.7	0	0	0	2.4	1.9	92	40
C1	80.1	4.5	80	.05	4.0	3	.7	.4	1.6	128	1.4	2.2	173	75
C2	39.1	2.2	78	.05	2.0	3	.7	.7	1.4	107	.4	1.4	110	47
C3	49.6	2.8	84	.1	5.0	3	.7	0	0	0	.5	.4	34	15

1	2 (A)	3 (A%)	4 (PDM)	5 (FPAL)	6 (PAL)	7 (DCC)	8 (FSC)	9 (FWD)	10 (IPAL)	11 (MPDM)	12 (PIAL)	13 (IPALI)	14 (MPDMI)	15 (MPGE)
C4	37.3	2.1	64	.1	3.8	3	.7	0	0	0	.2	.2	10	4
C5	16.0	.9	44	.05	.8	3	.7	.2	.2	7	.2	.3	12	5
C6	48.0	2.7	48	.1	4.8	3	.7	.5	2.4	115	2.6	3.2	153	66

Explanation of the columns:

1   Symbol of a broad soil region in a continent.

2 (A)   Area of a broad soil region (10^6 ha).

3 (A%)   Area (A) in percentage of the total area of the continent.

4 (PDM)   Potential production of dry matter (10^3 kg $\times$ ha^{-1} $\times$ year^{-1}).

5 (FPAL)   Fraction of potential agricultural land.

6 (PAL)   Potential agricultural land (10^6 ha).

7 (DCC)   Development cost class.

8 (FSC)   Reduction factor caused by soil conditions.

9 (FWD)   Reduction factor caused by water deficiency.

10 (IPAL)   Imaginary area of PAL with potential production, without irrigation (10^6 ha).

11 (MPDM)   Maximum production of dry matter without irrigation (10^6 tons $\times$ year^{-1}).

12 (PIAL)   Potentially irrigable agricultural land (10^6 ha).

13 (IPALI)   Imaginary area of PAL with potential production, including irrigation (10^6 ha).

14 (MPDMI)   Maximum production of dry matter, including irrigation (10^6 tons $\times$ year^{-1}).

15 (MPGE)   Maximum production of grain equivalents, including irrigation (10^6 tons $\times$ year^{-1}).

Table 7-7.   Totals of the Continents and the World

	A	PAL	PIAL	MPGE
S. America	1,780	616.5	17.9	11,106
Australia	860	225.7	5.3	2,358
Africa	3,030	761.2	19.7	10,845
Asia	4,390	1,083.4	314.1	14,281
N. America	2,420	628.6	37.1	7,072
Europe	1,050	398.7	75.9	4,168
Antarctica	1,310	0	0	0
Total	14,840	3,714.1	470.0	49,830

A = area (million hectares).
PAL = area of potential agricultural land (million hectares).
PIAL = area of potentially irrigable land (million hectares).
MPGE = maximum production of grain equivalents (million tons per year).

Table 7-8.   Crop Performance Indexes

Index	Name
0.1	Minimum crop performance
0.2	Very low crop performance
0.3	Low crop performance
0.4	Medium crop performance
0.5	High crop performance
0.6	Very high crop performance
0.7	Maximum crop performance
1.0	Photo synthetic maximum yield

Index 0.1 is typical for traditional farming; 0.2 and 0.3 for somewhat improved and improved farming; 0.4 and 0.5 for semimodern and modern farming; 0.6 for very modern farming; and 0.7 and more for optimal farming.

The conclusion is that enough food grains could be produced using very little fossil energy, that is, traditional subsistence farming were still applied. However, large areas of land would have been misused and damaged. The total yield would be much lower than calculated and the natural environment would have been seriously damaged.

This example demonstrates that the advances made in modern agriculture generally have not seriously disturbed the environment; on the contrary, large areas with natural vegetation still exist because of modern techniques. The natural environment can be better protected by introducing appropriate modern techniques than without them (see the section "Protecting the Natural Environment," above). Another assumed example shows that, if 65 percent of the present cultivated area (1,406 million hectares) is used for cereal crops, with a 70 percent crop intensity (640 million hectares harvested) and CPI equal to 0.4, the production then is 3,400 million tons. Here it is assumed that agriculture is on a rather (although not very) modern level, and still more than 2.5 times the present world cereal production would have been obtained.

Calculations presented here are purely theoretical. They can be made somewhat more realistic if applied to the various regions or countries of the world. In this section real figures on crop yields have been given, too. These figures clearly demonstrate the low level of farming in many countries in the world, especially in the tropics. Therefore, the conclusion is that food production in the world can be considerably increased, and there is no reason to believe that a double, triple, or quadruple production of human food is not possible. No indication has been given as to the costs; it is clear, however, that factories to manufacture fertilizers, chemicals, and machines have to be built, roads have to be constructed, and so on. Since so much money is spent for military purposes, one hardly can imagine that no money could be found to produce food for every human being in the world. People eat first to live; then they can start defending their freedom. One only can conclude that there will not be enough competent agronomists, extension workers, and soil-water and land-reclamation specialists to perform the job.

It is also stated that enough food can be produced on a rather low level of farm management. The consequence might be that various governments will decide not to change their agricultural policy, and then misuse of land will increase even on an accelerated scale, soil fertility will decrease, and soil degradation will continue. Indeed, the world can continue with robbery of the natural resources, particularly of potentially cultivable land and of natural vegetation. Such a policy would be a big mistake.

The philosophy behind all work to be carried out in the near future is that improvement of agriculture, and especially in management, in large parts of the world is necessary to produce some food. These improvements should be made step by step. This is also propagated by Papadakis (1975), Schuman (1973), and others, who indicate possibilities of low-cost techniques and intermediate technology, because the poor countries must actively encourage their agricultural development in order to become almost independent of food import.

Several economists and agronomists have already studied the food-shortage problem. It is technically not very difficult to raise low crop performance indexes by 0.1 or 0.2 points. Many regions at this moment have no direct need for introducing high-yielding varieties, applying large quantities of fertilizers, making new irrigation schemes, or the like. Maybe in some regions more advanced farm technology can be introduced. This is not the general opinion of most authors who have published information on the food problem. The main point, however, is that development of agriculture should start from the existing economic and social position of the farmers. These farmers are poor people, they are not in a hurry, and they can only be made aware of better economic possibilities after a long process of change. Therefore, it is important to strengthen local research institutes, extension services, education and rural development centers. Perhaps more attention can be given to pilot farms or to small-scale pilot schemes.

CONSTRAINTS AND BREAKTHROUGHS

Technical Constraints
It has already been proved that land for growing food crops is not a constraint. Cost of agricultural development has been discussed, and it is concluded that enough money can be made available if the governments do have the political will and take appropriate action. As far as reclamation costs are concerned, the MOIRA group has classified each of the 222 regions into one of the five reclamation cost classes. A summary is presented in Table 7-9, from which it can be concluded where land can be reclaimed at the lowest costs.

As has been mentioned, energy used for food production is approx-

Table 7-9. Potential Yield Classes and Development Costs (million hectares)

Potential Yield (metric tons/ha)	Development Cost Categories					
	1 Low	*2*	*3* Intermediate	*4*	*5* High	*Total*
I. Extremely high (25)	–	–	40	37	9	86
II. Very high (20-25)	–	56	313	160	20	549
III. High (15-20)	93	35	275	271	304	978
IV. Medium (10-15)	175	297	297	125	–	894
V. Low (5-10)	26	264	218	67	13	588
VI. Very low (5)	–	163	139	49	11	362
Total	294	815	1,282	709	357	3,457

Soil regions that are either attractive because of low estimated development costs, because if high potential yields, or because more than medium yields can be obtained at not more than average cost, are located above the broken line. These regions comprise 1.536 million hectares, 41 percent of total potential agricultural land. The location of those soils, by geographic areas, is shown in Table 7-3.

imately 5 to 7 percent of the total fossil energy consumption in an industrialized country. It can be no problem. The total energy problem is not discussed. Most energy is needed for fertilizer production, in particular for nitrogen-fixing. Various estimates have already been made on the availability of phosphate (P) and potassium (K). According to Gruhl (1975), there is a reserve of both minerals for at least 400 years if the annual consumption is 30 million and 20 million tons, respectively, per year. Even longer periods are mentioned by de Wit and van Heemst (1977). Schuffelen (1965) stated that 16 kilograms NPK-fertilizers are needed to produce food for one person for one year.

FAO (Dudal, 1969) estimates fertilizers used for 1962 at 2.6 million tons and for 1985 at 31.2 million tons. Wortman (1976) mentions 80 tons of chemical fertilizers used in 1976, half of it in synthetic fixed nitrogen. Almost 160 million tons will be needed in the year 2000 (Revelle, 1976). These are just a few examples. Estimates vary widely, depending on how and where agricultural development has to be performed.

Finally, in many countries the availability of water will become a factor limiting irrigated agriculture. Therefore, the increase of irrigation efficiency should have high priority. On the other hand farmers have to learn to make as good use as possible of rainfall. Water conservation, also at present on a small scale, is extremely important in regions with a long dry season. In such regions in the tropics poverty is extreme.

Firewood will be short within a few decades. Eckhol (1976) made clear statements on the importance of firewood for populations in the tropics. Very often there are no roads to bring fossil fuel, and poor people do not have money to buy it. Foresters should pay more attention to firewood production and should also prevent people from damaging natural forests. A good example can be seen on Java, where agrosylviculture in combination with firewood production (Caleandra) has been practiced for many years. Health constraints—for example, river blindness in Africa—probably can be solved in the near future, and consequently some large river valleys, which up till now have not been used, can be cultivated.

Economic, Social, and Political Constraints
From the foregoing it is clear that economic, social, and especially political constraints are considered to be the most important aspects in discussing world food production, food shortage, malnutrition, and hunger. This conclusion is the result of various studies, particularly the PSAC, the MOIRA, and Bareloch group studies. The economic part of the MOIRA study (de Hoogh, 1976; Linnemann, ed., 1977) is

interesting, but will not be dealt with here. Reference is also made to the books by Brown (1974), Eckholm (1976), Dumont (1973), and Schumacher (1973); the articles in *Scientific American* (September 1976); and various other publications on such subjects as marketing, cooperation, credit, extension, infrastructure, price politics, land value, land ownership, risk, farm management, and so on. These and other factors often limit food production. Locally, regionally, and nationally, the conditions are different; thus it hardly is possible to discuss such problems in general. Most authors therefore, give examples.

What has been said for economic constraints also fits for sociological factors, such as the attitude of the farmers, the situation of the farmer's family, education, organization, customs, religion, the contrasts between rural and city families and between the poor and rich part of the population. Some of these factors are also discussed in the literature cited in this paper and in the book by Hutchinson (1969). It seems too difficult to introduce social factors in computerized models.

Almost all constraints have political aspects and can only be solved if governments take the right measures; for this it is almost impossible to give general guidelines, although many recommendations have been formulated in various national and international conferences. Sometimes it seems almost impossible to find a solution because of the complex character of the problem. Unfortunately several people, who do not have responsibilities, think that only a few problems have to be solved to get an almost ideal situation. It is easy to blame governments of poor countries for not doing enough, or for not making the correct decisions, but it is very difficult to govern an underdeveloped poor country. In fact it probably is more difficult than to reign over a rich country, where organization is better, where large numbers of competent officers and specialists are available, where risks can be taken, and where the checking on observance of laws is better than in many poor countries.

It is no wonder that some authors refer to centrally directed and planned countries of Eastern Europe or China, where some problems are solved in a way that might be imitable by other countries. Whether the Chinese experience of transforming traditional farming is applicable in other countries is a debatable question. It is, however, clear from all studies that rich countries have an extremely high responsibility because they have to help unselfishly.

Political constraints are apparently the most important. Often it is concluded that the political will is present, but very often no political action is taken. Most political leaders generally have a short time horizon, and the food problem can only be solved in the long run. It therefore seems that an important constraint on the world food problem is the attitude that the rich countries have assumed toward the poor countries. It is everybody's responsibility to try to alter this attitude. This can be done in private discussions, meetings, conferences, and by going to the polls to vote.

Since the population is increasing so rapidly in many countries, unemployment will increase, too, because in modern advanced farms 20 to 40 man-hours are required to produce 1,000 kilograms of grain, against 1,200 man-hours in simple African farms (Allan, in Hutchinson, ed., 1969). Improving agriculture finally leads to fewer jobs.

Breakthroughs

In the various computations made, the basis has been the present known and applied technology. It has been pointed out that breakthroughs are not expected to solve the global problem of food, especially for poor countries, except where there is a possible breakthrough in political attitudes. Some scientists state that a new political will to deal with agricultural development is emerging (Wortman, 1976).

It seems possible that new technological discoveries will become available with the result that more food can be produced in the rich countries. For example, if crops could be grown that make a more efficient use of solar radiation, or that have a somewhat longer growing season, or that could fix nitrogen as do legumes, food production could be increased. Genetic and plant physiological research is being done in these fields. The number of food crops is rather small; probably some new food crops could be developed from wild species.

Soil heating in rather cold regions with a very short growing season, diversion of the course of rivers, as planned for some Siberial rivers in the USSR, improving irrigation efficiency, desalinization of sea water and of brackish drainage water, and similar technical measures also can have a great impact on future food production. Whether there will be a change in overall climate or whether local climate can be influenced by man in the future is not definitely known.

Research in many fields is going on also on the productions of unconventional foods. The results cannot be predicted. Unfortunately not enough research is carried out on the actual problem of increasing food production in countries in the tropics, although during the last decade a small number of important international research institutes are working hard on this problem and attaining much success.

REFERENCES

Baade, F. 1960. *Der Weltlauf zum Jahre 2000.* Oldenburg.

Baker, O. F. 1923. Land utilization in the United States: Geographical aspects of the problem. *Geogr. Rev.* 13: 1-26.

Breadfield, R. 1972. Maximizing food production through multiple cropping system centered on rice. In *Science and Man*, IRRI, Los Banos.

Breinjev, L. I. 1974. Un grand exploit du parti et du peuple. *Discours a Alma-Ata.* Moscou.

Brown, L.R., and P. Eckholm. 1974. *By Bread Alone.* New York.

Buringh, P.; H. J. D. van Heemst, and G. J. Staring. 1975. *Computation of the Absolute Maximum Food Production of the World.* Agr. Univ., Wageningen.

Buringh, P. 1977. Mondiaal bodemgebruik en voedselproduktie, Symp. Univ. of Surinam, Paramaribo, Dec. 1976.

Clark, J., and S. Cole 1976. Models of world food supply demand and nutrition. *Food Policy*, pp. 130-42.

de Hoogh, J. 1976. Voedsel voor een verdubbelde wereldbevolking, een studie over de wereldvoedselsituatie op langere termijn. In: Symposium *Voedsel voor allen, plaats en rol van de EEG, pp. 4-23. Utrecht.*

de Vries, C.A., et al. 1969. Choice of food crops in relation to actual and potential production in the tropics. *Neth. J. Agr. Sc.* 15/241-48.

de Wit, C. T., and A.T.J. Nooij. 1973. Over eten en over leven. Diesrede L.H., Wageningen.

de Wit, C. T., and H.D.J. van Heemst. 1977. Aspects of agricultural resources. In *Proc. World Congr. Chem. Engeneering*, Amsterdam, 1976. Elsevier, Amsterdam.

Dudal, R. 1969. Arable land. In *Annual Report 1969*, pp. 13-29. ILRI, Wageningen.

Dumont, R. 1973. *L'utopie ou la mort.* Paris.

Eckholm, E. P. 1976. *Losing Ground.* New York.

El Hakin, A. H. 1973. Das Dujailah Prohekt (Irak). *Ztschr. F. Ausl. Landw.* 12: 245-69.

FAO. 1969. *Provisional Indicative World Plan for Agricultural Development.* Vol. I. Rome.

FAO/Unesco. 1971/77. Soilmap of the World. Paris.

Ferwerda, J. D. 1970. Soil fertility in the tropics as affected by land use. Potassium Symposium.

Fundacion Bariloche, 1976, see A. O. Herrera et al.

Gifford, R. M., et al. 1975. Biophysical constraints in Australian food production: Implications for population policy. *Search* 6: 212-23.

Gruhl, H. 1975. *Ein Planet wird geplundert.* Frankfurt A.M.

Herrera, A. O., et al. 1976. *Catastrophe or New Society? A Latin American World Model.* IDRC-064 e, Canada.

Hopper, W. D. 1976. The development of agriculture in developing countries. *Scient. American* 235: 196-205.

Hutchinson, J., ed. 1969. *Population and Food Supply.* Cambridge.

IDRC. 1976. The tropical forest, overexploited and under used. Canada. Mimeo.

Jennings, P. R. 1976. The amplification of agricultural production. *Scient. American* 235: 180-95.

Kellogg, E. E., and A. C. Orvedal. 1969. Potential arable soils of the world and critical measures for their use. In *Advances in Agronomy*, Vol. 21, pp. 109-70. New York

Koppejan, A. W. G. 1976. "Linnemann and after": Het perspectief van de wereldvoedselvoorziening en de rol van de EEG. In Symposium, *Voedsel voor allen, plaats en rol in de EEG* pp. 60]65. Utrecht.

Korringa, P. 1972. Kan door "maricultuur" de productie van voedsel belangrijk worden opgevoerd? *Landbk. Tijdschr.* 84:41-49.

Kovda, V. A. 1974. *Biosphere, Soils and Their Utilization.* Moscow.

Linnemann, H., ed. 1977. MOIRA—A Model of International Relations in Agriculture. Amsterdam.

Loomis, R. S. 1976. Agricultural systems. *Scient. American* 235:98-105.

MacDonald, R. B. 1976. The large area crop inventory experiment (LASIE). Pectra Memorial Symposium, South Dakota, October 1976.

Meadows, D. 1975. Food and Population: Policies for the United States. New York.

Meadows, D., et al 1972. *The Limits to Growth.* New York.

Mesarovic, M., and E. Pestel. 1974. *De mensheid op een kruispunt.* Amsterdam, Brussel.

Nowland, J. L. 1975a. The Agricultural Productivity of the Soils of Ontario and Quebec. Ottawa.

Nowland, J. L. 1975b. The Agricutural Productivity of the Soils of the Atlantic Provinces. Ottawa.

Nix, H. A. 1976. Resource limitations: Land and water. In AIAS Nat. Conf., pp. 18-27. Camberra.

Papadakis, J. 1975. *The World Food Problem.* Buenos Aires.

PSAC. 1976. *The World Food Problem.* Vol. II. Washington, D.C.

Revelle, R. 1973. Will the earth's land and water resources be sufficient for future population? World Population Conference, Stockholm.

Revelle, R. 1976. The resources available for agriculture. *Scientific American* 235:165-178.

Russel, E. J. 1954. *World Population and World Food Supplies.* London.

Schuffelen, A. C. 1965. Kunstmest voor voedsel. Diesrede, L.H., Wageningen.

Schumacher, E. F. 1973. Small is Beautiful. London.

Simonson, R. W. 1967. Present and potential usefulness of soil resources. *IILC Annual Report 1967*, pp. 7-25. Wageningen.

Wellhausen, E. J. 1976. The agriculture of Mexico. *Scient. American* 235: 128-53.

Wortman, S. 1976. Food and Agriculture, *Scient. American* 235:30-39.

Young, A. 1976. *Tropical Soils and Soil Survey.* Cambridge.

Chapter Eight

Discussion of "The Natural Environment and Food Production," by P. Buringh

Glenn W. Burton

I must enthusiastically commend Professor Buringh for his very interesting paper. We are most fortunate that Professor Buringh was a member of the Dutch team that developed the fourth world model—Model of International Relation in Agriculture (MOIRA)—and that he has shared some of its findings with us. Dividing the world's land area into 222 regions and studying each individually seems to me to be an excellent approach to studying the world food problem. I appreciate Professor Buringh's frankness in emphasizing the weakness in the reliability of the data on which their study had to be based. I agree that much work is needed, but I think they have made a good start and for that I am grateful.

I like the optimism in his report. I am pleased that both the PSAC and the MOIRA studies agree "that economic, social and in particular, political conditions in the world are limiting food production and not the availability of cultivatable land or its productivity." I suppose those of us in agricultural research could conclude from this statement that we have done our part in feeding the hungry world. We could sit back and say "Let George do it," but I don't think we should.

It is good to know that the world has twice as much cultivatable land as it now cultivates. However, I believe Professor Buringh would agree that we are already cultivating the better half. I spent a month in South America last fall looking at some of this "cultivatable land." It had a pH of 4 or less, a high level of aluminum toxicity, deficiencies in several nutrients essential for crop production, and most of it was highly erodable.

I wonder what you thought when you heard Professor Buringh state that the theoretical "upper limit of food production is 30 times the present production when the production is expressed as grain equivalent"? Did you think, "Great, we've got nothing to worry about for a long time"? I hope you kept on listening as he explained some of the assumptions on which this estimate is based. I shall not dwell on his "reduction factors in order to get realistic" data, but I will remind you that the economists in the MOIRA group concluded that solving the world food problem by 2010 is "hardly possible."

It is good to be reminded that if "the 1,270 million metric tons of grain would be equally distributed over the world, nobody would be hungry." I would like to add that if it were equally distributed, no one would eat as well as you and I eat today.

When our American Plant Studies Delegation was traveling in the People's Republic of China in September 1974, we learned that the average Chinese diet was 78 percent cereals, potatoes, and other starchy foods. About 8 percent of their diet was meat, eggs, and milk, and only 12 percent of their diet could be the other things that add zest to our eating. The diet of the average American consists of 23 percent cereals, 35 percent meat, eggs, and milk, and 37 percent other things. No wonder we eat too much. The Chinese caloric intake averages only about two-thirds that of the American, yet the thousands of Chinese that we saw showed no evidence of malnutrition. Neither did we see any fat people. The Chinese people are smaller than Americans and do not need as many calories. Many of us would enjoy better health if we ate less.

Eating is one of our greatest pleasures, and as our economic status improves, diet is modified to include more meat, milk, eggs, and other foods. It takes more land to feed a person with these foods than it does with a cereal diet. As the poor in the world improve their economic lot, they will demand more of the world's land to produce their improved diets.

In emphasizing the importance of the cereal grains, Dr. Buringh states: "The cultivated grains (mainly wheat, rice, and corn) provide 75 percent of the energy and protein needs of man." I hope we can say this one day, but I don't believe we can today. The cereals do supply about 75 percent of humanity's energy, but only about half its protein. Most of the cereals are deficient in protein content and one or more of the essential amino acids. Thus millions of people restricted to a cereal diet suffer from malnutrition associated with protein deficiencies. One major objective of the cereal breeders today is to increase the quantity and quality of the protein in the cereal with which they work. The potential of such research can be found in the Lancota variety of hard red winter wheat recently released in Nebraska. Culminating 20 years of cooperative USDA-state research, Lancota combines 10 to 20 percent more protein with the yield, disease resistance, and milling and baking qualities of leading varieties in Nebraska. Replacing other varieties grown in Nebraska with Lancota would produce 45 million kg more protein per year at no extra cost. I can think of no cheaper or better way to solve the world's protein problem.

I agree that "the modernization of farming cannot be obtained in a few years." It took 25 years to increase by 4.6 times peanut yields on 213,000 ha of land in Georgia. For years before 1950, yields had averaged 800 kg/ha. Then research learned how to control late blight *Sclerotium rolfsii* Sacc. and use herbicides to control weeds. An outstanding young county agent, J. Frank McGill, became extension specialist for peanuts in 1954 and set about to overcome the resistance to change among Georgia's peanut farmer. Using many different educational tools, including outstanding peanut production schools in each peanut county every year, and by enlisting the cooperation of research, extension, teaching, government, industry, and growers, McGill served as the catalyst for improving peanut production in Georgia. His expertise and untiring efforts earned the grower's confidence, which led to rapid adoption of constraint-removing practices coming from research. The combined effort increased average peanut yields in Georgia from 800 to 3,700 kg/ha in 25 years. Perhaps more important, it demonstrated what the world must do if it is to feed itself.

How many of you realized before today that "post-harvest losses in most tropical countries are 40 percent or more"? Even in the United States, these losses amount to 10 percent of the food produced. Surely the world can and must do something to reduce these losses.

I was glad that Dr. Buringh considered the role of muscle power in the world. At the Human Survival Seminar at North Carolina State University last month, Dr. Calvin Schwabe from the University of California at Davis told us that animals provide 98 percent of the draft power for agriculture in India, China, Korea, and Indochina. For the world as a whole, the value drops to 85 percent. He also said that if the world were to use petroleum energy in agriculture as farmers in the United States do, its known petroleum reserves would last only 13 years. In China, weeds pulled from crop fields, grass cut from every square foot of land not cropped, and crop residues supply most of the energy for draft animals. When these animals can no longer work in the fields, they are slaughtered to make food, shoes, and a host of things by the population.

Anyone who has traveled in India knows that dung from the sacred cows is the fuel used to cook the food for half the people in that country. Dr. Schwabe told us that the fuel energy supplied by the sacred cow of India exceeded the draft energy that it produces. These animals consume crop residues, weeds, and sparse vegetation from land not suited to crop production and thus compete very little with the population.

In the People's Republic of China, I took a picture of a solar cooker that could cook 3 pounds of rice in 40 minutes. Back home, I made a simpler model that could be built by almost anyone for less than $10. As I shared the plans for this simple solar cooker with H.D. Johns, our agricultural missionary in Vikarabad, India, I asked, "How much more food could India produce if she used solar cookers to cook her food on sunny days and used the dung saved to fertilize her crops?"

Professor Buringh indicated that "50 percent of the timber cut in the world is used for firewood"—and in the tropics 80 percent of the annual cut is firewood. How much forest land now producing firewood could be used for food production if humans used solar energy to cook most of their food?

I am concerned that 0.5 to 1.0 percent of the world's cultivated land is lost annually because of nonagricultural land use. It is sobering to realize that another half million ha of cropland is being misused. I wonder how much longer the world can let me do as I please with the land that I own.

The FAO Indicative World Plan caused Professor Buringh to conclude that most of the annual increase in food production in the world results from cultivating land not cultivated before, and that a much smaller increase is the result of improving farm technology. I find this hard to believe and want to share with you information in the Foreign Agriculture Economic Report Number 98, published in 1974. This report divides the world's land for grain production about equally between the developed and the developing countries. The developed countries have had no increase in land area, but have had a 63 percent increase in yield per ha over the past 20 years. During the same period the developing countries have had a 32 percent increase in land area for grain production and a 32 percent increase in yield per ha. These data suggest to me that well over half of the increase in food produced from 1950 to 1970 must be credited to the use of superior varieties, more fertilizer, and improved technology, all of which increased yields on existing cultivated land. I am pleased that Professor Buringh sees increasing yields on existing cultivated land as a means of protecting the environment.

Professor Buringh states that because the world's 4 billion ha of grazing land contribute only 2 percent to total world food production, they can be ignored in global models. The PSAC report concludes that 3.6 billion ha of the world's land could be used to graze livestock, but that this grazing land could only provide "a few grams of animal protein per person per day for the estimated world population in the year 2000." Even though this may be true, I do not believe that animals should be excluded from our plans to protect and improve the environment as we also strive to improve humanity's diet.

Converting plant foods (grains) to animal foods before they are fed to people does reduce materially the number of people that can be fed. But most of the earth's 4 billion ha of grazing land is too dry, too rough, or too cold to grow food crops. These lands can feed people only as people consume the animals that feed on the plants that grow there. Straw and other crop wastes can feed animals that, in turn, can help feed people even as they furnish draft power and fertilizer (dung and urine) to grow crops and produce meat, milk, and fuel (dung) to cook their food. Ruminants could produce substantial amounts of food for people if they were fed only crop wastes and high-quality forages bred to grow on land too rough for crop production. These forages, largely grasses and legumes, as they produce food for people through agriculture, could also control soil erosion, conserve water, greatly reduce the sedimentation of rivers, lakes, and irrigation reservoirs, and help to beautify the environment.

Replacing the native forages with well-fertilized improved cultivars can increase the yields of forage and meat many times. The native range of the southeastern United States, with an annual rainfall of 125 cm, produces about 13 kg/ha/yr of liveweight gain (LWG). Coastal Bermuda-grass planted on the same land and fertilized with 224 kg/ha of N plus adequate P and K can produce 650 kg/ha of LWG during the warm season. A clover such as crimson or arrowleaf seeded on the grass in the fall can add another 300 kg/ha of LWG during the winter and spring. Thus the total animal production from such a pasture can be 80 times the production of the native range.

In the People's Republic of China, silt washed from the hillsides and carried in rivers to lakes and reservoirs threatens to seriously damage and ultimately destroy the irrigation system so essential for her food production. The soil on most of these hills could be stabilized if the open vegetation growing there was replaced with good sod-forming grasses such as Coastal and Coastcross-1 bermudagrass. If well fertilized, these grasses could materially increase the production of scarce meat.

I was delighted to learn last year that sprigs of Coastcross-1 bermudagrass that we sent to Professor Lee in Canton, China were being increased for experimental plantings on some of these hills. Is it too much to dream that one day the hills of southeastern China will be covered with a carpet of green grass that will beautify the environment as it protects the soil from erosion, reduces silt in the streams, and feeds cattle that can supply meat, milk, cheese, butter, and ice cream to enhance the Chinese diet? I don't think so.

Professor Buringh tells us that with "so much money spent for military purposes, one can hardly imagine that no money could be found to produce food for every human being in the world." I agree. It would be a different world if the leaders of the world's governments would also agree and act accordingly.

I am glad that Professor Buringh devoted the last section of his paper to a consideration of breakthroughs. I believe they are tremendously important. Most of the world's resources used to grow food are limited because they are nonrenewable. Most cultivars used today recover less than half the fertilizer used to grow them. I believe cultivars that are more efficient in fertilizer use can and must be bred.

Professor Buringh tells us that of the land presently cultivated in the world today, only 14 percent is irrigated. Of the 3.2 billion ha of potentially cultivatable land, only 400 million (12.5 percent) are potentially irrigable. Thus water will set the ceiling for potential crop yields on most of the world's cropland. Increasing water use efficiency on these lands should be one of the major objectives of agricultural research. Breeding cultivars with greater drought tolerance that can utilize water more efficiently offers one of the best solutions to this problem. Coastal bermudagrass that yielded 6 times as much as common bermudagrass in a very dry season (twice as much in normal years) is proof that it can be done.

New cultivars and technologies may first be used in rich countries, but they can also help to solve the food problems in the poor countries. New high-yielding semidwarf wheats with a package of recommended production practices and the leadership of Norman Borlaug quadrupled wheat yields in Mexico in 20 years. I believe that significant breakthroughs can help to increase food production anywhere in the world if they can be introduced by people like Norman Borlaug and Frank McGill. It requires the cooperation and support of research, extension, industry, government, the growers, and leaders like Borlaug and McGill to get it done.

Professor Buringh said that "building up larger food reserves and increasing foreign aid for agricultural development in the poor countries will be needed for many years to come." I agree. But I also know it is difficult to help people without hurting them. I believe, therefore, that food reserves should only be used for disaster relief and that aid should be directed toward helping the poor countries increase food production on their own lands. We must remember that we help people most when we help them help themselves.

Again I must thank Professor Buringh for his stimulating and optimistic paper. I too am optimistic. Much can be done to increase food production in the world. Professor Buringh emphasized the need for both political will and political action. I believe the world need for food today and certainly tomorrow demands the will and the action of everyone who has a responsibility for feeding the world.

Chapter Nine

Discussion of "The Natural Environment and Food Production," by P. Buringh

James E. Halpin

The second discussant has been labeled as the person who is supposed to agree with the speaker or the first discussant.

In that capacity, one can arbitrate the differences, and if necessary heal the wounds should they have led to fisticuffs. Or one can attempt to provide a somewhat different perspective to the material that has been brought forward, rehash it if necessary, fill up allotted time, and then sit down.

I feel very fortunate sharing the programs with the two gentlemen that have preceded me on the platform this morning. I think I'm a little more inclined to agree with Dr. Burton and his position than I am with that of Professor Buringh. Nevertheless, I am an optimist on world food and the potential for the future. There is one note of caution I would stress on this topic. Let's not make it look to be so very automatic!

I got the impression this morning, listening to the previous speakers, that things are just going to happen. For example, we are going to have more food. I would say that the automatic aspect we can assume is that we are going to have more people! I would hope that another automatic aspect is that we will have more longevity, a longer life span for the people we have. I do not feel, however, that this is quite so automatic. It is more problematical. In either case, more food will be required.

As Dr. Burton has brought out, the crops we are raising today are not the same crops that either our forefathers brought to this continent or that they found growing here. They have been altered extensively by genetics, by management, and by various economic and engineering practices, and these alterations are extremely important. The alteration process continues. While the alteration process continues, we at the same time are concerned with protecting a gene pool of wild gene sources of our economically important plants throughout the world. Gene pools are important because they are the sources of future genetic alterations which we recognize we will have to be able to make in order to cope with changes in environment, pests, and practices.

Let me give you a case in point. When the Rockefeller Foundation expanded their corn program in Guatamala, they entered into a country where corn was basically an open-pollinated crop. The Guatamalan farmer went out and picked the best ears grown, and saved those for the next harvest year. The farmers grew what was basically a wild crop under cultivation. They got quite good yields. The Rockefeller Foundation's program brought to them hybrid corn. As a result, yields increased dramatically. And as a result of this, the farmers in turn discarded native lines of corn. This is fine, except in the process of inadvertently destroying the genetic lines maintained for so long, these lines were lost for the future use of the plant breeder. And consequently there is a very real movement in the world today to search out natural lines—genetic lines of important crops—and see to it that we have them available for crop improvement. We just cannot go into a factory and manufacture them.

I refer to something like this as the General Motors Syndrome—a situation where agriculture is so very different from much of our world. I am not picking on General Motors, but it does serve as an example. General Motors can decide to make Chevrolets—a thousand different models and colors and combinations of accessories of Chevrolets at a plant in Janesville, Wisconsin; or, if they see fit, they can decide to stop making Chevrolets at the plant in Janesville, Wisconsin. They can take the dies, they can move them to another plant—say Atlanta, Georgia—and they can proceed after a startup period to turn out these same Chevrolets. There is no need for continuity. They can start and stop at will. But agriculture and our food supply is based on living systems. It is essential that we have continuity. If you break the continuity, you lose it.

I might also add, too, that we must remember that agriculture—and this refers to agricultural research—operates under certain constraints. I would like to express it this way. Engineers can have the plans for a building that would ordinarily take 21 months to build. They, however, can increase the amount of workers during construction, can go from one shift a day to two or three shifts a day, and possibly can compress the construction time so that the building is now erected and available for occupancy within 12 or 13 months. That's great! But no one has yet figured out a mechanism whereby a cow can have a calf in less than 9 months! And this holds true for much of what we are talking about. There are time restraints—biological time restraints that are imposed upon our agriculture and our food systems. These we cannot ignore.

I would say that Professor Buringh is more traveled, around the world, than I am, and is more optimistic. I do not mean to say that I'm a pessimist. I'm not that. I maintain that I think one of the points we have to face is the point of how humanity perceives this whole food issue. In this country we have basically a cheap food policy. Our readily available food supply and an absence of shortages has placed an automatic concept into the food issue here so that we do not really feel any food pressure. Looking down the road, I think we are inclined to believe that massive infusions of money and personnel can accomplish anything. If we need a satellite to orbit the earth in a short period of time, we can put a massive program together and we can place a satellite in orbit. And I don't really mean to downgrade this type of achievement. It is fantastic, and the world admires us for it. But within a biological constraint system, often it is not the quantity of the magnitude of personnel, but it is the capability of that personnel to function within the system that makes the results successful.

I would like to bring out one important point. We must protect our quality of life and try to achieve it for others elsewhere for the future. There are some major shifts that have taken place, especially in the United States, that have potential for the world, and they have occurred very recently. Dr. Buringh pointed out that the United States appeared to be at the point where there were a little over three million horses in the country. However, their population is on the increase. The 1975 figure is 6.7 million horses in this country. The unfortunate part, however, is that these horses are not working for us. We are using them as pleasure and companion animals. They are part of our pet syndrome. And so we have an increase in our companion animal population competing with our food supply for domestic human use and for potential exportation overseas.

We must also remember, too, that we have had a major increase in longevity for people in this country, and we have a potential for an even greater increase in longevity within the short life span of one, or two at the most, generations. These people will want to eat daily.

The other point is that there are areas of the world where the population pressure is very low. The country of Belize in Central America is a case study. That is a country where the average population is four people per square mile. The population is distributed basically one-third in the capital city, one-third in small outlying villages, and one-third in the rural country hacking out the jungle trying to produce food. Imagine a country with four people per square mile, and yet it imports 34 percent of its food supply! That is Belize today. Not a very productive use of apparent resources.

Why is there not greater production? Partly it is because the type of agriculture that could operate there, one that could eliminate the jungle and increase production almost instantly, is the type of agriculture that also requires a ready-made available market at a price—and a country with only 150,000 people just does not have that type of market to stimulate that type of agriculture. And so we get, in the world of agriculture, country by country, a situation where there is a need for incentives for people to produce—where they can do so at a cost that would permit them to put their results of production on the market, and have the essential resources to get the results of that production to market.

I would remind you that the majority of the people of the world continue to live near the peripheral areas of the continents because of the availability of the oceanic transports—ocean traffic and shipping. Yet, if this world is to be one with only a few areas as the sources of our surpluses, the ports for exportation may become clogged as the shipping capacity is not there to move the food that must be moved in world commerce. We have already seen this happen in the United States with the food-laden barges backed up the Mississippi River trying to get to the port of New Orleans to transfer their loads to ocean-going vessels, which are likewise stacked up trying to load. The world must expand its production locally to supply people where they are.

That's enough of the pessimistic side; I'm not a pessimist. Let us look to other aspects; the optimistic side. Our topic is natural resources. I feel there are natural resources which have not really been covered in this symposium, and I think they are worthy of mention.

The first is new plant and animal resources. The animals and plants we utilize for food production today have been domesticated by humanity because they showed promise, and in turn did actually provide a return on the investment of time, labor, and capital. The net result was favorable. Obviously, on this globe there are other plants and animals suitable for study and potential domestication. Agricultural researchers can find these others if they seek them out. We have active projects in progress right now looking for new plant and animal resources. For example, I like to joke about the alligator. My friends tell me that Halpin has the alligator syndrome. But I maintain that the alligator *might be* a very desirable animal to domesticate and utilize for a food source. It tastes like chicken. The hide is desirable for shoes and other leather products. So here we have an animal to which we could feed our garbage—garbage that in many areas we are burying or we are burning, and a resource we are losing. We could pass this garbage through an animal system and provide food in a new form for people.

The second is new innovative animal feed systems. Dr. Burton covered the area of forage crops. The figures I have for the United States is that 81 percent of the calories consumed by the red meat industry today come from grasses and not from the fattening grains. Most of the grass comes from land not suitable for row crops. Our use of grasses will increase; it already has. It has already increased because the time that beef animals are spending in the feed lot and being fed grain has been greatly reduced due to the high price of corn. It is a basic market principle: as corn goes up and people resist the increased price of red meat, then we move to more leaner and less expensive grass-fattened beef. I think this is a step in the right direction, because obviously our number one disease in this country is being overweight. We do not need the fat that excess corn will add to it.

But there are other resources to be considered in animal feeding as well. As a result of our animal production systems in this country, and the types of systems being devloped elsewhere, our animals are producing tremendous quantities of manure—animal waste. Now this is, in the eyes of some people, a dirty topic. I maintain it is a unique and valuable resource. It is a new type of resource, and one that is available in concentration as a result of current agricultural management practices. And this new resource is natural in view of its background. Most important, it has potential for increased food production.

In studies going out at the Alabama Agricultural Experiment Station and elsewhere, agricultural scientists are studying various combinations of manures with grasses, corn stalks, and other non-human-competitive food sources. Unique forms of silage are being developed. The scientists are feeding our livestock these unique rations and obtaining meat supplies that are very, very adequate. Good-quality economical beef is the result. This type of energy and nutrient cycling permits the poultry industry to feed the grain to the chickens the first time and remove a certain proportion of the diet; the chicken manure is restructured into the ration for the steer. The initial food for poultry helped create chicken meat, eggs, and later beef, as well. This may be repugnant to you, but nevertheless it is a very natural process, because animals have historically often consumed a certain amount of manure in their daily living. Particularly is this true in the wild. Consequently, we have a new resource.

We can carry this one step further. After we have obtained from this resource the food energy it contains, and has been wasted in the past on microorganisms and insects in the soil, we can pass the residue through another process and make pressboard from it. What was originally manure now is a component of the lumber trade, and as such will conserve trees, another natural resource we must not remove excessively.

Or we can utilize the same process to make lumber out of sugar baggasse, which is currently being burned. (Unfortunately, it is being burned to create an energy source for the production of sugar through the sugarcane manufacturing process.) Or we can even take the paper out of the garbage and produce another type of paneling out of that material. A wide variety of products can be developed, all useful.

Such imitation materials may not look very good when on the walls of your house. Nevertheless, it can be used in the construction trade in many places that only use lumber one time or where appearance is of no importance. Obviously it will take paint or some other type of surface coating such as the plastic types. New products can be the result of new uses of unusual resources.

The third is unique biological resources in this world of plants. Green plants represent a unique resource because of their photosynthetic capacity. I think one of the hopeful things being worked on through agricultural research is the concept of photosynthetic efficiency in important crops. Agricultural scientists are literally making food-producing plants more efficient in their use of sunlight. For example, the leaf of the corn plant is basically horizontal. As such, it is approximately seven cells thick and literally thousands of cells long and wide. The people of Illinois, through plant genetics, have restructured the corn plant so that the leaves of these experimental plants are held more perpendicular, more upright. The net result is that the rays of the sun, instead of having only five effective cells to go through to be captured from a photosynthetic standpoint, now have thousands more.

Research results show an increase in the chance for capturing the sunlight and improving its photosynthetic efficiency. Comparisons with normal lines of corn demonstrate an increase of approximately 15 percent in these experimental lines over the conventional corn lines from which they are derived. But there is a second improvement as well. Because the leaves of these experimental corn plants are now more upwardly inclined, and the plants require less space, you can move the plants closer together and increase the number of plants per acre. The real key to this was brought up in the symposium earlier. It's not how many more acres we bring in production, but how much do we produce per acre—that's what may really feed the world.

I do want to emphasize a fourth component of what both Dr. Buringh and Dr. Burton have said. Modern agriculture provides a mechanism to protect the environment. It consists of its efficient production systems. Modern agriculture requires inputs from the biological scientists, the horticulturists, agronomists, the physical scientists such as soil science, the agricultural engineers, and from the economists who work with the production and the movement to markets. I do not think there is any place on earth where the "systems approach" has been brought together quite so well as has been done in American agriculture. It is important for us, therefore, to improve our systems approach and study mechanisms whereby we can move these systems into other countries. We must provide these other countries with essential modifications, however, that will meet their needs, but which are based on what we can show to be correct for their condition and not necessarily for ours.

I might add that there are other parameters that I want to state one more time before we leave. These must be considered. One is the reluctance of many governments to properly support food and agricultural research. Unfortunately, often in the underdeveloped countries of the world the emphasis in food reseach has not been "food for the people" of that country, but has been on export items—coffee, tea, cocoa, jute, and the like. There are exceptions. (One of the pleasures of having been with the Rockefeller Foundation Program is the realization that its program philosophically gave a chance for countries to realize they have needs at home and the opportunities they can develop there.) There is a need to reduce distribution costs and improve food quality in much of the world. This is not only from the standpoint of food itself but from the energy utilized or the energy lost. Certainly there is a need to be able to maintain the continuity of food production because we are talking about people who must eat continuously throughout the year in spite of the fact that agriculture historically, at least in the temperate zone, has been a system based on planting once a year—harvesting once a year—with intervening periods of either growth and development or periods of no production. The tropics are somewhat different, but as of yet we still do not have in the tropics a good, continuous system whereby you plant every day and you harvest every day. The tropics do have potential for coming close to this, however, at least for some crops.

I think the most important question that must be raised is, How much pressure should humanity put on this globe? It is actually finite in size; we share it with other organisms, some of which are available to us. If we are to speak of averages, as has been done throughout this symposium, and seek increases on such potential averages, we must remember that brief shortages can lead to malnutrition and death.

And my final point is that a low cost food policy may reduce incentives to produce. If there is anything that agriculture needs, it's incentives. We need to develop a philosophy of food from the standpoint of its overall worth, coupled with the care of our important and available resources. I hope, through research, we may develop means to acquire such incentives.

Part IV

Demographics

Chapter Ten

Migration, Urbanization, Resources, & Development

Andrei Rogers

WORLD URBANIZATION AND THE PROBLEMS OF HUMAN SETTLEMENTS

Representatives from 132 nations assembled in Vancouver in June of last year to convene Habitat, the United Nations Conference on Human Settlements. The conference was a global inquiry into solutions of the critical and urgent problems of human settlements created by the convergence of two historic events: unprecedentedly high rates of population growth and massive rural-to-urban migration.

World population in 1975 numbered about 4 billion and exhibited a growth rate of just under 2 percent a year. At this rate of growth the world's population would double in about 35 years and would total approximately 6.5 billion by the end of this century.

Figure 10-1 illustrates the enormous increase in the speed with which world population has grown during the past three centuries. From the beginning of human time to 1650, world population grew to a total of about a half billion. The second half billion came by 1830, and the second billion was added in only another hundred years. It took just 30 years to increase this total to 3 billion and the fourth billion came a little over 15 years later.

Urban population growth has been even more explosive (Figure 10-2). Roughly 1.6 billion people—40 percent of the world's population—live in urban areas today. At the beginning of the last century

The author is indebted to Frans Willekens for programming and carrying out the computer-generated urbanization scenarios described in this paper.

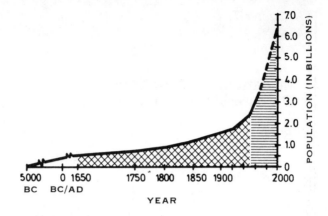

Source: Berelson (2) (1974), p. 4.

Figure 10-1. World Population through History

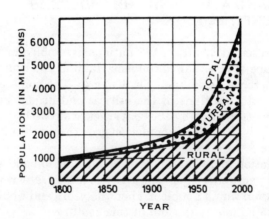

Source: United Nations (34) (1976), p. 3.

Figure 10-2. Growth of the World's Urban and Rural Populations: 1800-2000 (in millions).

the urban population of the world totaled only 25 million. The United Nations estimates that about 3.1 billion people, twice the size of today's urban population, will be living in urban areas by the year 2000.

Rapid rates of population growth and urbanization occurred first among nations that first experienced modernization. Thus, for two-thirds of the world these rates did not reach significant levels until very recently, generally after World War II. It is convenient, therefore, to examine the population situation separately for the developed and the less developed parts of the world.

Urbanization in Developed and Less Developed Countries

Less than one-third of the world's population lives in developed parts of the world, defined by the United Nations to comprise all of Europe, Northern America, Japan, Temperate South America, Australia and New Zealand, and the Soviet Union. The rest of the world's people, about 2.9 billion of them, live in the economically poorer, less developed world.

Birth rates in less developed countries are, on the average, about twice as high as those in developed countries. Although death rates in the former also exceed those in the latter, the gap is smaller and becoming narrower. The difference between births and deaths is natural increase, and rates of natural increase in the less developed world far exceed those in the developed nations. Consequently, the population growth rate of the less developed countries is two and a half times that of the developed (2.4 percent against 0.9 percent); and their share of the global population total is rapidly increasing and is expected to exceed three-fourths by the year 2000 (Figure 10-3).

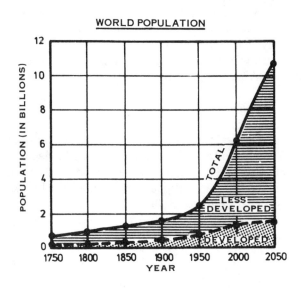

Source: Keyfitz (1976), p. 29.

Figure 10-3. Population Growth of Today's Developed and Less Developed Countries.

A large proportion of the population of the less developed world is engaged in agriculture. In consequence, a relatively small fraction of this population is urban—only about one-fourth. The corresponding fraction for the developed world is close to seven-tenths (Figure 10-4). But because of their considerably larger share of the world's population, less developed countries today have as large an urban population as do the developed countries, each having an urban population of just under four-fifths of a billion people.

Urban populations are growing much more rapidly than the total populations of which they are a part. Table 10-1 shows that this is specially true in the less developed world. Between 1950 and 1970 the total population of the developed countries increased by 26 percent, and that of the less developed countries by 54 percent; during the same period the urban population of the developed countries grew by 57 percent, while that of the less developed countries increased by over 146 percent.

The latest United Nations projections of urban populations up to the year 2000 for seven major areas of the world are graphed in Figure 10-5. These are drawn on a logarithmic scale so that parallel slopes depict equal rates of growth. They indicate that urban growth rates in Europe, Northern America, and the Soviet Union are likely to slow down to relatively moderate levels, whereas those of East and South Asia, Latin America, and Africa are likely to continue to be comparatively high. Between 1975 and the year 2000 the urban population of Europe is likely to increase by a third, that of Northern America and the Soviet Union by one-half. It may double in East Asia, treble in South Asia and Africa and grow two and a half times in Latin America.

Historically, urban growth and urbanization have occurred together, but they do not measure the same attribute to national population. Urban growth refers to an increase in the number of people living in urban settlements. Urbanization refers to a rise in proportion of a total population that is concentrated in urban settlements. The latter measure, therefore, is a function not only of urban growth but also of rural growth (Figure 10-6). Thus urban growth can occur without any urbanization if the rural population increases at a rate equal to or greater than that of the urban population.

Table 10-2 traces the urbanization process in the world's developed and less developed regions and in eight of its major geographical areas. In striking contrast to the substantial differences among urban growth rates in Table 10-1 and Figure 10-5, differences in the rates of urbanization are relatively minor, except in three instances. The Soviet Union and Latin America exhibit above-average rates of urbanization; in Oceania the pace of urbanization is below average. Urbanization in

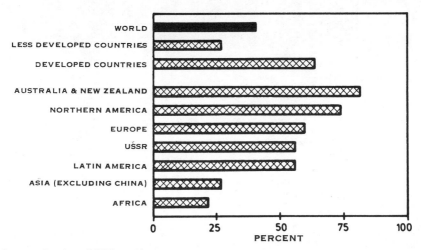

Source: Berelson (1974), p. 14.

Figure 10-4. Percentage Population Urban in Major World Regions, 1970.

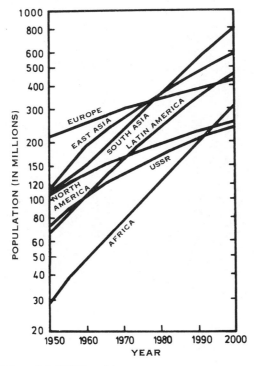

Source: United Nations (34) (1976), p. 21.

Figure 10-5. Urban Population, 1950-2000, in Seven Major Areas.

Table 10-1. Population Estimates and Projections (Medium Variant) and Average Annual Rate of Growth: World Total, Regions, Countries or Areas, Urban and Rural, 1950-2000

Regions, countries or areas	Total: T Urban: U Rural: R	Total population (in thousands) Annual rate of growth (percentage)												
		1950	Rate	1960	Rate	1970	Rate	1975	Rate	1980	Rate	1990	Rate	2000
(1)		(2)	(3)	(4)	(5)	(6)	(7)	(8)	(9)	(10)	(11)	(12)	(13)	(14)
World Total	T	2,501,243	1.8	2,985,937	1.9	3,609,600	1.9	3,967,005	2.0	4,373,210	1.9	5,279,041	1.7	6,253,135
	U	714,681	3.4	1,006,942	2.9	1,350,032	2.9	1,557,685	2.9	1,799,528	2.8	2,385,646	2.6	3,103,214
	R	1,786,562	1.0	1,978,995	1.3	2,259,568	1.3	2,409,320	1.3	2,573,682	1.1	2,893,395	0.9	3,149,921
More Developed Regions	T	857,305	1.3	975,748	1.1	1,084,018	0.9	1,131,715	0.9	1,181,072	0.8	1,277,570	0.6	1,360,557
	U	457,339	2.5	586,192	2.0	717,626	1.7	782,582	1.6	849,670	1.5	983,935	1.1	1,106,942
	R	399,966	-0.3	389,556	-0.6	366,393	-1.0	349,133	-1.0	331,402	-1.2	293,635	-1.5	253,615
Less Developed Regions	T	1,643,938	2.0	2,010,189	2.3	2,525,582	2.3	2,835,290	2.4	3,192,138	2.3	4,001,471	2.0	4,892,579
	U	257,342	4.9	420,750	4.1	632,407	4.1	775,103	4.1	949,858	3.9	1,401,711	3.5	1,996,272
	R	1,386,596	1.4	1,589,439	1.4	1,893,175	1.7	2,060,187	1.7	2,242,280	1.5	2,599,760	1.1	2,896,307
Africa	T	218,833	2.2	272,753	2.5	351,594	2.6	401,138	2.8	460,686	2.9	613,714	2.8	813,119
	U	28,878	5.1	47,991	4.7	76,997	4.8	98,059	4.8	124,789	4.7	199,300	4.3	306,780
	R	189,955	1.7	224,762	2.0	274,597	2.0	303,079	2.1	335,897	2.1	414,414	2.0	506,339
Europe	T	391,968	0.8	425,154	0.8	459,085	0.6	473,128	0.6	486,611	0.5	513,779	0.5	539,812
	U	214,751	1.6	251,785	1.6	296,903	1.4	317,700	1.3	338,548	1.2	381,799	1.1	424,996
	R	177,217	-0.2	173,369	-0.7	162,182	-0.9	155,428	-1.0	148,063	-1.1	131,980	-1.4	114,816
America, North	T	218,633	2.0	267,577	1.7	318,008	1.5	342,609	1.6	371,480	1.7	440,143	1.5	513,373
	U	125,371	3.0	168,589	2.4	214,936	2.1	239,241	2.2	267,408	2.2	334,545	2.0	408,618
	R	93,262	0.6	98,988	0.4	103,072	0.1	103,368	0.1	104,072	0.1	105,598	-0.1	104,755

America, South	T	111,365	2.8	146,662	2.7	191,401	2.6	*218,324*	2.6	248,984	2.5	320,578	2.3	402,755
	U	47,371	4.6	74,725	4.2	113,845	3.8	*137,825*	3.7	165,587	3.4	232,133	2.9	311,050
	R	63,994	1.2	71,937	0.8	77,556	0.7	*80,499*	0.7	83,397	0.6	88,445	0.4	91,705
Asia	T	1,367,737	1.8	1,643,691	2.1	2,027,420	2.1	*2,255,458*	2.2	2,513,851	2.0	3,068,977	1.7	3,636,335
	U	219,284	4.6	348,495	3.5	496,462	3.6	*595,268*	3.6	713,856	3.5	1,008,499	3.2	1,385,689
	R	1,148,453	1.2	1,295,196	1.7	1,530,958	1.6	*1,660,190*	1.6	1,799,995	1.4	2,060,478	0.9	2,250,646
Oceania	T	12,632	2.2	15,771	2.0	19,323	2.0	*21,308*	1.9	23,482	1.8	28,109	1.5	32,715
	U	8,142	2.4	10,396	2.7	13,561	2.4	*15,262*	2.3	17,156	2.2	21,298	1.8	25,584
	R	4,490	1.8	5,375	0.7	5,762	1.0	*6,046*	0.9	6,326	0.7	6,811	0.5	7,131
USSR Union of Soviet Socialist Republics	T	180,075	1.7	214,329	1.3	242,768	1.0	*255,038*	1.0	268,115	0.9	293,742	0.7	315,027
	U	70,884	3.9	104,961	2.7	137,328	2.3	*154,330*	2.2	172,185	1.9	208,071	1.5	240,498
	R	109,191	0.0	109,368	−0.4	105,440	−0.9	*100,708*	−1.0	95,930	−1.1	85,671	−1.4	74,529

Source: United Nations (1976), pp. 22-49.

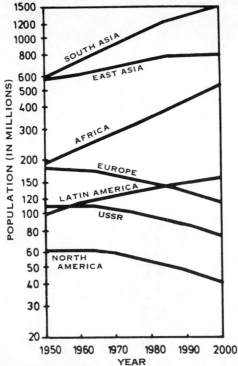

Source: United Nations (1976), p. 23.

Figure 10-6. Rural Population, 1950-2000, in Seven Major Areas.

Table 10-2. Estimated and Projected Percentage of Population (Medium Variant) in Urban Areas: World Total, Macro Regions and Regions, 1950-2000

Macro regions and regions	Percentage of estimated and projected population in urban areas						
	1950	*1960*	*1970*	*1975*	*1980*	*1990*	*2000*
(1)	*(2)*	*(3)*	*(4)*	*(5)*	*(6)*	*(7)*	*(8)*
World Total	28.57	33.72	37.40	*39.27*	41.15	45.19	49.63
More Developed Regions	53.35	60.08	66.20	*69.15*	71.94	77.02	81.36
Less Developed Regions	15.65	20.93	25.04	*27.34*	29.76	35.03	40.80
Africa	13.20	17.60	21.90	*24.45*	27.09	32.47	37.73
Latin America	40.90	48.51	56.85	*60.42*	63.76	69.74	74.80
Northern America	63.65	69.83	74.15	*76.53*	78.78	82.88	86.41
East Asia	16.55	24.63	28.53	*30.66*	32.90	37.73	43.19
South Asia	15.53	18.05	21.09	*22.96*	24.97	29.59	35.04
Europe	54.79	59.22	64.67	*67.15*	69.57	74.31	78.73
Oceania	64.46	65.92	70.18	*71.63*	73.06	75.77	78.20
USSR	39.36	48.97	56.57	*60.51*	64.22	70.83	76.34

Source: United Nations (1976), p. 54. (34)

the remaining regions, however, may be seen to be proceeding at a relatively similar pace, with percentage urban shares increasing by approximately one-half of a percent every year. The differences are a consequence of variations in rates of rural growth.

The Problems of Human Settlements

Problems of urbanization are problems of national human settlement systems: those networks of spatially dispersed concentrations of people and economic activities. Cities, towns, and urban agglomerations are nodal centers of life in modern societies, and changes in urbanization trends appear as changes in the spatial and hierarchically structured patterns of such centers.

The major problems of urbanization arise because urban growth is polarized and spatially imbalanced. Growth does not generally occur proportionally at all nodes of a national settlement system. Particularly in less developed countries, it usually falls unequally on the larger (20,000 or more) and often already overcrowded centers of urban life (Table 10-3).

Regional disparities in rates of urban growth are even more dramatic at the level of the individual urban settlement. Table 10-4 sets out recent United Nations projections of the growth of some of the less developed world's largest urban centers. The size of the population growth multiplier, the urban momentum, for some cities is truly awesome. During the 25 years between 1975 and 2000, Lima, Mexico City, Jakarta, and Teheran all are expected to triple their populations; Sao Paulo and Seoul are projected to grow by a factor of 2.5; and Addis Ababa, Nairobi, Lagos, and Kinshasa are to increase fourfold.

As with rapid population growth in general, rapid urban growth increases the difficulties of providing a population with the necessary sustenance, employment, services, and infrastructure. A rapidly burgeoning urban population strains health and education budgets, complicates the reduction of unemployment levels, and exacerbates problems connected with provision of adequate supplies of food, energy, housing, water, and transport and sanitary facilities. The "demographic investment" needed just to maintain present doubling or tripling of institutional plant within the next 25 years. That these areas are to be found mostly in countries least able to afford such an investment only multiplies the difficulties associated with the resolution of human settlement problems.

The magnitude of the accumulating demands for services and infrastructure in less developed countries may be illustrated with data on the provision of housing. According to the 1965 United Nations estimate (Table 10-5), the less developed regions of Africa, Asia, and Latin America required the construction of 392 million housing units

Table 10-3. Average Annual Growth Rates in Total, Urban, and Rural
Populations: Selected Countries, 1950-1960

Major area and country	Total population	Reported rural population	Reported urban population[a]	Urban population in localities of		
				20,000 or more	100,000 or more	500,000 or more
South Asia	2.1	1.8	3.4	4.3	4.6	4.8
India	1.9	1.8	2.3	3.5	3.9	4.0
Turkey	2.8	2.3	4.7	6.8	6.6	7.4
Philippines	3.0	2.2	5.1	4.0	4.1	3.8
Thailand	3.0	2.2	8.3	6.9	5.3	4.9
Iraq	2.9	2.0	4.3	6.6	6.9	N.A.
Latin America	2.8	1.3	4.5	5.5	5.5	5.8
Brazil	3.0	1.5	5.2	6.3	5.8	6.8
Mexico	3.0	1.5	7.8	6.9	7.8	7.3
Colombia	2.8	1.2	5.0	6.6	7.5	9.4
Chile	2.3	−0.2	3.7	4.7	4.1	5.1
Peru	2.3	1.2	3.7	6.0	5.3	4.7
Africa	2.1	1.6	4.5	5.4	6.5	5.3
Egypt[b]	2.4	1.5	4.1	4.1	4.9	3.5
Nigeria	2.6	2.1	5.4	7.6	11.6	N.A.
Algeria	2.3	1.1	5.5	7.1	6.3	3.4
Zaire	1.9	1.1	4.9	10.8	6.9	N.A.

N.A. = Not applicable.
[a]According to the national definition of an urban area.
[b]United Arab Republic.
Source: Farooq (1975), p. 137. (9)

during the fifteen-year period 1960-1975, with almost three-fourths of
this total being required in Asia. This means that an average annual
construction of 19.4 million housing units had to be built to satisfy
demands arising from population increase, replacement of obsolescent
stock, and elimination of existing shortages. Translated into per capita
terms, the estimated requirement for this region is about eleven units
per thousand population. Available statistics indicate that in most
countries in Asia less than two housing units per thousand population
were built each year during the 1960s (Mok, 1975, p. 98).

Rapid rates of urban population increase are but one element of the
demands generated by growth. Increased consumption arising out of a
growing per capita income also plays an important role. Continued urban growth at an annual rate of 4 to 5 percent, accompanied by a

Table 10-4. Population Estimates and Projections for Fifteen Large Cities

City	Population (millions)			Multiple Increase over Base Year	
	1950	*1975*	*2000*	*1950-1975*	*1975-2000*
Cairo, Egypt	2.4	6.9	16.4	2.9	2.4
Addis Ababa, Ethiopia	0.2	1.1	4.2	4.8	3.9
Nairobi, Kenya	0.1	0.7	3.4	5.5	4.5
Lagos, Nigeria	2.9	2.1	9.4	7.2	4.6
Kinshasa, Zaire	0.2	2.0	9.1	12.5	4.4
Mexico City, Mexico	2.9	10.9	31.6	3.8	2.9
São Paulo, Brazil	2.4	10.0	26.0	4.1	2.6
Bogota, Colombia	0.7	3.4	9.5	5.2	2.8
Guayaquil, Ecuador	0.3	1.0	3.1	4.0	3.1
Lima, Peru	0.6	3.9	12.1	6.4	3.1
Jakarta, Indonesia	1.6	5.6	16.9	3.6	3.0
Teheran, Iran	1.0	4.4	13.8	4.3	3.1
Seoul, Korea	1.0	7.3	18.7	7.1	2.6
Karachi, Pakistan	1.0	4.5	15.9	4.3	3.6
Bangkok, Thailand	1.0	3.3	11.0	3.4	3.4

Source: United Nations (1976), pp. 77-83. (34)

growth rate of urban per capita income of a similar level, means an annual growth rate of total urban income and demand for goods and services of about 9 percent. Compounded over the 30 years from 1970 to the end of the century, such a rate leads to a thirteenfold increase in throughput of materials and services.

This rate of increase is hard to comprehend. It means, for example, that the metropolitan area of Mexico City, which in 1970 generated about $8 billion in total income (assuming that per capita income was $1,000 and population 8 million), would have a total income of $104 billion in the year 2000. This figure is greater than the total income today of any country in the world with the exception of the United States, the Soviet Union, West Germany, Japan, France, and the United Kingdom.[Ridker and Crosson, 1975, p. 217.]

An examination of future prospects for world population growth and urbanization reveals very forcefuly that the twin historic developments that have combined to create the problems of human settlements today will continue for the rest of this century and beyond in most parts of the world. The rate of world population growth, though apparently declining, will still be considerable for some time to

Table 10-5. Estimated Housing Needs of Africa, Asia, and Latin America, 1960-1975 (millions of dwelling units)

Housing required to provide for:	Average Annual Requirements						Total Requirements, 1960-1975	
	1960-1965		1965-1970		1970-1975			
	Urban	Rural	Urban	Rural	Urban	Rural	Urban	Rural
Population increase								
Africa	0.4	0.9	0.5	1.0	0.7	1.1	7.8	14.7
Asia	2.2	4.0	2.7	4.2	3.2	4.5	41.0	62.1
Latin America	0.9	0.4	1.3	0.3	1.5	0.3	18.7	4.8
Subtotal	3.5	5.3	4.5	5.5	5.4	5.7	67.5	81.6
Replacement of obsolescent stock								
Africa	0.1	1.1	0.1	1.1	0.1	1.1	1.8	16.1
Asia	1.1	6.3	1.1	6.3	1.1	6.3	16.5	94.0
Latin America	0.3	0.7	0.3	0.7	0.3	0.7	4.1	10.3
Subtotal	1.5	8.1	1.5	8.1	1.5	8.1	22.4	120.4
Elimination of existing shortages								
Africa	0.1	0.7	0.1	0.7	0.1	0.7	1.8	10.7
Asia	0.7	4.2	0.7	4.2	0.7	4.2	14.6	62.6
Latin America	0.2	0.5	0.2	0.5	0.2	0.5	3.4	6.9
Subtotal	1.0	5.4	1.0	5.4	1.0	5.4	19.8	80.2
Total	6.0	18.8	7.0	18.0	7.9	19.2	109.7	282.2

Source: Mok (23) (1975), p. 99.

come, and rural-urban migration shows no signs of abating in most of the less developed world. Therefore, the number of people in the world will continue to increase in the near future, as will the proportion of people living in urban settlements. Populations in urban centers will continue to grow at an alarming rate, particularly in the larger urban agglomerations of the less developed world. The problems created by this transformation are manifold and involve large private and social costs. But there are obvious benefits too, and it is important to keep these in mind when considering policies for intervening in the urbanization process. A better understanding of the dynamics and consequences of urban-rural population growth and economic development appears to be an essential ingredient of such considerations, and this requires a focus on the *processes* of change together with their manifestations. We now turn to such an examination in the remainder of this paper.

THE DEMOGRAPHIC TRANSITION

Accelerated rates of population growth and urbanization are direct consequences of higher rates of natural increase (births minus deaths) and rates of net urban migration (urban immigration minus urban out-migration). Explanations of temporal and spatial variations in the patterns exhibited by these two sets of rates generally have taken the form of descriptive generalizations phrased in terms of transitions or revolutions. Specifically, the *vital revolution* is commonly held to be the process whereby societies with high birth and death rates move to a situation of low birth and death rates. The *mobility revolution* is the transformation experienced by societies with low migration rates as they advance to a condition of high migration rates. These two revolutions occur simultaneously and they jointly constitute the demographic transition.

The Vital Revolution
As traditional, largely illiterate, rural and agricultural-based populations have become transformed into modern, largely literate, urban, industrial-service dominated societies, they have at the same time moved from high levels to low levels of mortality and fertility. The belief that such a transition inevitably follows modernization has fostered the now often-voiced view that "development is the best contraceptive."

The general description of the vital revolution was originally developed some fifty years ago as an explanation of the demographic experiences of nineteenth-century Europe. This revolution begins with the control of deaths. Improvements in health care, in sanitation, in general standards of living, in nutrition, and in personal cleanliness all act to postpone death and to reduce mortality rates.

Control over deaths is followed, after some lag, by control over births. The principal factor underlying the reduction of the birth rate appears to be the voluntary regulation of fertility. The lag between the onset of mortality decline and that of fertility decline creates an asymmetry that leads to rapid population growth due to natural increase (Figure 10-7).

The changes in fertility and mortality that constitute the vital revolution are more readily understood if developed and less developed countries of the world are considered separately. The birth rate in the less developed world in 1960 was approximately 42.8 per thousand, while that in the developed world was half that. The death rate in the less developed regions also was higher than that of the developed regions, but the magnitude of the difference was roughly half of that

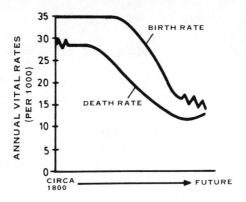

Source: Coale (4) (1969), p. 66.

Figure 10-7. Dependency Burden, Annual Rate of Increase, and Relative Size of Population Aged 15 to 64 Years: Two Alternative Projections.

between the two birth rates. As a result the population of the developed countries in 1960 was growing at a rate of 12.5 per thousand, whereas that of the less developed countries was increasing at the rate of 22.5 per thousand.

Because of their much higher fertility, less developed nations have a much "younger" age composition than developed countries, and therefore a far greater built-in tendency for further growth. A country with a recent history of high birth rates, such as Mexico, for example, exhibits an age pyramid with a broad base that tapers off sharply at the older age groups. A country with a history of low birth rates, such as Sweden, on the other hand, has an age composition that yields an almost rectangular age pyramid (Figure 10-8).

Populations in which children outnumber parents potentially have a larger number of parents in the next generation than today and therefore acquire a built-in *momentum* for further growth, even if their fertility immediately drops to bare replacement level. Bare replacement level under conditions to modern mortality means that each family reduces its fertility to about 2.1 to 2.3 children on the average. If average family size in developing countries dropped to bare replacement immediately, this would produce a zero growth population only after 80 years or more and one that would then be about two-thirds larger than the current one (Figure 10-9). If the drop were to take about 70 years to achieve, then this increase would be 450 percent. In other words, the momentum with the immediate fertility decline is about 1.66, and with delayed decline it is approximately 5.5.

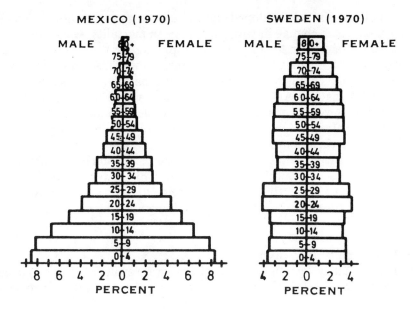

Source: Berelson (1974), p. 12.

Figure 10-8. Young and Old Population Age Compositions.

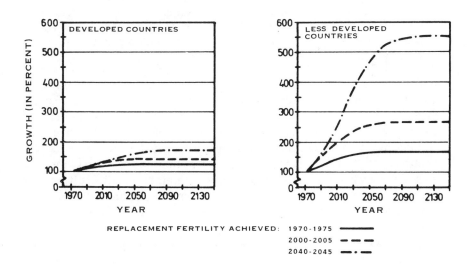

Source: Berelson (1974), p. 13.

Figure 10-9. Momenta of Population Growth for Developed and Less Developed Countries.

Populations in all developed countries have gone through a process of demographic change in which a decline in mortality eventually was followed by a drop in fertility. Demographers refer to this transformation as the demographic transition, and associate it with socioeconomic changes that arise during a nation's industrialization and modernization. Although the process has been far from uniform, and its linkages with changes in socioeconomic variables have not been clearly identified, the universality of this revolution in developed countries is nevertheless quite impressive.

The vital revolution deals only with vital rates and neglects internal displacements attributable to migration. This latter contributor to spatial demographic change also exhibits a historical pattern—one that is described by the generalization known as the *mobility revolution.*

The Mobility Revolution

The primarily *temporal* aspect of the vital revolution has a *spatial* counterpart that Zelinsky has called the mobility transition or revolution, describing it in the following terms:

> There are definite, patterned regularities in the growth of personal mobility through space-time during recent history, and these regularities comprise an essential component of the modernization process. . . . A transition from a . . . condition of severely limited physical and social mobility toward much higher rates of such movement always occurs as a community experiences the process of modernization. [Zelinsky, 1971, pp. 221-22.]

Zelinsky's hypothesis is that for any specific community the vital and the mobility revolutions follow a parallel transitional sequence. He argues that as humanity has extended its control first over deaths and then over births, it also has increased people's ability to move from one community to another. Thus, whereas in premodern societies opportunities for territorial movement were limited, in most modern societies many individuals can migrate without major difficulties. The transition from the premodern to the modern condition is the mobility revolution, and its three principal phases appear to be:[1]

I. *Premodern Society.* High fertility and mortality, low natural increase, and little geographical mobility.

---

[1]This three-way division essentially collapses Zelinsky's five phases. The first is his premodern traditional society; the second combines his early and late transitional societies; and the third represents his advanced and superadvanced societies.

II. *Transitional Society.* A decline in mortality in the early stages of this phase is followed, after a lag, by a corresponding decline in fertility. The lag produces a rapid increase in population. This increase is accompanied by massive rural-to-urban migration, which gradually rises to a peak and then slackens.

III. *Modern Society.* Low fertility and mortality. Vigorous urban-to-urban migration and intraurban commuting. Net rural-to-urban migration declines and may even take on negative values as the population increasingly shifts outward from metropolitan agglomerations toward smaller communities.

In the premodern traditional societies of medieval Europe, early nineteenth-century Japan, and most of pre-World War II Asia and Africa, individually motivated migration over substantial physical distances was relatively uncommon. Difficulties of long-distance transportation, low levels of communication exchange between spatially distant localities, minimal disposable per capita incomes, and strong social ties all contributed to the evolution of communities whose demographic growth was relatively undisturbed by migration. Such societies were in Phase I of the mobility revolution.

Phase II begins with the onset of industrialization and modernization. Physical and social barriers to internal migration decline and the incentives for territorial movement increase. Rapidly growing rural populations experiencing the second phase of the vital revolution and structural changes in the technology of agricultural production combine to impel increasing numbers of individuals to migrate in search of improved social and economic opportunities. This geographical shift is directed mostly toward the larger urban centers.

During the final phase of the mobility revolution, urban-to-urban migration and commuting are the predominant forms of territorial movement. Rural-to-urban migration declines and its decrement to rural population may be more than offset by the size of the reverse flow. This late stage of Phase III has been called counterurbanization, and it appears to be occurring today in the United States, in Sweden, and in the Federal Republic of Germany (Morrison and Wheeler, 1976).

The hypothesis that rates of internal migration rise in the course of national socioeconomic development has been proposed on several occasions and has received empirical support in a number of empirical studies (e.g., Zelinski, 1971; Parish, 1973; and Long and Boertlein, 1976). Residential mobility in Japan, for example, has increased from a 1-year rate of 9.5 percent in 1960 to 12.8 percent in 1970. Kuroda (1973) reports a parallel rise in Japan's interdistrict migration rate from about 5.8 percent in the early 1950s to approximately 8 percent in 1970. A simple plot of these rates against per capita income as a proxy for development and modernization suggests a decidedly positive association.

Data for nations in the late stages of modernization indicate that rates of geographical mobility ultimately tend to stabilize and perhaps even decline. For example, annual migration data for the United States between 1948 and 1971 exhibit insignificant year-to-year variations in the rate of residential mobility (U.S. Bureau of the Census, 1976). Figure 10-10 shows that a slight *decline* may have occurred in the United States during the decade of the 1960s.

Rising income and declining family size give households more freedom to move. Thus increased economic development and reduced fertility levels should raise rates of internal migration. But other factors push in the reverse direction. Economic development stimulates the labor force participation of wives, and working wives reduce the ease with which couples can relocate. Low fertility populations have a comparatively high proportion of the aged, whose rates of migration are relatively low. This compositional effect acts to reduce aggregate movement rates. The gradual reductions of regional differentials in well-being that seem to follow modernization dampen some of the stimulus for migration. Finally, the improved locational accessibility characteristic of modern societies allows people to increasingly substitute commuting for migration.

The transitional society of Phase II of the mobility revolution experiences the particular form of population redistribution that is urbanization. As Kingsley Davis has observed, this is a new and relatively recent step in the social evolution of human society.

> Although cities themselves first appeared some 5,500 years ago, . . . [b]efore 1850 no society could be described as predominantly urbanized, and by 1900 only one—Great Britain—would be so regarded. Today, . . . all industrial nations are highly urbanized, and in the world as a whole the process of urbanization is accelerating rapidly. [Davis, 1965, pp. 41-53.]

Urbanization is a finite process all nations go through in the course of their transition from an agrarian to an industrial society. Such urbanization transitions can be depicted by attenuated S-shaped curves (Figure 10-11). These tend to show a swift rise around 20 percent, a flattening out at a point somewhere between 40 and 60 percent, and a halt or even a decline in the proportion urban at levels above 75 percent.

Nations that are still predominantly agricultural and rural have a built-in tendency for continued urbanization. This "urbanization

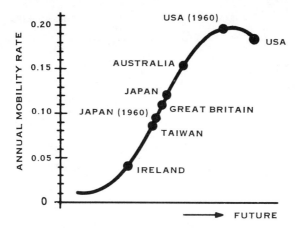

Source: L.H. Long and C.G. Boertlein (1976), pp. 3 and 17.

Figure 10-10. Residential Mobility Rate in Six Countries Around 1970 (and 1960 Where So Identified).

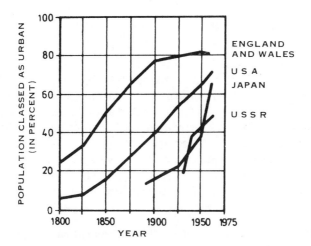

Source: Davis (1965), p. 47.

Figure 10-11. Historical Evolution of Population Classed as Urban.

momentum" is the spatial counterpart of the growth momentum that was described as part of the vital revolution. In most instances the size of the former is considerably larger than that of the latter. Figure 10-12 documents this for the case of India today. The principal spatial dynamics that contribute to such urbanization momenta are examined next.

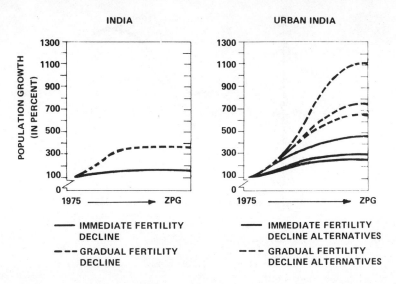

Source: Rogers and Willekens (32) (1976), p. 32.

Figure 10-12. Urbanization Momenta of India's Population.

The Demographics of Urbanization

Urbanization results from a particular spatial interaction of the vital and the mobility revolutions. It is characterized by distinct urban-rural differentials in fertility-mortality levels and patterns of decline, and by a massive net transfer of population from rural to urban areas through internal migration.

The few theoretical statements that have sought to explain the urbanization process seem to concur that this social phenomenon generally evolves physically in the following sequence (e.g., Gibbs, 1963):

1. During the initial period of city formation the rate of urban growth is exceeded by the rate of rural growth.
2. At some point in the history of the nation or region, a reversal occurs and the urban growth rate outstrips the rate of increase of the rural population, thereby initiating the growth of urbanization.
3. Eventually a "turning point" is reached as the proportion of the population that is urban exceeds 50 percent for the first time.
4. With the continuous decline in agriculture's share of the total labor force, the rural population ceases to grow and begins to decline.

5. In the late stages of industrialization, a decentralization of urban population occurs within urban centers and beyond, producing a more dispersed spatial pattern of population. In some instances rural (nonfarm) growth overtakes and once again exceeds urban growth.

Figure 10-3 illustrates the path followed by urban and rural growth rates in the United States as the nation was transformed from a 5 percent urban population in 1790 to a 70 percent urban population in 1960. Already in the second stage of the above sequence in 1790, the nation reached the "turning point" just before 1920 and entered the fourth stage in the late 1940s. It currently is well into the fifth stage and recently has experienced the second reversal in growth rates: rural growth rates once again are higher than urban rates of growth (Morrison and Wheeler, 1976).

The pattern illustrated in Figure 10-13 for the United States seems to have some generality and apparently has also occurred in other countries, such as the Soviet Union:

> After more than a century of rising rates of increase in the urban population, from an average of 1.3 per cent per annum early in the 19th century to 6.5 per cent per annum average for the period between the censuses of 1926 and 1939, the Soviet Union is now experiencing declining growth rates. The highest rates of urban growth were achieved . . . when the proportion of urban population was still low . . . [and] the peak was reached in 1938 with an increase of 12.2 per cent in one year. . . . But the long-range trend has been downward with average annual increases of 4.1 per cent, 1950-1959, and 2.8 per cent, 1959-1970. A study of individual years, reveals a drop from 4.6 per cent in 1958 to 2.3 per cent in 1969, or a decline of one-half in a dozen years. [Harris, 1975, p. 77.]

If urbanization is a finite process, what are the spatial population dynamics that underlie it? How do urban and rural birth, death, and migration rates vary over time to produce the paths taken by urban and rural growth rates in countries such as the United States? We shall examine the three components of population change in turn, starting with mortality. Since the necessary data are very scarce and, in many instances, nonexistent, much of our discussion must necessarily be speculative.

Factors affecting mortality are likely to differ between urban and rural areas. Health care facilities, for example, are more readily available in urban areas. The number of deaths attributed to contagious diseases or automobile accidents, on the other hand, is apt to

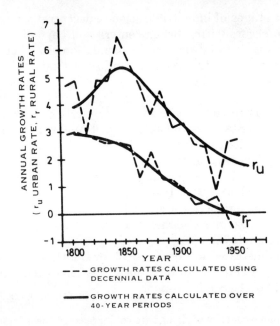

Source: Eldridge and Thomas (8) (1964), p. 194.

Figure 10-13. Annual Growth Rates of Urban and Rural Populations in the United States: 1790-1960.

be lower in rural areas. On balance it appears that post-1930 rural mortality exceeds urban mortality levels, although in developed countries the differences have been narrowed considerably (Table 10-7). A recent United Nations calculation estimates the urban death rate around 1960 to have been "almost 8 points less than the rural in Africa, about 6 points less in East Asia and South Asia, and considerably less also in Oceania; in Europe and Northern America, on the other hand, the difference, if any, could have been only slight" (United Nations, 1974, pp. 17-18).

The fertility of urban women is lower than that of rural women virtually everywhere (Table 10-7). The principal factors associated with lowered birth rates—such as education, income, labor-force participation of women, age at marriage—are all correlates of urbanization. Thus fertility decline has tended to spread from city to village and from village to farm. United Nations estimates of urban and rural crude birth rates around 1960 revealed that "the urban crude birth rate was in general considerably below the rural crude birth rate. Only in Northern America was the difference rather slight. In Europe the rural birth rate exceeded the urban by 4 points, in East Asia and South Asia by about 7 points, in Latin America by 9 points, and in Oceania by 14 points" (United Nations, 1974, p. 18).

Table 10-6. Component Rates of Population Growth: World Total and Regions, 1960 (percentages)

Regions	Growth rate r	Birth rate b	Death rate d	Natural increase rate n
World	*19.2*	*35.8*	*16.6*	*19.2*
More developed regions	12.5	21.5	9.0	12.5
Less developed regions	22.5	42.8	20.3	22.5
Africa	*22.9*	*46.7*	*23.8*	*22.9*
Western Africa	22.8	48.8	26.0	22.8
Eastern Africa	22.3	46.7	24.4	22.3
Northern Africa	25.7	46.5	20.6	25.7
Middle Africa	18.2	45.1	26.9	18.2
Southern Africa	23.1	41.1	18.0	23.1
Northern America	*16.5*	*24.4*	*9.1*	*15.3*
Latin America	*28.0*	*39.9*	*11.8*	*28.1*
Tropical South America	29.3	41.4	12.1	29.3
Middle America (Mainland)	32.6	45.0	12.4	32.6
Temperate South America	18.9	27.2	9.2	18.0
Caribbean	22.2	37.9	12.3	25.6
East Asia	*17.4*	*35.2*	*17.8*	*17.4*
China	17.7	37.4	19.7	17.7
Japan	9.6	17.3	7.7	9.6
Other East Asia	28.7	40.8	12.1	28.7
South Asia	*23.9*	*45.8*	*21.9*	*23.9*
Middle South Asia	23.0	45.9	22.9	23.0
South East Asia	25.6	45.9	20.3	25.6
South West Asia	27.3	45.4	18.1	27.3
Europe	*8.8*	*19.4*	*10.1*	*9.3*
Western Europe	11.4	18.5	10.8	7.7
Southern Europe	.8.2	21.3	9.3	12.0
Eastern Europe	7.4	20.0	9.4	10.6
Northern Europe	6.4	17.4	11.0	6.4
Oceania	*21.7*	*27.2*	*10.3*	*16.9*
Australia and New Zealand	20.9	23.6	8.6	15.0
Melanesia	23.0	42.8	19.8	23.0
Micronesia and Polynesia	29.1	41.4	12.3	29.1
USSR	*16.2*	*23.7*	*7.5*	*16.2*

Source: United Nations (34) (1976), p. 50.

The difference between the birth rate and the death rate is natural increase, and rural natural increase exceeded the urban in most parts of the world in 1960 (Table 10-7). Yet urban areas have been growing much more rapidly than rural areas. Clearly, the component of change fostering this growth is migration.

The urban population of the Soviet Union was growing at an annual rate of approximately 2.5 percent during the early 1970s. At the same time its rural population was declining at the annual rate of 1.1 percent. The urban growth rate was the sum of a rate of natural increase of 0.9 and a net migration rate of 1.6 percent. The urban rate of natural increase, in turn, was the difference between a birth rate of 17 per thousand and a death rate of 8 per thousand. The net migration rate was the difference between an inmigration rate of 27 per thousand and an outmigration rate of 11 per thousand. Expressing these rates on a per capita basis, we have the fundamental accounting identity (Rogers, 1976):

$$r_u = (b_u - d_u) + (i_u - o_u) = n_u + m_u$$

$$= (0.017 - 0.008) + (0.027 - 0.011) = 0.009 + 0.016 \qquad (10.1)$$

$$= -0.025$$

The corresponding identity for the rural population was:

$$r_r = (b_r - d_r) + (i_r - o_r) = n_r + m_r$$

$$= (0.019 - 0.009) + (0.014 - 0.035) = 0.010 - 0.021 \qquad (10.2)$$

$$= -0.011$$

We may contrast the above data for the Soviet Union, which is about 56 percent urban, with corresponding data for India, which is only 20 percent urban. The two accounting identities for India in the late 1960s were, respectively (Rogers and Willekens, 1976):

$$r_u = (0.030 - 0.010) + (0.027 - 0.010) = 0.020 + 0.017$$
$$= 0.037 \qquad (10.3)$$

and:

$$r_r = (0.039 - 0.017) + (0.002 - 0.007) = 0.022 - 0.005$$
$$= 0.017 \qquad (10.4)$$

Observe that the outmigration rates from urban areas in both countries are almost identical (0.011 and 0.010), and note that the rural outmigration rate in India is *lower* than its urban outmigration rate. The latter at first glance seems to contradict the view of a massive net

Table 10-7. Component Rates of Urban and Rural Population Growth: World Total and Regions, 1960 (percentages)

Macro regions, regions, urban and rural	Urban Population			Rural Population		
	Growth rate r_u	Birth rate b_u	Death rate d_u	Growth rate r_r	Birth rate b_r	Death rate d_r
World	*33.0*	*27.7*	*11.6*	*12.5*	*39.8*	*19.1*
More developed regions	23.5	20.1	8.9	−2.6	23.3	9.3
Less developed regions	45.5	37.9	15.4	16.5	44.1	21.7
Africa	*44.8*	*41.6*	*18.0*	*18.0*	*47.8*	*25.1*
Western Africa	49.9	41.1	20.0	17.9	50.2	27.1
Eastern Africa	49.9	44.6	18.9	20.1	46.9	24.8
Northern Africa	42.3	43.8	17.1	18.5	47.4	22.1
Middle Africa	58.6	47.2	20.6	13.0	44.8	27.7
Southern Africa	32.9	32.1	15.1	16.3	47.6	20.1
Northern America	*24.3*	*24.2*	*8.9*	*−1.2*	*24.8*	*9.3*
Latin America	*44.6*	*35.1*	*10.8*	*12.7*	*44.2*	*12.6*
Tropical South America	49.6	31.1	11.2	11.7	45.0	12.8
Middle America (Mainland)	47.0	42.7	11.5	21.1	47.0	13.0
Temperate South America	30.2	24.3	9.1	−9.1	34.3	9.5
Caribbean	34.2	30.8	11.3	15.1	41.9	12.9
East Asia	*48.6*	*29.8*	*12.9*	*8.6*	*36.7*	*19.3*
China	50.3	33.9	15.4	9.7	38.2	20.7
Japan	29.2	15.8	6.6	−5.9	18.5	8.6
Other East Asia	56.2	35.8	9.0	14.9	43.3	13.6
South Asia	*36.7*	*40.0*	*17.2*	*21.2*	*47.1*	*22.9*
Middle South Asia	32.6	39.6	17.9	21.1	47.2	23.9
South East Asia	43.3	42.2	16.2	21.9	46.7	21.1
South West Asia	46.4	38.0	15.1	18.6	48.9	19.5
Europe	*17.9*	*17.8*	*10.2*	*−4.2*	*21.8*	*10.0*
Western Europe	19.5	17.4	10.6	−6.5	20.9	11.2
Southern Europe	21.0	19.3	9.1	−2.2	23.0	9.4
Eastern Europe	19.2	17.3	9.6	−3.8	22.6	9.3
Northern Europe	11.2	17.4	11.0	−6.4	17.6	11.1
Oceania	*26.2*	*22.5*	*8.9*	*13.2*	*36.3*	*13.1*
Australia and New Zealand	25.8	22.2	8.9	1.8	29.0	7.5
Melanesia	47.9	45.8	13.8	22.4	42.7	19.8
Micronesia and Polynesia	47.6	35.5	9.1	25.8	42.6	12.9
USSR	*34.5*	*20.8*	*6.5*	*−1.4*	*26.5*	*8.4*

Source: United Nations (34) (1976), pp. 51-52.

transfer of people from rural to urban areas, but a closer examination of the fundamental accounting identity in Equation (10.1) readily shows that no such contradiction is implied.

Return migration and the much larger base population in rural India together account for much of the level of observed outmigration from urban areas. To see this more clearly we may rewrite Equation (10.1) as:

$$r_u = b_u - d_u + \frac{1-v}{v} o_r - o_u \tag{10.5}$$

where v is the fraction of the population that is urban. Since India's population is about 20 percent urban and o_r is 0.0007, we find that:

$$i_u = \frac{1-v}{v} o_r = \frac{0.80}{0.20} 0.007 = 0.028 \tag{10.6}$$

which is what we had in Equation (10.3) (except for a unit difference in the third decimal place due to rounding).

Equation (10.5) may be rearranged to give:

$$o_u = \frac{1-v}{v} o_r + (n_u - r_u) \tag{10.7}$$

a relationship which reveals that so long as v is small, o_u is likely to be large. Thus, for India, we have:

$$o_u = 4(0.007) + (-0.017) = 0.010 \tag{10.8}$$

whereas the corresponding data for the Soviet Union give:

$$o_u = 0.78(0.035) + (-0.016) = 0.011 \tag{10.9}$$

Curiously, both sets of data yield nearly identical values[2] for o_u and $n_u - r_u$.

---

[2]This near equivalence suggests the potentially more useful alternative rearrangement of Equation (10.5):

$$o_r = \frac{1}{1-v} \left[o_u + (r_u - n_u) \right] \tag{10.10}$$

In both the Soviet Union and in India the quantity in the square brackets is 0.027. When this quantity may be assumed to be approximately fixed (which is likely to hold only for countries not yet over 60 percent urban), then one can crudely estimate the rural-to-urban migration rate to be about 0.027 u/1 − u. This would give Mexico, for example, which in 1970 was roughly 59 percent urban, a rural-to-urban migration rate of 0.039. With a birth rate of 44 per thousand and a death rate of 10 per thousand, Mexico's urban population should then have been increasing at an annual rate of approximately 7.3 per annum. The reported rate for the 1950-1960 decade was 7.8 percent (Table 10-3).

ALTERNATIVE PROJECTIONS OF URBANIZATION

In a now classic analysis of the demoeconomic consequences of fertility reduction, Ansley Coale (1969) examined some of the ways in which the population characteristics of less developed countries are related to their poverty and how alternative demographic trends might affect their modernization.

Coale focused on nations rather than regions within nations, and consequently could ignore population gains or losses arising through migration. Moreover, he assumed that widespread famine could be averted, at least in the short run, and therefore posited only a single future course for mortality—a reduction that could be achieved and maintained. Thus fertility was left as the sole population-change variable considered to be responsive to government policy.

> We shall be concerned here with the implications, for the growth in per capita income and for the provision of productive employment, of alternative possible future courses of fertility. The specific alternatives to be considered are the maintenance of fertility at its current level and, as the contrasting alternative, a rapid reduction in fertility, amounting to fifty per cent of the initial level and occupying a transitional period of about twenty-five years. [Coale, 1969, p. 63.]

After generating the two alternative projections or "scenarios," Coale went on to examine what effects these contrasting fertility trends would have on three important population characteristics:

> ... First, the burden of dependency, defined as the total number of persons in the population divided by the number in the labor force ages [fifteen to sixty-four]; second the rate of growth of the labor force, or, more precisely, the annual per cent rate of increase of the population fifteen to sixty-four; and third, the density of the population, or, more precisely, the number of persons at labor force age relative to land area and other resources. Then we shall consider how these three characteristics of dependency, rate of growth, and density influence the increase in per capita income. [Coale, 1969, p. 63.]

In this section we shall adopt Coale's scenario-building approach to focus on some of the demoeconomic consequences of rapid urbanization. Because this requires a view of urban and rural regions with interacting populations, we cannot ignore the impact of migration. We begin by describing the construction and evolution of four alternative population scenarios and then go on to examine the implications that these alternative trends in migration and fertility would have on

Coale's three important population characteristics: the dependency burden, the growth rate of labor force "eligibles," and the density of the population.

The Dynamics of Urbanization: Four Scenarios

Multiregional population projections translate assumptions about future trends in mortality, fertility, and migration with respect to a specific initial population into numerical estimates of the future size, age composition, and spatial distribution of that population. Tables 10-8 and 10-9 present several such illustrative projections. As in the Coale paper, a hypothetical initial population of one million persons with an age composition and fertility-mortality rates typical of a Latin American country is projected one hundred and fifty years into the future. To his two alternative projections (*A*—Fertility unchanged; and *B*—Fertility reduced), however, we have added two others by vary-

Table 10-8. Alternate Projections of the Population of a Less Developed Country: Migration Unchanged[a]

A. Fertility Unchanged

		Population (thousands)							
Projection Aa	*Year*	*0*	*10*	*20*	*30*	*40*	*50*	*60*	*150*
Urban	0-14	89	147	241	378	583	902	1,377	54,145
	15-64	104	168	275	420	656	1,005	1,536	60,897
	65+	7	8	12	20	31	52	83	3,360
	Total	200	323	518	817	1,270	1,959	2,996	118,402
Rural	0-14	394	511	745	1,084	1,587	2,352	3,481	122,989
	15-64	378	534	731	1,042	1,531	2,252	3,313	117,276
	65+	29	29	38	58	84	116	181	5,926
	Total	800	1,073	1,514	2,184	3,202	4,721	6,974	246,191

B. Fertility Reduced

		Population (thousands)							
Projection Ba	*Year*	*0*	*10*	*20*	*30*	*40*	*50*	*60*	*150*
Urban	0-14	89	127	151	185	235	285	339	1,432
	15-64	104	168	259	369	487	618	754	3,195
	65+	7	8	12	20	31	52	83	463
	Total	200	302	422	574	754	955	1,176	5,090
Rural	0-14	394	461	545	592	663	783	886	3,213
	15-64	378	534	718	940	1,188	1,419	1,662	6,014
	65+	29	29	38	58	84	116	181	821
	Total	800	1,023	1,302	1,590	1,934	2,318	2,729	10,048

[a]Column values do not always sum exactly to given totals because of independent rounding.

Table 10-9. Alternative Projections of the Population of a Less Developed Country: Migration Increased[a]

A. Fertility Unchanged

		Population (thousands)							
Projection Ab	*Year*	*0*	*10*	*20*	*30*	*40*	*50*	*60*	*150*
Urban	0-14	89	174	356	667	1,161	1,940	2,958	75,126
	15-64	104	193	375	710	1,270	2,128	3,293	85,388
	65+	7	9	14	24	44	84	157	5,146
	Total	200	376	745	1,402	2,475	4,152	6,408	165,661
Rural	0-14	394	482	617	751	886	1,034	1,331	46,645
	15-64	378	508	622	750	896	1,046	1,325	45,280
	65+	29	28	37	53	71	84	108	2,459
	Total	800	1,018	1,276	1,554	1,852	2,164	2,764	94,384

B. Fertility Reduced

		Population (thousands)							
Projection Bb	*Year*	*0*	*10*	*20*	*30*	*40*	*50*	*60*	*150*
Urban	0-14	89	150	226	334	475	625	738	1,982
	15-64	104	193	368	630	954	1,318	1,633	4,487
	65+	7	9	14	24	44	84	157	709
	Total	200	352	607	988	1,473	2,028	2,529	7,178
Rural	0-14	394	435	452	409	368	340	334	1,216
	15-64	378	508	610	675	694	664	668	2,330
	65+	29	28	37	53	71	84	108	338
	Total	800	971	1,099	1,138	1,133	1,088	1,109	3,884

[a]Column values do not always sum exactly to given totals because of independent rounding.

ing our assumptions about internal migration (*a*—Migration unchanged; and *b*—Migration increased). This gives the following four possible combinations:

	a. Migration unchanged	*b.* Migration increased
A. Fertility unchanged	Projection *Aa*	Projection *Ab*
B. Fertility reduced	Projection *Ba*	Projection *Bb*

Coale's assumptions about initial and future patterns of mortality and fertility were a crude birth rate of about 44 per 1,000 and a crude death rate of 14 per 1,000, giving rise to a population growing at 3 percent per year. Starting with an expectation of life at birth of approximately 53 years, he assumes that during the next 30 years it will rise to about 70 years, at which point no further improvement will occur. In Coale's Projection *A*, current age-specific rates of childbearing are fixed for 150 years; in Projection *B* they are reduced by 2 percent each year for 25 years (reducing fertility to half of its initial level), at which point they too are fixed for the remainder of the projection period.

For our four urbanization scenarios we have spatially disaggregated Coale's data and assumptions in the following manner. Twenty percent of the initial population of a million persons is taken to be urban. The initial values for birth and death rates are assumed to be lower in urban areas than in rural areas (40 against 45 per thousand for the birth rate, and 11 against 15 per thousand for the death rate). Mortality and fertility are reduced as in the Coale projections, but the declines are accomplished ten years sooner in urban areas (25 instead of 35 years for the decline in mortality, and 20 instead of 30 years for the decline in fertility).

A multiregional population projection also requires a specification of the initial values and future course of internal migration (see Rogers, 1975). To generate the four scenarios, initial rates of outmigration were set equal to those prevailing in India in 1960 (Bose, 1973); that is, a crude outmigration rate from urban areas of 10 per thousand and a corresponding rate from rural areas of 7 per thousand. The age-specific rates of outmigration from urban areas are held fixed in all four projections, as are the corresponding rates from rural areas in the two *a* projections. Outmigration from rural areas in the two *b* projections, however, is assumed to increase sixfold over a period of 50 years, and then to drop to a half of its peak value over the following 30 years, after which it is held unchanged for the remaining 70 years of the projection period (Figure 10-14).

Table 10-10 lists the principal parametric assumptions that generated Coale's two illustrative projections and contrasts them with those that produced the four scenarios summarized in Tables 10-8 and 10-9. The assumptions appear to be reasonable in that the hypothetical urbanization paths charted by them are plausible. For example, the percentage-urban paths for the *b* projections in Figure 10-15 resemble the general shape of the observed urbanization paths set out earlier in Figure 10-11, and Figure 10-16 shows that the trajectories of urban and rural growth rates for these projections are in general similar to those exhibited by the U.S. data graphed in Figure 10-13.

As in Coale's scenarios, the initial population and the future regime of mortality are the same for all of the four population projections summarized in Tables 10-8 and 10-9. The major impact of the drop in

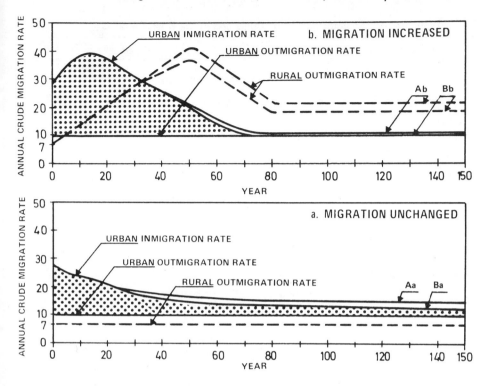

Figure 10-14. Migration Rates: Alternative Mobility Transitions

fertility appears in the projected totals: the *A* projection totals are about 24 times as large as the *B* projection totals after 150 years. Migration's impact, on the other hand, appears principally in the spatial distribution of these totals: the *a* projections allocate approximately a third of the national population to urban areas after 150 years, whereas the *b* projections double this share.

Recently published statistics show population declines in the larger metropolitan regions of many major industrialized nations (Vining and Kontuly, 1977). In the United States, for example, net migration into metropolitan areas has been negative since the early 1970s. Thus, whereas the average annual growth rate of metropolitan populations exceeded the nonmetropolitan rate by 1.6 percent to 0.4 percent in the 1960s, a reversal occurred between 1970 and 1973 which transformed these rates to 0.9 percent and 1.3 percent, respectively (Morrison, 1975, p. 10).

The dynamics leading to the decline of metropolitan rates of growth are reflected in Table 10-11, which describes the evolution of Projection *Bb* in greater detail. Note that the rural growth rate declines and

Table 10-10.   Assumptions in the Coale and in the Rogers Models

	Coale	*Rogers*	
		Urban	*Rural*
Initial Values			
Population	1,000,000	200,000	800,000
Death Rate	14/1,000	11/1,000	15/1,000
Birth Rate	44/1,000	40/1,000	45/1,000
Outmigration Rate	–	10/1,000	7/1,000
Future Paths			
Mortality	Decline over 30 years to level with an expection of life at birth of 70 years; unchanged thereafter	Decline as in Coale's model, but over 25 years; unchanged thereafter	Decline as in Coale's model, but over 35 years; unchanged thereafter
Fertility	*A.* Unchanged	*A.* Unchanged	*A.* Unchanged
	B. Reduction of 50 percent over 25 years; unchanged thereafter	*B.* Reduction as in Coale's model, but over 20 years; unchanged thereafter	*B.* Reduction as in Coale's model, but over 30 years; unchanged thereafter
Migration		*a.* Unchanged	*a.* Unchanged
		b. Unchanged	*b.* Increase of 500 percent over 50 years followed by a reduction to half of that peak level over 30 years; unchanged thereafter

even takes on negative values for a 15-year period, then increases gradually and ultimately overtakes the urban growth rate. Observe that this does not occur at the intervals in which net migration to urban areas is negative.

Demoeconomic Consequences of Growth and Urbanization

Figure 10-17 shows that the three population characteristics examined by Coale vary in their relative significance in the short, medium, and long runs, respectively. Changes in age compositions appear as changes in the dependency burden during the first 30 years and constitute the first principal impact of reduced fertility. After the first generation, however, the etablished difference in dependency burdens remains relatively fixed for the rest of the projection period. The varia-

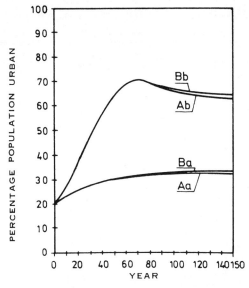

Figure 10-15. Alternative Urbanization Paths: Four Scenarios

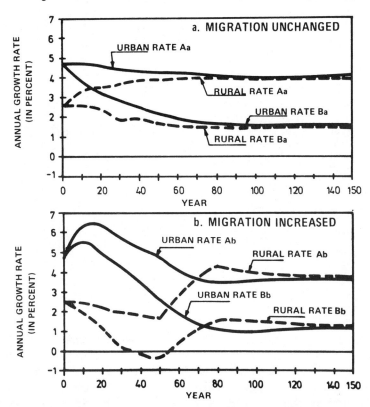

Figure 10-16. Urban and Rural Growth Rates: Four Alternate Scenarios

Table 10-11.   Annual Component Rates of Change and Urbanization Levels: Scenario Bb

Year	Component Rates of Change (per thousand)						Percentage Regional Share	
	Natural Growth		Net Migration		Growth Rate			
	Urban	Rural	Urban	Rural	Urban	Rural	Urban	Rural
0	29.00	30.00	18.00	−4.50	47.00	25.50	20.00	80.00
5	28.47	29.76	24.81	−7.36	53.28	22.40	22.89	77.11
10	26.52	29.56	28.47	−10.32	54.99	19.24	26.61	73.39
15	23.86	28196	29.49	−13.21	53.35	15.75	30.94	69.06
20	20.35	26.92	28.17	−15.56	48.52	11.36	35.58	64.42
25	21.56	23.84	24.76	−17.14	46.32	6.70	40.91	59.09
30	21.10	20.20	20.98	−18.22	42.09	1.98	46.48	53.52
35	20.20	20.40	18.11	−19.34	38.31	1.05	51.65	48.35
40	19.12	19.12	15.44	−20.08	34.57	−0.96	56.53	43.47
45	17.95	17.38	12.84	−20.10	30.79	−2.72	61.02	38.98
50	16.78	15.66	10.50	−19.57	27.28	−3.91	65.08	34.92
55	15.52	14.69	6.81	−14.32	22.33	0.37	67.77	32.23
60	14.43	14.41	4.41	−10.04	18.84	4.37	69.50	30.50
65	13.40	14.26	2.69	−6.43	16.09	7.83	70.47	29.53
70	12.37	14.22	1.40	−3.40	13.77	10.82	70.83	29.17
75	11.43	14.52	0.36	−0.87	11.80	13.65	70.67	29.33
80	10.71	15.19	−0.53	1.25	10.17	16.44	70.05	29.95
85	10.24	15.65	−0.22	0.51	10.01	16.15	69.41	30.59
90	9.92	15.92	0.05	−0.11	9.97	15.81	68.79	31.21
95	9.78	16.13	0.30	−0.64	10.08	15.49	68.20	31.80
100	9.81	16.29	0.52	−1.09	10.33	15.20	67.65	32.35
105	9.81	16.29	0.72	−1.47	10.53	14.82	67.15	32.85
110	9.87	16.21	0.88	−1.77	10.76	14.44	66.71	33.29
115	9.81	15.97	1.02	−2.01	10.83	13.96	66.33	33.67
120	9.86	15.84	1.14	−2.21	11.01	13.63	66.00	34.00
125	9.97	15.78	1.24	−2.39	11.21	13.39	65.73	34.27
130	10.07	15.75	1.33	−2.53	11.40	13.22	65.50	34.50
135	10.14	15.72	1.41	−2.65	11.54	13.07	65.30	34.70
140	10.16	15.68	1.47	−2.75	11.63	12.94	65.14	34.86
145	10.17	15.64	1.52	−2.83	11.70	12.81	65.01	34.99
150	10.19	15.61	1.57	−2.90	11.76	12.71	64.89	35.11

tion between the annual growth rates of labor-force agegroups begins to appear after 15 years, and widens to a maximum difference in about 70 years, that is, 45 years after fertility stabilizes at its reduced value. Once established, this difference continues essentially unchanged forever after in the two scenarios. Finally, the long-run effect of reduced fertility starts to become significant after 70 years; at this point

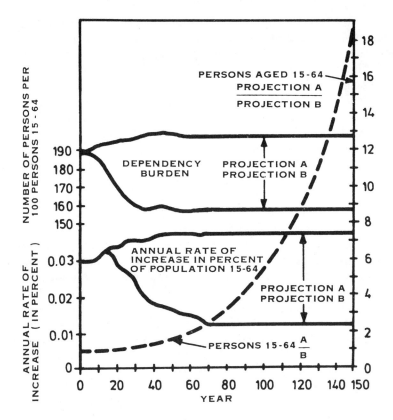

Source: Coale (1969), p. 66.

Figure 10-17. Dependency Burden, Annual Rate of Increase and Relative Size of Population Aged 15-64 Years: Two Alternative Projections.

the two alternative projections assume essentially fixed differences in age compositions and in rates of growth, and vary primarily in their relative sizes. This variation assumes enormous dimensions after 150 years, when the total size of the population in the 15 to 64 year age bracket in the population with constant fertility is about 18 times larger than the corresponding number in the population with reduced fertility.

The process of national modernization and development depends in a very direct way on the capacity of a national economy to increase its level of net investment. Recognizing that this is only a *necessary* and not a *sufficient* condition, Coale argues that the low fertility population is in a better position to divert resources away from production for current consumption to net investment aimed at the enhancement of future productivity.

The two projected populations in the labor-force agegroups in

Figure 10-17 differ by only 4 percent after 25 years. It is not unreasonable, therefore, to assume that national income is at that point the same for the two scenarios. The pressure for allocating a much higher proportion of the national product for consumption then would be greater in the higher fertility population because of its higher dependency burden. Families with a large number of children, it is frequently argued, save less than those with fewer children, and the capacity of their governments and economies to raise the level of net investment, therefore, will be seriously impaired.

The short-run depressing influence of high dependency on savings and investment is exacerbated in the middle run by a high growth rate of the labor-force population. A larger labor force requires a larger capital stock to achieve the same productivity per capita. Adopting as a rule of thumb a capital-output ratio of 3, Coale concludes that with net investment growing at the respectable rate of 15 percent of national income, a "population with a rate of growth of three percent in its labor force can, with such a level of investment, add about two percent per year to the endowment of capital per worker" (Coale, 1969, pp. 70-71). It therefore will be able to add less to the productive capacity of the economy than a population experiencing a less rapid rate of labor-force growth. Thus, reduced fertility not only generates, in the short run, a population with fewer consumers among whom to divide a given output, it also helps, in the middle run, to generate a larger national output to divide.

Finally, the concern with excessive density of people to available resources—that is, with "overpopulation"—stems from the belief that per capita output declines above some ratio of workers to resources. It is argued that at some point an excessively large population produces a depressing effect on per capita output.

As Coale points out, however, the usefulness of the density concept in diagnosing population problems of less developed countries is limited. Politically feasible and realistic policies to influence the size of a national population are largely limited to fertility control, and such policies can affect the relative density of the labor force to resources only in the long run, that is, after changes in dependency and labor-force growth rates have already produced their major economic effects. Also, density is relevant primarily in economies that do not participate in international trade or that are principally organized around extractive activities such as mining, agriculture, and forestry.

The principal demographic impacts of reduced fertility described above are not altered substantially by the introduction of migration as a component of change and the concomitant spatial subdivision of the national population into urban and rural sectors. Figure 10-18 and

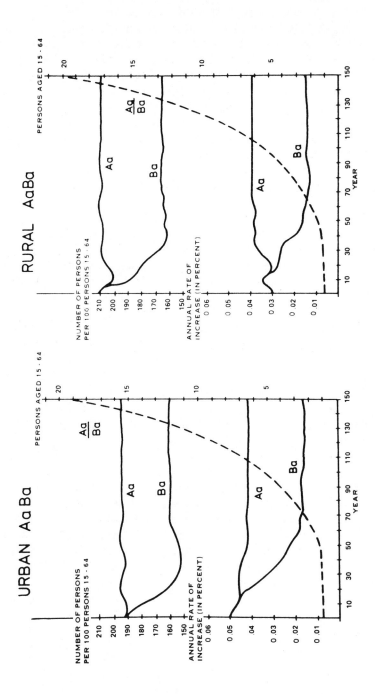

Figure 10-18. Dependency Burden, Annual Rate of Increase, and Relative Size of Population Aged 15-64 Years: Alternative Urban-Rural Projections

10-19 show that for a given regime of migration (*a* or *b*), the major impacts of reduced fertility are, as in the Coale model, a decline in the burden of dependency in the short run, a lowering of the growth rate of the labor-force population in the medium run, and a very much smaller density of people to resources in the long run. The spatial model does, however, bring into sharp focus urban-rural differentials: (1) differentials in dependency burdens and in the relative magnitudes of their decline following fertility reduction; and (2) differentials in initial growth rates of the labor-force population and the paths of their gradual convergence in the long run.

The dependency ratio in urban areas is 19 points lower than its rural counterpart at the start of the projection period. With constant fertility, the regional dependency burdens remain essentially unchanged. Declining fertility, however, narrows these differentials to almost a third of their original values, as the urban drop of 33 points is matched by a corresponding decline of 45 points in rural areas.

The annual growth rates of the labor-force population in urban and rural areas initially are 0.05 and 0.03, respectively. For both migration regimes, however, they converge to approximately the same values in the long run: 0.04 in the constant fertility scenario and slightly above 0.01 in the reduced fertility projection.

The major demographic impacts of increased rural-urban migration for a given regime of fertility are set out in Figures 10-20 and 10-21, in which are graphed the *a* and *b* projections for each of the two fertility regimes: fixed and reduced. These diagrams show that the influence of migration patterns in our particular scenarios is negligible with respect to dependency burdens, and is of paramount importance, in the short and medium runs, with regard to the growth rate of the population aged 15 to 64. In the long run, migration also has a moderately powerful impact on the density of workers to resources in rural areas.

Perhaps the most interesting observation suggested by Figures 10-20 and 10-21 is the transitory nature of high rates of urban growth. In the *b* projections, urban growth rates in excess of 6 percent per annum occur only in the short run, as the national population experiences its early phases of urbanization. This sudden spurt of growth of urban areas in the short run declines over the medium run, and in the long run it levels off at a rate below that generated by the fixed migration regime. The growth curve of rural areas, of course, assumes a path that reverses this trajectory, with the growth of the rural working population declining to relatively low—even negative—levels before increasing to stabilize at about the same level as that prevailing in the urban population.

Increased migration into cities reduces the size of rural populations

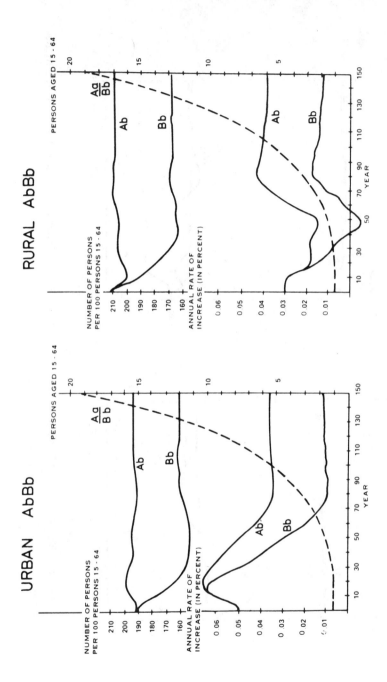

Figure 10-19. Dependency Burden; Annual Rate of Increase, and Relative Size of Population Aged 15-64 Years: Alternative Urban-Rural Projections

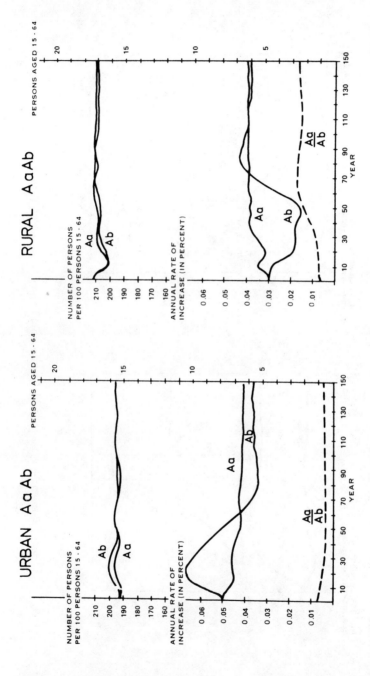

Figure 10-20. Dependency Burden; Annual Rate of Increase, and Relative Size of Population Aged 15-64 Years: Alternative Urban-Rural Projections

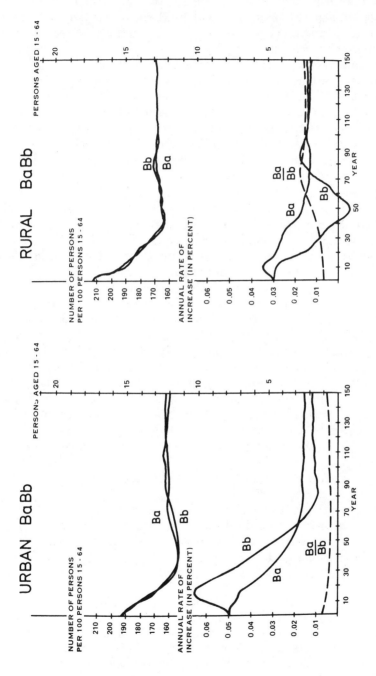

Figure 10-21. Dependency Burden, Annual Rate of Increase, and Relative Size of Population Aged 15-64 Years: Alternative Urban-Rural Projections

and hence their density with respect to rural resources such as agricultural land. Figures 10-20 and 10-21 show that the relative size of the rural population aged 15 to 64 is over 2.5 times larger under the fixed migration schedules of projections *a* than under the increased rural-urban migration rates of projections *b*. Thus the *b* scenarios create rapid urban growth and exacerbate human settlement problems, but at the same time reduce the density of rural populations to land and other rural resources. The *a* scenarios, on the other hand, give urban areas more time to cope with growth, but do so at the cost of increasing rural population densities. "Hyperurbanization" and "rural overpopulation," therefore, are the two sides of the fundamental policy question regarding development.

The economic implications of the spatio-temporal behavior of dependency, growth, and density in the urbanization scenarios are much the same as those described by Coale (1969), but they now include a spatial dimension. First, it is commonly believed that urban households save a larger fraction of their income than rural households. Thus the rapid urbanization arising out of increased rural-urban migration could have a positive impact on the national savings rate. But increased rural-urban migration creates rapid urban growth, thereby reducing the per capita endowment of capital and infrastructure in cities and contributing to high rates of unemployment in exploding urban centers. Finally, rapid urban growth in less developed countries tends to be concentrated in a few very large cities, and "city bigness" is viewed by many as a negative feature of development. The argument is that urban agglomerations become inefficient once they pass a certain size threshold, and thereafter the social costs of further growth begin to exceed the corresponding social benefits. However, several economists have maintained that large urban agglomerations generate more benefits than costs and that efforts to retard their growth, therefore, are likely to reduce national economic growth rates (for example, Gilbert, 1976).

Until recently, research on the economic influences of rural-urban migration in less developed countries has been largely ignored by national economic planners who have tended to emphasize "traditional economic variables such as output growth rates, terms of trade, savings and investment, and relative efficiency."

The efficient allocation of human resources between sectors, if discussed at all, has been assumed to be a natural out-growth of a self-adjusting mechanism which functioned to equate sectoral marginal productivities. Rural-urban migration was portrayed as a manifestation of this self-adjusting mechanism (with its implicit full-employment assumptions) and, as such, was not deemed to be of sufficient intrinsic importance to warrant detailed theoretical and empirical investigation. [Todaro, 1975, p. 367.]

Growing levels of urban unemployment and underemployment in less developed countries have sharply underlined the danger of ignoring the impacts of migration on development, and have exposed to question the applicability of the traditional economic models as descriptors of the practical socioeconomic realities of today's less developed world. The determinants and consequences of rural-urban migration and the relationships between such migration and the economic development of urban and rural areas are currently subjects of utmost importance and warrant careful scholarly examination. Agreement on this seems to be widely shared. What is less evident is the conceptual framework one could profitably adopt in such an endeavor. Can the Coale-Hoover (1958) paradigm and its successors, which have served as an economic framework for examining the probable consequnces of a drastic decline in the fertility rates of low-income countries such as India, be generalized and extended to serve as a framework for examining the probable consequences of significant increases in rural-urban migration levels and urbanization rates of such countries?

Migration and Development
In developed countries, high levels of urbanization and high rates of urban growth have historically been associated with high and increasing levels of per capita income. Figure 10-22, for example, indicates that the higher the percentage of a national population that is urban, the higher is the national per capita gross national product (GNP). This positive association is generally attributed to factors such as rapid industrialization, increases in productivity, widespread literacy, improved nutrition, and advances in health services.

Figure 10-23 illustrates that it is important to distinguish the effects of high levels of urbanization from those of high rates of urban population growth. The positive relationship between per capita GNP and urbanization level is difficult to discern in the plot of urban growth rates and per capita GNP growth rates that appear there. Indeed there seems to be a lack of any association whatsoever. We conclude, therefore, that although high proportions of national populations in urban areas are conditions that appear to be positively associated with high levels of per capita GNP, one cannot infer from this that rapid urban growth fosters rapid increases in a nation's wealth or productivity.

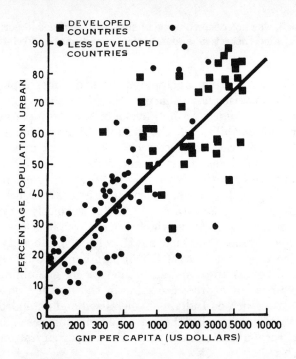

Source: United Nations (1976), p. 27.

Figure 10-22. Degree of urbanization compared with GNP per capita, 1973.

Most nations of the developing world are currently less urbanized than the developed countries, but are urbanizing more rapidly. With a few notable exceptions, their per capita income is growing slowly relative to their population increase, and their development is much too complex to be studied with the aid of simple plots such as those found in Figures 10-22 and 10-23. A fuller understanding of the important relationships that are hidden in these graphs requires the specification and estimation of a model that interconnects the principal contributing sectors of demoeconomic growth.

Figure 10-24 sets out the underlying structure of such a macrodemoeconomic model. Here changes in population are allowed to influence the level of output directly, and the contribution of natural resources (such as land) can be included in the same aggregate production function. Ideally the demoeconomic growth model should disaggregate population into urban and rural components and distinguish agricultural from nonagricultural production.

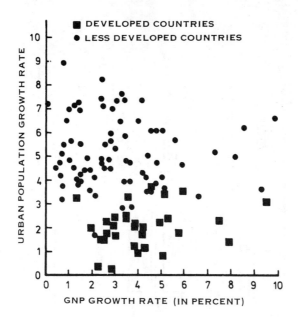

Source: United Nations (34) (1976), p. 28.

Figure 10-23. Comparison of Annual Average Percentage Rates of Growth of Urban Population and Annual Percentage Rates of Growth in GNP per Capita, 1965-1973.

Dualistic Models of Demoeconomic Growth

A large number of studies have concluded that migration usually is a response to economic differentials and that the individual migrant generally improves his or her well-being by moving. The net benefits of this move to society, however, are much more difficult to determine. Since the relationships between migration and development are multidimensional and complex, evaluations of their interaction and their societal impacts call for a general equilibrium systems framework.

Migration between rural and urban areas changes population and labor-force growth in both regions. It also changes savings-investment behavior and the growth of capital stock. It alters labor-force productivity, and both affects and is affected by rural-urban income differentials. A focus on the behavior of only one of these aspects while holding the others unchanged can lead to erroneous policy conclusions.

A fuller set of social consequences of rural-urban migration can be

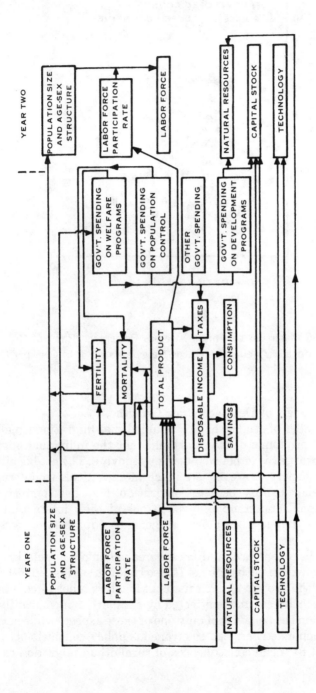

Figure 10-24. An Interactive Economic-Demographic Macro Model

Source: Robinson (28) (1975), p. 20.

captured with a model framework that explicitly incorporates relatio@-
ships between demographic and economic change. But progress in the
development of such macroeconomic models has been slow, with the
result that we have not advanced much beyond the pioneering
framework provided by Coale and Hoover two decades ago.
Nonetheless, the outlines of a profitable and robust paradigm are
emerging out of the experiences of studies that have tried to exploit
the natural intersection within economics of dualistic growth theory,
general equilibrium analysis, and quantitative economic history. The
utility of such dualistic models of modern economic growth can be
defended with an argument based not solely on their usefulness "as
abstract analytical constructs, but rather on their usefulness as quantitative tools for interpreting the historical experience of developing
countries" (Kelley and Williamson, 1973, p. 450).

Dualistic models of modern economic growth typically divide a low-
income economy into an agricultural-rural sector, which produces a
single consumption good, and an industrial-urban sector whose output
is divided between consumption and investment. Both sectors employ
labor and capital to produce their outputs; the agricultural sector, in
addition, utilizes land. Cobb-Douglas production functions are normally adopted for the agricultural sector, and CES production functions
are often assumed for the industrial sector. Technological change is
specified differentially to capture dualism in production, and urban
and rural residents are assumed to differ in their consumption and savings behavior. Growth of the labor force is given exogenously, in most
instances, whereas the growth of the capital stock is determined en-
dogenously by means of a savings-investment equation.

Several future directions for dualistic model development were suggested by Kelley (1973) in a recent review of the role of population in
models of modern economic growth. Heading the list of revisions of
the "standard" model was the desirability of endogenizing population
growth:

> Models in which population is endogenous are particularly relevant for
> two specific policy-oriented reasons. First, if population growth
> responds to economic conditions, then typical theoretical and empirical
> estimates of population's impact will be biased. For example, if popula-
> tion growth exerts a negative impact on the level and the pace of
> economic progress, and if family size varies inversely with economic con-
> ditions, then population growth will *decline* in response to its own
> hypothesized negative impact on the economy. Its *net* adverse impact on
> growth will therefore be quantitatively less than in the case where
> population growth is assumed to be exogenously given.... Second, if
> population growth is endogenous and sensitive to the variables used to

assess its impact—pollution, economic growth, social stability, employment—then policy recommendations should be formulated in a framework analyzing population's *net* impact. The relevant research issues include the speed of adjustment of population growth to policy objectives—and the extent to which the adjustment level is in some sense "appropriate." [Kelley, 1973, p. 40.]

We shall refer to such models as dualistic models of demoeconomic growth.

Kelley also emphasizes the importance of sectoral disaggregation. He argues that because the rate of economic development is associated with the rate of structural change, along such dimensions as degrees of industrialization and urbanization, models used for policy purposes should incorporate sectoral disaggregations. Such disaggregations should include, for example, the impact of population growth on the *composition* of demand as between urban and rural goods and the response of population growth to the rate of structural economic change when urban areas are assumed to foster a lower family size than is found in rural areas. The latter has already received some attention in the preceding section of this paper; the former will be examined in the next section. Here we shall return to our discussion of dualistic models of demoeconomic growth and closely examine a recent prototype of such a model in which the most important endogenous population variable is internal migration.

A Prototype Model of Migration and Development

Population's role in models of economic growth has been substantially enlarged in recent years. Most of the well-known models developed thus far have focused on impacts of population growth on per capita output (or income). Only a few models have also taken into account the influences of economic variables on population growth. Fewer yet have included internal migration as an endogenous variable affecting growth and development.

A prototype model of macrodemoeconomic growth should sketch out the main relationships determining the demographic and economic evolution of a nation experiencing modernization and development. It should contribute to the understanding of population's principal impacts on socioeconomic change and of the consequences of such change on demographic growth and distribution. In order to deal with questions of urbanization, such a model should distinguish between agricultural and nonagricultural production sectors and between rural and urban populations. Differential patterns of fertility, mortality, and internal migration should be incorporated explicitly, the government policy variables should constitute an important part of the model.

Instead of reviewing the several existing demoeconomic models that in general satisfy these criteria, we shall describe a single prototype model that resembles and draws on the others.[3] The model outlined below was developed by Lorene Yap as part of a doctoral dissertation and is described in greater detail in Yap (1976). It is representative of a growing class of dualistic demoeconomic models that could contribute to an improved understanding of the societal consequences of rural-urban migration in developing countries.

Yap presents a three-sector neoclassical model of rural-urban growth, with internal migration explicitly specified as an endogenous variable that both influences and is influenced by regional differentials in economic well-being. The model describes a disequilibrium process of growth in which firms maximize profits and individuals maximize utility. Migration between urban and rural sectors is viewed as a means of equalizing factor returns.

> . . . Rural-urban sectoral differences are emphasized in the model. In particular, there are higher capital and labor productivity and rates of technological change in the modern urban than in the rural and traditional urban sectors; higher rates of natural population growth for the rural than for the urban population; and higher marginal savings propensities for urban workers and businesses, and higher tax rates for urban workers, than for their rural counterparts. Urban population growth also generates pressures for more urban investment by the government, as well as for higher per capita public service expenditures in urban than in rural areas. With these sectoral differences a transfer of population from rural to urban areas will change the productivity of both labor and capital in the two areas, the growth of both factors, and therefore, the growth potential of the sectors. [Yap, 1976, p. 122.]

The Yap model was estimated using 1950-1965 data for Brazil, and simulation techniques were used to assess the impact of rural-urban migration on the growth of the Brazilian national product during that fifteen-year period. A historical growth path and two alternative paths of the Brazilian economy were simulated, each with different rates of internal migration. The differences between the historical simulation and simulations using a lower migration flow than the historical one were assumed to reflect the importance of migration in the determination of the growth rate of GNP during the period 1950 to 1965.

Table 10-12 sets out the principal results of Yap's three simulations. Run R1 is the historical simulation with observed migration levels. Runs R2 and R3 are the two "counterfactual" simulations: the first

---

[3]Several reviews and assessments of demoeconomic modeling have been published. Among the best are those of Robinson (1975), Robinson and Horlacher (1971), Arthur and McNicoll (1975).

Table 10-12. Simulation Runs with Alternative Migration Levels

Variables	Run R1 (actual migration level) Average Growth Rate (%)	Initial Year	Final Year	Run R2 (migration parameters reduced by 0.5) Average Growth Rate (%)	Final Year	Run R3 (migration parameters set to zero) Average Growth Rate (%)	Final Year
1. Migration as proportion of urban population		0.03	0.02		0.02		0
2. Urban population (mill.)	5.1	17.5	37.3	4.1	32.0	2.4	25.0
a. Proportion of total population		0.35	0.47		0.39		0.31
3. Income per capita ($)	2.7	300	441	2.4	418	1.9	391
a. Rural	1.5	162	200	1.3	193	1.0	186
b. Urban	1.9	557	716	2.2	759	3.0	852
4. Income or value added ($bill.)	5.9	15.0	35.2	5.6	33.6	5.2	31.7
a. Agriculture	3.3	5.3	8.4	3.9	9.3	4.7	10.4
b. Modern	7.1	9.2	25.6	6.5	23.4	5.7	20.9
c. Traditional	4.9	0.5	1.2	2.9	0.9	−2.1	0.4
5. Capital stock ($bill.)	5.4	37.0	79.5	5.2	77.5	4.9	75.1
a. Agriculture	3.3	13.1	21.1	3.4	21.5	3.6	22.0
b. Modern sector	6.3	23.9	58.4	6.0	56.0	5.6	53.1
6. Sectoral employment as proportion of total employment							
a. Agriculture	1.8	0.65	0.53	2.7	0.60	3.7	0.69
b. Modern	5.2	0.26	0.35	4.5	0.31	3.5	0.27
(1) skilled	5.5	0.10	0.15	4.6	0.12	3.3	0.10
(2) unskilled	5.0	0.16	0.20	4.4	0.19	3.6	0.17
c. Traditional	4.9	0.09	0.12	2.9	0.09	−2.1	0.04
7. Wage differentials							
a. Rural-urban		0.37	0.36		0.33		0.29
b. Rural-urban: Unskilled only		0.59	0.57		0.53		0.47
c. Urban unskilled-urban skilled		0.33	0.35		0.34		0.34
8. Sectoral wage inequality		3.43	4.34		4.63		6.93

Source: Yap (38) (1976), pp. 133-34.

assumed that migration was half as sensitive to regional wage differentials as it actually was; the second assumed that migration did not occur at all.

An examination of the major economic consequences of the two counterfactual experiments reveals four significant impacts occasioned by the reduction in rural-urban migration:

1. Reducing migration reduces the growth rates of total and per capita GNP.
2. Reducing migration increases agriculture's share of total output.
3. Reducing migration reduces the accumulation of capacity for future growth.
4. Reducing migration increases sectoral inequalities.

Yap's simulations indicate that migration made a positive contribution to Brazil's postwar development. A 50 percent reduction in the values taken on by the parameters of the migration function lowers the average annual growth rate of GNP from 5.9 to 5.6 percent. A further drop to 5.2 percent follows from a complete prohibition of migration. A similar decline occurs in per capita terms, with the annual per capita GNP growth rate declining from 2.7 to 2.4 and 1.9 percent, respectively.

A reduction in rural-urban migration increases the growth of agricultural output from 3.3 to 3.9 percent annually, as migration's sensitivity to wage differentials is reduced to half of its previous level, and to 4.7 percent annually as migration drops to zero. At the same time the annual growth rate of the modern sector's output decreases from 7.1 to 6.5 to 5.7 percent, respectively. The output of the traditional sector also declines, and actually contracts at the rate of −2.1 percent per year in the run with zero migration.

A reduction in migration lowers the capacity for future growth, according to the counterfactual simulations reported in Table 10-12. Growth capacity, measured in terms of physical and human capital stocks, declines with reduced migration. Terminal stocks of physical and human capital (the latter measured by the fraction of skilled workers)—which are $79.5 billion and 15 percent, respectively, in the historical simulation—drop to $77.5 and $75.1 billion and to 12 and 10 percent, respectively, in the two counterfactual simulations with lowered migration levels.

Finally, the counterfactual simulations indicate that migration contributes positively to a reduction in the growing inequality between the urban and rural sectors. Yap's model shows that the extent of wage inequality in the labor force and the differential in per capita income between sectors both increase when rural-urban migration is reduced below its historical level. More wage inequality and a larger differential in per capita income are reported in Table 10-12 for the final year of the two counterfactuals than for the historical simulation.

The principal results of the prototype model of migration and development described above add further weight to arguments directed against major efforts to curb rural-to-urban migration in the less developed world. The powerful private incentives and the apparently substantial social gains associated with such migration are apt to make policies to restrict rural-urban migration very costly. Urbanization policies in the less developed nations, therefore, are likely to be more socially beneficial if their focus is on managing rapid urban growth and reducing urban poverty rather than curtailing the flow of migrants to cities. Such a policy perspective leads naturally to an interest in the resource and service demands of rapid urbanization.

RESOURCE AND SERVICE DEMANDS OF A RAPIDLY URBANIZING POPULATION

What are the resource and service demands of urbanization likely to be during the next 30 to 50 years in the less developed nations of the world? How important will urban *population* growth be relative to urban *economic* growth as a generator of increased levels of demand? To what extent would the management problems associated with meeting these demands be eased if urbanization rates were significantly reduced? These and related questions are receiving increasing attention as part of a general concern over whether population increase will ultimately outstrip the growth in food supplies and exhaust the world's stock of natural resources.

Resources and services are demanded by people; hence, if all else is fixed, the level of demand should be approximately proportional to population size. Demand above this level may be attributed to affluence. For example, Keyfitz (1976) calculates that U.S. energy consumption would have risen from its 1947 level of 1.21 billion tons of coal equivalent to 1.77 billion tons in 1973 if it merely kept pace with population increase. The fact that energy consumption rose beyond that total to 2.55 billion tons in 1973 was due to affluence, according to Keyfitz. Thus of the total increment of 1.34 billion tons, 0.56 billion was due to population growth and 0.78 billion to affluence (Figure 10-25).

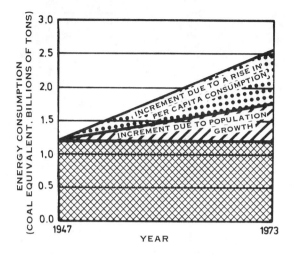

Source: Keyfitz (20) (1976), p. 32.

Figure 10-25. U.S. Energy Consumption, 1947-1973.

The association between energy consumption and affluence is more explicitly shown in Figure 10-26, which plots per capita energy consumption against per capita income for 96 nations of the world. The correlation is striking and it reflects the fact that as a poor country develops, it requires a larger throughput of energy resources to run its economy and supply the needs of its population.

The relationships between demoeconomic change and patterns of resource and service demand are imperfectly understood. The demographic and economic determinants of the level and composition of demand are several, but a satisfactory first approximation may be obtained by considering only the impacts of changes in the size of a given population and in the total income that is at its disposal.

If relative prices and tastes remain stable, then the demand for a given commodity or service may be shown to grow approximately at a rate equal to the sum of: (1) the income demand elasticity times the growth rate of per capita real income; and (2) the population demand elasticity times the rate of population growth (Kaneda, 1968, p. 6):

$$\frac{\dot{D}}{D} = \xi \frac{\dot{P}}{P} + \eta \frac{\dot{Y}}{Y} \qquad (10.11)$$

where D denotes demand, Y is real income, P is population, σ is the elasticity of demand with respect to income, ξ is the elasticity of demand with respect to population, and where the dots indicate time

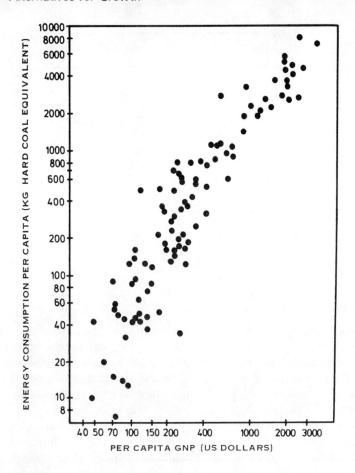

Source: Fisher and Potter (10) (1971), p. 237.

Figure 10-26. Per Capita-Energy Use and GNP, 1965

derivatives (that is, changes in the value of the variable over time).[5] If, in addition, the postulated demand function is homogeneous of degree one; that is, if there are no scale economies of demand, then $\xi = 1 - \sigma$ and (10.11) simplifies to:

$$\frac{\dot{D}}{D} = \frac{\dot{P}}{P} + \eta \left(\frac{\dot{Y}}{Y} - \frac{\dot{P}}{P} \right) \qquad (10.12)$$

---

[5]Elasticities of demand measure the percentage change in demand generated by a unit percentage change in a variable thought to be influencing the level of that demand. For example, if an additional dollar of income raises the demand for food by 50 cents, we say that the income elasticity of demand for food is 0.5

Equation (10.12) may be used to infer the income elasticity of demand for food from data on income, population, and agricultural production. For example, taking as given a 1 percent annual population growth rate, a 3.8 percent rate of growth of per capita income per year, and a 1.6 percent annual growth rate of rice available for consumption, Kaneda used Equation (10.12) to infer that the income elasticity of demand for rice in Japan must have been $\sigma = 0.21$ (Kaneda, 1968, p. 7). Thus, approximately half of the observed percentage increase in the amount of rice demanded was due to growth in per capita income, and the other half was attributable to population increase.

The Influence of Spatial Distribution:
The Demand for Food

Patterns of food consumption undergo considerable change during the process of a country's urbanization and development. Two fundamental shifts are: (1) a decline in the fraction of total per capita income that is spent on food (Engel's law); and (2) the change in the composition of the per capita food bundle. The share of food in private consumption expenditures (the so-called Engel ratio) declines from levels as high as 75 to 80 percent in traditional poor societies to levels less than half of that in modern developed societies. The composition of the per capita food bundle also changes, as consumers substitute "preferred" food products, such as animal protein foods, for "inferior" food products such as starchy staples.

Rapid urbanization has helped to shape new food consumption patterns in developing nations. Electric kitchen appliances have expanded the range and variety of methods for preparing food. Increasing affluence in urban centers has led to a growing importation of exotic foods and such essential food items as meat and dairy products.

Urbanization influences the level and composition of food consumption in a number of related ways. First, urban and rural populations typically have different consumption patterns. Thus a rapid change in the geographic distribution of a national population is bound to alter the aggregate demand for food. Second, an important consequence of rural-urban migration is a change in the pattern of income distribution, as migrants gradually improve their income status. This change influences aggregate food consumption patterns; for example, an improvement in the income level of lower income groups would be expected to increase aggregate food demand more rapidly than otherwise. Finally, changes in tastes induced by urban development processes would be expected to further increase the aggregate elasticity of food demand.

Recently published data for Japan indicate very clearly the substantial reduction in urban and rural Engel ratios that has followed the high growth rates of per capita income during the postwar years (Figure 10-27). For each of the three years included in Figure 10-27, the Engel ratio for urban households is lower than that for farm households. This in part reflects the higher per capita income of urban households. The fraction of total expenditure that is devoted to starchy staples (cereals, potatoes, and so on) is also lower for the urban population. As increasing income permits urban households to modify their dietary habits, they tend to consume ever larger quantities of animal protein foods such as meat, dairy products, eggs, and fish.

The differences in urban and rural food consumption patterns illustrated in Figure 10-27 also may be observed in the recent estimates of income elasticities developed by Kaneda (1968). These are set out in Table 10-13 and reveal that, as in the case of Engel ratios, the elasticities for all food, starchy staples, and animal proteins are smaller for the urban population than for the rural (farm) population. A possible explanation of this result is the greater variety and availability of alternative goods in urban centers. As a consequence, income expansion among farm households would increase aggregate food consumption more than a similar growth in income among urban households.

Sector-specific income elasticities such as those presented in Table 10-13 may be combined with urban and rural versions of Equation (10.12) to yield crude estimates of food demand over time and space.

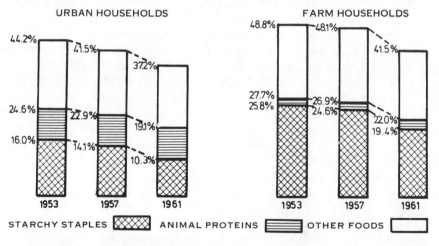

Source: Kaneda (1970) (16), p. 423.

Figure 10-27. Percent of Total Household Expenditures Devoted to Specified Food Groups by Urban and Farm Households in Japan

Table 10-13. Measured Income Elasticities Based on Household Budget Surveys, Urban Workers' Households, and Farm Households, 1953, 1957, and 1961

Year	Total food	Starchy staples[a]	Animal proteins[b]	Other food
		Urban Workers' Households[c]		
1953	0.481	0.196	0.750	0.590
	(.015)	(0.32)	(.012)	(.017)
1957	.456	.062	.773	.602
	(.011)	(.012)	(.032)	(.018)
1961	.472	.075	.700	.585
	(.004)	(.012)	(.008)	(.012)
		Farm Households[c]		
1953	0.529	0.466	1.117	0.412
	(.036)	(.080)	(.220)	(.084)
1957	.531	.363	1.156	.507
	(.044)	(.089)	(.181)	(.069)
1961	.529	.159[d]	1.087	.720
	(.040)	(.091)	(.236)	(.072)

Source: Kaneda (16) (1968), p. 22. Estimates were derived by weighted logarithmic regressions; observations were weighted according to the number of households represented in each group.

[a]Cereals and starchy roots (such as potatoes) for farm households represented in each group.
[b]Meat, dairy products, eggs, and fish.
[c]Figures in parentheses are standard errors of estimate.
[d]Not significantly different from zero at 5 percent.

Assume, for example, that the income elasticity for starchy staples is 0.1 in urban areas and 0.4 in rural areas. Let the annual growth rates of urban and rural incomes be 6.5 percent and 3.3 percent, respectively. (The latter are roughly the values presented for Brazil in Table 10-12.) Finally, assume that projection *Bb* in Table 10-11 describes the demographic evolution of the population under study. Then, during the initial years, demand for starchy staples in urban areas will be growing at an annual rate of about:

$$\frac{\dot{D_u}}{D_u} = 0.047 + 0.1(0.065 - 0.047) = 0.049$$

whereas the corresponding demand in rural areas will increase at the annual rate of:

$$\frac{\dot{D_r}}{D_r} = 0.025 + 0.4(0.033 - 0.025) = 0.028$$

If the only changes after fifty years are increases in the annual growth rates of urban income to 10 percent and of rural income to 4 percent, then the growth rate of demand for starchy staples should decline to 0.034 in urban areas and to 0.014 in rural areas. Since during this period the urban share of the total national population increased from 20 percent to 65 percent, the aggregate national demand for starchy staples should decline from an initial annual growth rate of about 3.2 percent to one close to 2.7 percent. (If, as is likely, the income elasticities decline with increasing income, then this reduction should be, of course, even greater.)

Equations (10.11) and (10.12) provide crude approximations of demand changes stimulated by population and income growth in settings where the assumption of stable tastes and relative prices is not seriously violated. However, when food consumption patterns change rapidly, as they did in postwar Japan, for example, then the impacts of possible shifts in tastes and relative prices should be taken into account. Kaneda (1968) attempts to do this by adopting the following generalization of Equation (10.11):

$$\frac{\dot{D}}{D} = \frac{\dot{A}}{A} + \xi \left(\frac{\dot{P}}{P}\right) + \eta \left(\frac{\dot{Y}}{Y}\right) \tag{10.13}$$

in which the intercept term is interpreted as a measure of *changes* in the structure of demand defined by the parameters ξ and σ. Using household budget data for Japan and relaxing the assumption that ξ must equal $1 - \sigma$, he obtains the partial elasticities of food demand for family income and also for *family size*. Table 10-14 presents his estimated elasticities, and reveals the following two important points:

1. Urban and rural partial *size* elasticities for total food expenditures do not differ nearly as much as partial *income* elasticities (0.405 against 0.455, for the former; and 0.462 against 0.555, for the latter). This suggests that differences in urban and rural household consumption behavior may be attributed much more to differences in income levels than to variations in family size.
2. The ranking of food groups in terms of partial *income* elasticities is, in descending order of magnitude: animal proteins, other foods, total food, and starchy staples. The corresponding ranking in terms of partial *size* elasticities is essentially the reverse. The first ordering reflects consumers' preferences; the second ranking reflects the effects of family size on food consumption. For example, animal proteins are preferred to starchy staples, but an increase in family size makes its members relatively poorer and increases the basic "need" for food energy. As family size for farm households increases, their consumption of animal proteins is reduced.

A widely observed regularity associated with urbanization, development, and modernization is the decline of agricultural production and

Table 10-14.   Estimated Elasticities with Respect to Family Size and Total Expenditure, Postwar Years

Category of expenditure	Size elasticity	Income elasticity
	Urban Workers' Households[a]	
Total food	0.405	0.462
	(.083)	(.024)
Cereals	.461	.216
	(.168)	(.050)
Animal proteins	.327	.722
	(.130)	(.038)
Other foods	.394	.591
	(.097)	(.029)
	Farm Households[a]	
Total food	0.455	0.555
	(.022)	(.016)
Starchy staples	.921	.343
	(.036)	(.026)
Animal proteins	−1.125	1.299
	(.089)	(.065)
Other foods	.274	.579
	(.037)	(.027)

Source: Kaneda (16) (1968), p. 24.
[a]Figures in parentheses are standard errors of estimate.

the corresponding rise in the importance of industrial production. The conventional explanation for this regularity points to the declining importance of food expenditures as income rises. But as Kelley (1969) observes, Engel curve analysis—with its primary focus on expenditure and income elasticities—can serve only as crude first approximation in any assessment of the influence of aggregate demand on industrial patterns: "Systematic changes in the rate of population growth, of ages, of average family size, and of urbanization (internal migration) are all part of economic development . . . each of these factors exerts an impact on the size and composition of demand . . ." (Kelley, 1969, p. 111).

The Influence of Age Composition: Demand
for Personal Health Services
In discussing the determinants of the demand for health care, we shall focus on personal health services only, that is, "those provided for individuals by doctors, nurses, and health technicians . . . to treat illness, prevent disease or disability, or facilitate such normal processes as human reproduction" (Corsa and Oakley, 1971, p. 372). Thus

we shall exclude from consideration societal environmental health activities and such services as public information, education, vital registration, and health surveillance.

Crude estimates of personal health-care demands may be obtained by using appropriate service utilization ratios. Thus, for example, current ratios of health personnel and facilities to population may be applied to alternative population projections to develop estimates of the requirements for future health needs. However, as in the case of energy consumption in Figure 10-25, greater demands for health personnel and facilities arise not only from a growing population but also from an increasing level of income. Figure 10-28 indicates that this relationship, which is very evident in the less developed countries, may not persist in such a simple form once the countries reach a relatively high level of development.

The spatial distribution of a population also needs to be taken into account in studies of health-service requirements. Health-service ratios in less developed countries, for example, are generally much higher in the major cities than in the rest of the country (see, for example, Table 10-15). As a result, most developing countries are striving to narrow the gap that exists between urban and rural areas in the availability of health services, so current rural service ratios are inadequate norms with which to scale levels of future health-care needs for the rural population.

To obtain a more complete assessment of the impacts of different population trends on resource and service demands it is necessary to go beyond simple per capita ratios and examine the effect of changing population age composition on such demands. Figure 10-29 illustrates the relationships between age composition and demands for a number of services. These data show that demands for educational services, for example, occur largely between the ages of 5 and 20, with a peak at age 10. Housing requirements, on the other hand, increase during the later years of childbearing and hold steady until the age of retirement. Jobs are in demand during the labor-force participation ages of 15 to 65. Food requirements increase until the late teens, peaking at about age 18; after a slight decline they then level off and remain constant. Finally, health-service demands are relatively high for infants and older adults. These agegroups have the highest incidence of illness and require the most hospitalization.

Illness and hospitalization rates tend to be higher among adults at all ages above 50 than among children in the 0-5 agegroup. Nevertheless, because of their relatively large numbers in high fertility populations, young children generate a significant proportion of the total health-service demand. A decline in fertility does not reduce total

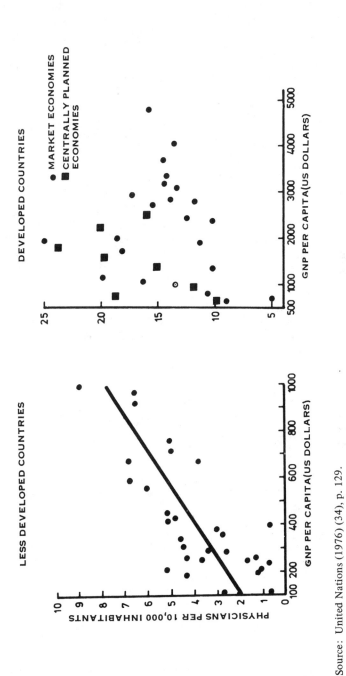

Source: United Nations (1976) (34), p. 129.

Figure 10-28.   Gross National Product per Capita in Relation to the Number of Physicians per 10,000 Inhabitants, 1970

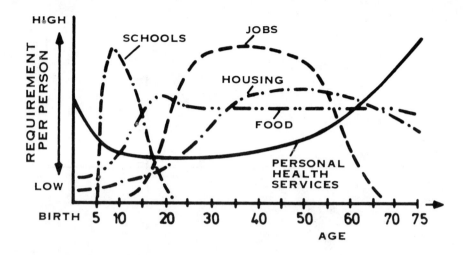

Source: Corsa and Oakley (6) (1971), p. 370.

Figure 10-29. Time Relationships between a Birth and Future Service Requirements

Table 10-15. Projected Service Ratios per 10,000 Population, Thailand, 1970 (service ratios in Bangkok and rest of Thailand separately)

Personnel and facilities	Service ratios in Thailand as a whole	Bangkok	Rest of Thailand
Hospital beds	9.14	41.55	5.86
Physicians	.90	7.27	.32
Nurses	2.03	14.24	.92
Practical nurses	1.29	3.76	1.01
Midwives	.88	.57	.91
Sanitarians	.70	.71	.66
Dentists	.098	.71	.043

Source: Jones (15) (1975), p. 119.

health-care requirements, however, because the corresponding decline in the proportion of young children is offset by the increase in the proportion of older adults.

Much of the variability in rates of illness (morbidity) and death (mortality) among different age and sex groups in a population can be attributed to differences in their underlying cause-of-illness or cause-of-death structure. By way of illustration, Table 10-16 presents death rates among U.S. and Swedish males, by cause of death, for three broad age groups. These data reveal a striking variation of mortality with age.

Teenagers and young adults in the United States are, on the average, very healthy, and their probabilities of dying of diseases are extremely small. Their probabilities of dying in accidents, however, are not that small, especially for males. Table 10-16 indicates that out of 100,000 U.S. males at age 15, over 1,100 will die in accidents before reaching age 25. More than half of these will lose their lives in automobile accidents. Combining these totals with deaths attributable to suicide and homicide, we find that deaths caused by violence in one form or another accounted for three out of every four male deaths in the 15-24 agegroup. This is in marked contrast to the corresponding aggregate rate for all U.S. males, which is one in every ten.

Heart diseases become the major cause of death from about age 35 on according to Table 16. Approximately one out of every hundred

Table 10-16. Expected Number of Deaths, by Cause, per 100,000 Males at Various Ages: United States, 1968, and Sweden, 1967

	United States (white males only)			Sweden		
Cause of Death	*15-24*	*35-44*	*55-64*	*15-24*	*35-44*	*55-64*
Heart diseases	28	999	9,940	22	369	5,293
Neoplasms	103	507	4,697	110	343	3,159
Cerebrovascular disease	–	–	1,196	6	76	950
Cirrhosis of liver	–	188	645	–	50	204
Other accidents	310	321	508	228	287	426
Influenza and pneumonia	29	79	505	25	30	310
Motor accidents	807	351	382	335	197	285
Suicide	113	232	348	140	427	520
Homicide	75	98	62	9	4	9
All causes	1,690	3,458	21,902	1,045	2,286	13,410

Source: Fuchs (11) (1974), pp. 41-45.

white American males dies of a heart attack or related disease in the 35-44 age group. Neoplasms, especially lung cancer, and cirrhosis of the liver, both become important causes of death among American males starting at age 35. Thus the combined impact of smoking and drinking on health is considerable.

The probabilities of dying during the ten-year period between ages 55 and 64 are substantially higher than during the entire forty-year period between ages 15 and 55. The principal reason is the striking increase in the probabilities of dying from a heart attack. According to Table 10-16, the death rate of this cause is then times greater during late middle age than it is at ages 35-44, and over half of all deaths in the former agegroup are attributable to it. The chances of dying from lung cancer also increase to more than ten times the rate observed at ages 35-44.

A comparison of the U.S. and Swedish male death rates (Table 10-16) sheds some light on the character of health problems among American males. Largely because of the high rate of violent deaths, the U.S. rate at ages 15-24 is more than 60 percent higher than the corresponding rate in Sweden. The number of violent deaths per 100,000 individuals is 83 percent higher in the United States than in Sweden, whereas the corresponding differential in nonviolent deaths is only 16 percent.

The pattern changes in the 35-44 age group as the differential in deaths from violence declines and the differential in deaths from heart diseases increases substantially. Between ages 55 and 65 the U.S. death rate is 63 percent higher than the corresponding rate in Sweden, and the U.S. rate for heart diseases is approximately double the Swedish rate.

As better control over such diseases as typhoid fever, diphtheria, whooping cough, and measles leads to major declines in mortality levels, death rates provide an increasingly incomplete description of a national population's general health status. Illnesses and disabilities associated with arthritis, mental illness, and sight and hearing problems are not reflected in mortality statistics, yet much of a nation's requirements for health care are connected with such illnesses and disabilities. Moreover, as more people survive to older ages, chronic degenerative diseases, including heart disease, cancer, and stroke, become more common. Finally, it is important to recognize that future demands for health services also depend on the combined influences of a number of factors besides population. These include national decisions about the importance of health goals relative to other goals, national decisions regarding the health-service functions that should be carried out by various kinds of health personnel, world technological developments, and levels of intenational technical assistance (Corsa and Oakley, 1971).

POLICY ISSUES AND CONCLUSIONS

Scholars and policymakers often disagree when it comes to evaluating the desirability of current rates of rapid urbanization and massive rural-urban migration in the less developed world. Some see these trends as effectively speeding up national processes of socioeconomic development, while others believe their consequences to be largely undesirable and argue that both trends should be slowed down.

Those taking the negative view argue that most developing countries are "over-urbanized" in the sense that urban growth rates have greatly outdistanced rates of industrial development and economic growth. This has created an imbalance that finds cities in the less developed world perpetually struggling with crisis. Despite substantial gains in industrial production, new jobs do not appear at anywhere near the rates required to employ a significant portion of the growing urban labor force. Despite impressive improvements in urban housing, food availability, educational services, and transportation facilities, squatter settlements proliferate, hunger and illiteracy are in evidence everywhere, and traffic congestion is worse than before. And, most important, resources that could otherwise be applied to more directly and immediately productive uses instead must be diverted to satisfy the ever-growing demands for urban social services and infrastructure.

Supporters of current urbanization and migration patterns in developing countries point to the modernizing benefits of urbanization and to the improved well-being of most rural-urban migrants. They contend that urbanization transforms people's outlook and behavioral patterns, while broadening their skills and fostering in them the greater acceptability of innovations and rationality necessary for generating sustained wealth and power in a modern society. They also argue that concern on welfare grounds is probably misplaced, because despite job insecurity and squalid living conditions, most rural-urban migrants are better off than they were prior to their move. Their transfer from the farm to the city enables them to raise their personal income and to obtain social services of a much wider variety and superior quality than were available to them before.

The three population-related policies most frequently suggested for dealing with the urbanization problems of less developed nations are fertility reduction, economic development, and a redistribution of the urban population away from the largest cities. Countries that have achieved a high standard of living, it is pointed out, also have experienced significant declines in their birth rates. And sustained reductions in birth rates have not been accomplished without significant economic growth. Moreover, there is also some evidence that costs of services and environmental damages increase markedly with city size. Yet, although there is evidence to support all of these points, it is by no means irrefutable. Fertility declines have occurred without economic growth. Economic growth has occurred alongside population growth. And convincing arguments have been put forward against a narrow cost-minimization perspective in the debate on city size.

In this paper we have outlined what we believe to be three major components of any complete analysis of human settlement problems: (1) the demographics of rapid urbanization; (2) its demoeconomic development aspects; and (3) the resource-service demands that it generates. A great deal more needs to be learned about these three processes before convincing evidence can be marshaled for or against rapid rates of urbanization. This evidence could shed some light on the following three important policy questions:

1. Is it high fertility or high rural-urban migration that is the principal cause of current rapid rates of urbanization and urban growth in less developed countries, and which of these two components of population change should receive the major attention of national population policy?
2. Is a strategy of rapid industrialization, with its predominantly urban bias, the appropriate model for most developing countries, or should agricultural and rural development programs play a much larger role than they do today?
3. Are the major urban agglomerations in the less developed world too large and do they consume a disproportionately large share of national resources and services, or is the problem one not of urban size but of urban growth management?

The countries of the less developed world are currently faced with the problem of accommodating more people in urban areas within a shorter period of time than did the developed countries. The dimensions of the task confronting the cities of developing nations are, therefore, truly gargantuan. But there are grounds for optimism, since accelerating population increases in urban areas have been absorbed at rising income levels in a number of developing countries. What is sorely needed, however, is enlightened management of the urbanization process to remove systemic inefficiencies and inequalities, and simultaneous preparation of already growing cities for a very much larger increment of growth in the future.

REFERENCES

Arthur, W. B., and G. McNicoll. 1975. "Large-Scale Simulation Models in Population and Development: What Use to Planners?" *Population and Development Review* 1:251-65.

Berelson, B. 1974. "World Population: Status Report 1974." *Reports on Population/Family Planning*, No. 15. New York: The Population Council.

Bose, A. 1973. *Studies in India's Urbanization, 1901-1971.* Bombay: Tata McGraw-Hill.

Coale, A. J. 1969. "Population and Economic Development"; Office of Population Research, Princeton University, Princeton, N.J. Also in *The Population Dilemma*, P. M. Hauser, ed., 2nd ed. Englewood Cliffs, N.J.: Prentice-Hall.

_____ , and E. M. Hoover. 1958. *Population Growth and Economic Development in Low-Income Countries: A Case Study of India's Prospects.* Princeton, N.J.: Princeton University Press.

Corsa, L., Jr., and D. Oakley. 1971. "Consequences of Population Growth for Health Services in Less Developed Countries—An Initial Appraisal." In *Rapid Population Growth: Consequences and Policy Implications*, Vol. 2 *Research Papers*, pp. 368-402. Baltimore: Johns Hopkins Press for the National Academy of Sciences.

Davis, K. 1965. "The Urbanization of the Human Population." *Scientific American* 213:41-53.

Eldridge, H. T., and D. S. Thomas. 1964. *Population Redistribution and Economic Growth, United States 1870-1950*, Vol. 3: *Demographic Analyses and Interrelations.* Philadelphia: The American Philosophical Society.

Farooq, G. M. 1975. "Population Distribution and Migration." In *Population and Development Planning*, W. C. Robinson, ed., pp. 134-52. New York: The Population Council.

Fisher, J. L., and N. Potter. 1971. "The Effects of Population Growth on Resource Adequacy and Quality." In *Rapid Population Growth: Consequences and Policy Implications*, Vol. 2, *Research Papers*, pp. 222-44. Baltimore: Johns Hopkins Press for the National Academy of Sciences.

Fuchs, V. R. 1974. *Who Shall Live? Health, Economics, and Social Choice.* New York: Basic Books.

Gibbs, J. P. 1963. "The Evolution of Population Concentration." *Economic Geography* 39:119-29.

Gilbert, A. 1976. "The Arguments for Very Large Cities Reconsidered." *Urban Studies* 13:27-34.

Harris, C. D. 1975. "The Urban and Demographic Revolutions and Urban Population Growth: The Case of the Soviet Union." In *Urbanization in Europe*, B. Sarfalvi, ed., pp. 69-77. Budapest: Akademiai Kiado.

Jones, G. W. 1975. "Population Growth and Health and Family Planning." In *Population and Development Planning*, W. C. Robinson, ed., pp. 107-33. New York: The Population Council.

Kaneda, H. 1968. "Long-Term Changes in Food Consumption Patterns in Japan 1878-1964." *Food Research Institute Studies in Agricultural Economics, Trade, and Development* 8:3-32.

Kelley, A. C. 1974. "The Role of Population in Models of Economic Growth." *American Economic Review* 64:39-44.

_____ 1969. "Demand Patterns, Demographic Change and Economic Growth." *Quarterly Journal of Economics* 83:110-26.

_____ , and J. G. Williamson. 1973. "Modeling Economic Development and General Equilibrium Histories." *American Economic Review* 63:450-58.

Keyfitz, N. 1976. "World Resources and the World Middle Class." *Scientific American* 235:28-35.

Kuroda, T. 1973. *Japan's Changing Population Structure.* Tokyo: Ministry of Foreign Affairs.

Long, L. H., and C. G. Boertlein. 1976. "The Geographical Mobility of Americans: An International Comparison." *Current Population Reports,* Special Studies Series P-23, No. 64. Washington, D.C.: Bureau of the Census, U.S. Government Printing Office.

Mok, B. N. 1975. "Population Change and Housing Needs." In *Population and Development Planning,* W. C. Robinson, ed., pp. 95-106. New York: The Population Council.

Morrison, P. A. 1975. *The Current Demographic Context of National Growth and Development.* Rand Paper Series No. P-5514. Santa Monica: Rand Corporation.

_____ , with J. P. Wheeler. 1976. "Rural Renaissance in America? The Revival of Population Growth in Remote Areas." *Population Bulletin,* Vol. 3, No. 3. Washington, D.C.: Population Reference Bureau.

Parish, W. L. 1973. "Internal Migration and Modernization: The European Case." *Economic Development and Cultural Change* 21:591-609.

Ridker, R. G., and P. R. Crosson. 1975. "Resources, Environment and Population." In *Population and Development Planning,* W. C. Robinson, ed., pp. 202-22. New York: The Population Council.

Robinson, W. C., ed. 1975. *Population and Development Planning.* New York: Population Council.

_____ , and D. E. Horlacher. 1971. "Population Growth and Economic Welfare." *Reports on Population/Family Planning,* No. 6. New York: The Population Council.

Rogers, A. 1976. "Two Methodological Notes on Spatial Population Dynamics in the Soviet Union." RM-76-48. Laxenburg, Austria: International Institute for Applied Systems Analysis.

_____ . 1975. *Introduction to Multiregional Mathematical Demography.* New York: Wiley.

_____ , and F. Willekens. 1976. "The Spatial Reproductive Value and the Spatial Momentum of Zero Population Growth." RM-76-81. Laxenburg, Austria: International Institute for Applied Systems Analysis.

Todaro, M. P. 1975. "Rural-Urban Migration, Unemployment and Job Probabilities: Recent Theoretical and Empirical Research." In *Economic Factors in Population Growth,* A. J. Coale, ed., pp. 367-85. London: Macmillan.

United Nations. 1976. *Global Review of Human Settlements: A Support Paper for Habitat*. Vols. 1 and 2. Oxford: Pergamon Press.

————. 1974. *Methods for Projections of Urban and Rural Population, Manual VIII*. New York: Department of Economic and Social Affairs.

U.S. Bureau of the Census. 1972. "Mobility of the Population of the United States: March 1970 to March 1971." *Current Population Reports*, Series P-20, No. 235.

Vining, D. R., Jr., and T. Kontuly. 1977. "Increasing Returns to City Size in the Face of an Impending Decline in the Sizes of Large Cities: Which is Bogus Fact?" *Environment and Planning* 9:59-62.

Yap, L. 1976. "Internal Migration and Economic Development in Brazil." *Quarterly Journal of Economics* 90:119-37.

Zelinski, W. 1971. The Hypothesis of the Mobility Transition." *Geographical Review* 61:219-49.

Chapter Eleven

Discussion of "Migration, Urbanization, Resources, and Development," by Andrei Rogers

Robert Louis Clark

Professor Rogers has presented a detailed review of observed differences in urban and rural economic choices and status. He outlines potential problems associated with rapid rates of urban growth and urbanization. The principal focus of his examination is the direct and interactive effects of migration, urbanization, and resource utilization on the developmental process. The Rogers framework of analysis includes the influence of population growth on national and per capita income. In these comments, I will explicitly state the economic model of migration and examine it in light of Rogers's analysis. Next, the influence of population growth on the age structure and composition of the dependent population will be explored; and finally the use of dependency ratios to determine investment and economic growth is reviewed.

MIGRATION AND NATIONAL INCOME

An individual's decision to leave a current job and community to migrate to a new geographic region can be treated as an investment decision. The worker recognizes the future earnings pattern available in an existing location and compares this value to alternative estimates of income opportunities in other areas minus the cost of relocation. The following model, whose origins are attributed to Sjaastad,[1] indicates the present value in discrete time associated with a move from area j to area k:

$$PV = \sum_{t=0}^{T} \frac{Y_k(t) - Y_j(t)}{(1 + r)^t} - C$$

where $Y_k(t)$ is the expected earnings[2] in area k at time t; $Y_j(t)$ is the anticipated earnings in area j at time t; T is the remaining years of work; r is the discount rate the individual applies to the earnings streams; and C represents the direct cost of moving assumed to occur entirely in the first period. Of course, the model can easily be expanded to include the value of nonpecuniary returns to both areas. In addition, demand for services such as education and health for one's children may influence location decisions.

The implication of this migration model is that individuals, as Rogers states, "migrate in search of improved social and economic opportunities." Workers make locational decisions in an attempt to maximize the present value of their lifetime earnings or utility. This model clearly states that the individual operating with full information will have improved his or her economic well-being following migration. At various points, Rogers wonders whether individuals, regions, or the nation as a whole gain from migration. For example, he states:

> The problems created by this transformation [urban growth and urbanization] are manifold and involve large *private and social costs*. But there are obvious benefits, too, and it is important to keep these in mind when considering policies for intervening in the urbanization process. [Emphasis added.]

Can the individual who moves be made worse off by a decision to relocate? While imperfect information can produce ex post suboptimal outcomes, migration is expected to increase the well-being of movers[3] with informational networks, that is, friends and relatives, newspapers, and so on, arising to generate the needed flow of knowledge. The improved status of migrants does not, however, insure a positive net benefit to either the region or the nation as a whole. The improved status of the migrant is not a sufficient condition to provide a net gain to the economy due to the possibilties of externalities and returns to scale in the production of goods. Differences between social costs and returns and private expenditures and receipts might provide a rationale for a public policy aimed at increasing or decreasing migratory flows.

Externalities produced by expansion of city size may be either positive or negative. Rogers focuses on the negative aspects of urban growth such as pollution or congestion. His analysis would seem to imply ihat if new migrants were forced to pay the of urban growth such as pollution or congestion. His analysis would seem to imply that if new migrants were forced to pay the full social costs of their relocation, fewer people would be drawn to urban areas. Thurow states the problem in the following manner:

Private incomes may increase enough to more than make up for the costs of moving, but the social costs of accommodating people in a crowded urban area may exceed the net private gain. More public services must be provided, and congestion may increase.[4]

The magnitude and nature of externalities can be expected to depend on urban characteristics, perhaps, to the extent that generalities cannot be made.

For society to be made worse off from migration, the full social costs of relocation, including these externalities, would have to be greater than the social gain from increased production attributable to workers finding employment with higher productivity than in their old residences. To the extent that higher levels of social services are provided in the urban areas—welfare benefits, subsidized housing, schooling—the difference between private and social gains may be widened, and it is possible that people will give up employment in rural areas to draw these benefits in cities. This, however, begs the question of why such differentials exist. Political and social hypotheses may be put forward to explain the existence of state-supported urban-rural differentials in social services, such as greater likelihood of revolution among disgruntled masses, urban poverty is more visible, and the like. But there may be economic rationales influencing these government decisions. Public policy may be explicitly directed toward increasing urbanization in the belief that there is a positive codecisions. Public policy may be explicitly directed toward increasing urbanization in the belief that there is a positive correlation between these migrational flows and economic development. The government may also recognize economies of scale in the production and supply of these services.

If social services are financed by the local area, the inflow of new migrants may increase the tax load on the existing inhabitants relative to the benefits that the newcomer provides. The possibility then exists that the individual and the nation may benefit by migration while the previous inhabitants of a particular city or region might suffer. In the case of social services, the increased tax burden on the long-term residents arise because of a pricing policy that provides them below costs and thus implies income transfers to the newcomers. In way of summary, Greenwood stated in his review of the migration literature that "little empirical work has attempted to measure the magnitudes of externalities associated with migration."[5]

Henderson argues that if the social and private costs of externalities are equated, cities will reorder their production priorities away from the goods that are producing the pollution or other externality. The adverse effect of the reduction in the production of the polluting commodity "will be more than offset by the increase in output of other goods and the decline in pollution. Welfare of city residents will rise, and immigration to the city from the rest of the economy will then occur."[6] Thus, under certain conditions, an optimal taxing or pricing of an externality—pollution, congestion, and so on—may increase the well-being of the city dwellers at the existing urban population size, which will induce migration to the city, increasing its size.

Migration into large urban areas might also create additional burdens to a society if the production of social goods and services were characterized by decreasing returns to scale. In such a case the marginal and average costs of providing housing, education, and other services would increase as the population of the region rose. The inference is that it would have cost the society less to provide these services to new migrants in their old location. A recent study using U.S. data estimated that the production functions of urban services exhibited constant returns to scale across the entire sample.[7]

Arguing that urban production functions will exhibit increasing returns to scale, Goldstein and Moses conclude that the growth of urban areas "is intimately related to scale and agglomerative economies."[8] In his review of the internal migration literature, Greenwood concludes that "migration has historically been an important means by which these economies have been achieved in urban areas."[9] Kuznets, in his *Modern Economic Growth*, states that "urbanization is a necessary condition for industrialization and modern economic growth and essential to the economies of scale of modern industry."[10]

An additional concern stated by Rogers is that rural-to-urban migration increases city size, thus "reducing the per capita endowment of capital" in the urban area. Increases in the supply of labor in a particular region would be expected to generate downward pressure on wage rates; however, in the rural region wages should increase. Migratory flows that tend to equalize returns to capital and labor in the different areas within an economy are contributing to efficient allocation of resources. Therefore, reduced urban wages caused by the inflow of rural labor should not be considered an externality unless property rights on the existing capital stock and technology have been assigned to the initial urban workers.

These studies seem to indicate that the nation as a whole would tend to benefit from migration in the following manner: first, as workers move to areas where their productivity and earnings are greater, national and per capita income rise; second, the net negative values of externalities are typically not sufficient to offset these income gains, and if property taxed may contribute to increased city size; and finally, some evidence exists that indicates urban services are produced under constant or increasing returns to scale. This explanation is consistent with results of Yap[11] that are cited in detail by Rogers. I might add that in any theoretical economic framework, unrestrained movement of resources is a necessary condition for efficient production and the achievement of maximum output. Thus, a government policy to restrict or retard the flow of labor within a country might significantly impair the economy's ability to respond to economic fluctuations.

POPULATION GROWTH, AGE STRUCTURE CHANGES AND ECONOMIC WELL-BEING

Professor Rogers outlines a framework that links population growth, investment, and per capita income. His reasoning is that a nation with a rapidly increasing population "will be able to add less to the productive capacity of the economy than a population experiencing a less rapid rate of labor-force growth." This decline in investment occurs because "the pressure for allocating a much higher proportion of the national product for consumption then would be greater in the higher fertility population because of its higher dependency burden."

This is, of course, the traditional hypothesis of the interaction of population growth and economic well-being. It was stated forcefully by Spengler over two decades ago:

> Population growth is a major obstacle to economic betterment in most parts of the world. It is retarding capital formation, accelerating the rate of depletion of the world's limited store of nonreplaceable resources, augmenting the rise of costs in increasing cost industries, and decelerating the rate of increase of per capita income.[12]

The tenet that population growth retards and has slowed past economic growth is not, however, a uniformly accepted belief. Kuznets found that "no clear association appears to exist in the present sample of countries, or is likely in other developed countries, between rates of growth of population and product per capita."[13] In his examination of 76 less-developed countries over a period of ten years, Alfred Sauvy estimated no significant correlation between the rate of growth of population and national per capita income.[14]

Some researchers have outlined the economic advantages of population growth. These factors may include: existence of economies of scale in some industries; with fixed firm size, population growth may increase competition; higher proportion of capital stock is of a new vintage;[15] enhances vertical mobility of labor; and easier adaptability to economic change.[16]

While I do not wish to argue in favor of rapid population growth, I believe it would be useful in the framework of this conference to analyze the implication of population increases on the ability of the economy to generate investment. My examination will focus on: (1) relating fertility decisions to a family choice model; (2) expenditures on children as a form of investment; and (3) the use of dependency ratios to determine savings capacity.

HOUSEHOLD SAVINGS DECISIONS

Much of the analysis of the impact of children on aggregate saving concludes that increases in the number of children raises the number of consumers without increasing production; therefore, to maintain consumption standards, savings must be reduced.

Before continuing, we must reach agreement on the definition of investment. Expenditures that increase the ability of society to generate output in subsequent periods are described as investment, and these expenditures can be on either physical or human capital. Much of the public and private expenditures on children directly influence the income-generating capacity of the economy by increasing the stock of human capital. For example, educational expenditures provide children with the training and work skills that enable them to be more productive during their worklives. Thus, one must be cautious in describing the influence of children on household savings. The presence of children may induce the family to reduce its savings in the form of physical assets and bank accounts while it is increasing its investment in the human capital of the children.

Schultz estimated that the stock of education embodied in the labor force rose by 8.5 times from 1900 to 1956, compared to an increase of 4.5 times for reproducible capital.[17] Growth in national income is a function of physical capital accumulation and changes in its productivity, increases in per capita human capital, and changes in the aggregate stock of human capital due to population changes. Selowsky estimated that for the United States, improvements in the average level of educational attainment accounted for 0.52 percent of the annual growth rate between 1940-1965. Maintaining the same per capita educational levels with population growth contributed 0.33 percent to the rate of growth of national income.[18] Therefore, all public and private expenditures on children should not be allocated to consumption, but instead should include a definite investment component.

Kelley has argued that expenditures on children need not be substitutes for family savings, but may represent a reordering of the family consumption pattern. In addition, the presence of children may induce different patterns of market work (more or less) and might encourge the accumulation of assets, that is, add a bequest goal to the family objective function. He concludes that "hard evidence on the relationship between family size and household savings is almost nonexistent."[19] Household decisions about the number and quality of children and the consumption of other commodities have been analyzed in a utility framework by Becker and Lewis. Their model shows the interactive nature of family decisions about family size and levels of consumption.[20] Thus, the influence of children on family savings in both human and physical assets is not certain.

POPULATION AGE-STRUCTURE AND GOVERNMENT SPENDING ON DEPENDENTS

To examine the aggregate influence of alternative levels of population growth and the implied dependency burden, we employ age structure data developed by Coale and Demeny for a stable population of males exhibiting Western mortality rates. Five rates of population growth are shown in Table 11-1, along with the resulting age structure. Defining the labor force as 20-64, the proportion of the population in this agegroup is at its highest for a stable or slightly declining population. For a zero population growth rate, 57.43 percent of the population is in the working years while 15.95 percent would be retired and 26.63 percent were young dependents. By comparison, a nation growing at 2 percent per year has only 50 percent of its population in the labor force with 43 percent below age 20 and 7 percent age 65 and over.

Individuals outside the arbitrarily defined working ages are assigned to a dependent status presumably because they are adding to consumption but are not contributing to production. We must recognize that participation in the labor force is an individual decision, therefore not all those of working age will be in the labor force, while the entirety of those of dependent ages will not refrain from market participation. In addition, why should we call aged individuals dependents when they are living on the income from the assets that they have accumulated? Are those who have chosen to continue to invest in human capital formation dependents?

The conclusion of an increasing "dependency burden" with higher rates of population growth would seem obvious upon examination of Table 11-1. Two points, however, should be stressed: first, the reduction in the dependency ratio with decreased population growth is sensitive to the age of entry into the labor force and the retirement from it; and second, expenditures on young and old dependents might have a differential impact on the economy. Table 11-2 shows that if the age of entry into the labor force is lowered to 15, the difference between the proportion of the population in the labor force in the no-growth popula-

Table 11-1. Rate of Population Growth and Age Structure

	Rate of Growth in Stable Population (percent)				
Percent in Age Group	*−0.5*	*0*	*0.5*	*1*	*2*
0-14	16.99	19.99	23.20	26.60	33.73
15-19	5.94	6.64	7.33	7.99	9.14
20-54	45.08	45.62	45.66	45.22	43.07
55-59	6.64	6.09	5.50	4.91	3.76
60-64	6.40	5.72	5.04	4.39	3.20
65-69	5.91	5.15	4.43	3.76	2.61
65 and over	18.95	15.95	13.26	10.89	7.10
20-64	58.12	57.43	56.20	54.52	50.03
20-69	64.13	62.58	60.63	59.28	52.64
18-64	60.50	60.09	59.13	57.72	51.85

Source: A.J. Coale and Paul Demeny, *Regional Model Life Tables and Stable Populations* (Princeton, 1966), p. 168.

Table 11-2. Age Structure and Population Growth

Rate of Growth	*Percent of Total Population Aged:*						
	20-64	*20-59*	*20-54*	*20-69*	*15-64*	*15-59*	*15-54*
−0.5	58.12	51.72	45.08	64.13	64.06	57.66	51.02
0	57.43	51.71	45.62	62.58	64.07	58.35	52.26
0.5	56.20	51.16	45.66	60.63	63.53	58.49	52.99
1.0	54.52	49.48	44.57	59.28	62.51	57.47	52.56
2.0	50.03	48.83	43.07	52.64	59.17	55.97	52.21

Source: Table 11-1.

tion and one that is increasing is significantly narrowed. A decline in age of withdrawal from the labor force has a similar effect. For example, if the labor force is defined as the population 15-54, there is virtually no difference in the total dependency ratios for annual growth rates between 0 and 2 percent. This sensitivity of the relative size of the working-age population with changes in the ages of entry and retirement imply that generalizations about population growth and dependency ratios must be made with considerable caution. With economic development, two of the dominant labor-force participation trends are earlier retirement and later entry into the labor force. As previously stated, these patterns of labor supply exert conflicting pressures on the relative size of the dependent populations under alternative fertility assumptions.

The composition of the dependent population must also be examined if the impacts of changing age structures are to be related to national and per capita income. Let us once again define the labor force to be composed of individuals 20-64, with the remaining agegroups classified as dependents. The proportion of all dependents who are below the age of entry into labor varies directly with the population growth rate, as follows:

The changing composition of the dependent population raises the following two questions: (1) Is the cost of maintaining young dependents the same as that for older ones? (2) Are the public and private costs of supporting the two groups of the same nature? If the costs of supporting an older dependent is greater than that of maintaining children, the burden of dependency costs with increasing population growth rates may be reversed. Using U.S. data, Clark and Spengler have estimated that the annual public cost of supporting an older dependent is three times that of a youth; however, greater intrafamily transfers are usually made to children.[21] We can incorporate the higher costs of supporting the elderly to estimate an adjusted dependency burden in the following manner: let X represent the cost of supporting a child, and αX the cost of maintaining an older dependent. Then the adjusted dependency burden is $X + \alpha X$. A higher support cost of as low as 50 percent is sufficient to reverse the pattern of increased dependency burden with population growth. Of course these ratios are also sensitive to the definition of the working age population:

In addition to the differences in the level of transfers to the two groups, the very nature of the spending may be different. We have previously argued that to a significant degree the expenditures on children represents investment in human capital formation, while transfers to the elderly are more likely to be for current consumption. Thus, in a rapidly growing population, more of the dependency costs will be for investment than in a no-growth society.

This analysis leads one to conclude that researchers should not look only at dependency ratios based on a single definition of the labor force to assess the impact of population growth on the ability of an economy to generate investment and thus influence the capital-labor ratio and per capita income. I have attempted to illustrate several critical variables that must be considered in examining population growth and economic development, including sensitivity to the age boundaries of the labor force, cost of young versus old dependents, and the investment component of expenditures for youths. Shifts in the population age structure will also influence economic growth due to differential patterns of savings, productivity, and earnings over the life cycle.

* * *

I would like to contribute one final comment as it pertains to a statement about mobility of the dual career family. Rogers writes that "economic development stimulates the labor-force participation of wives, and working wives reduce the ease with which couples can relocate." While the few existing studies provide weak support of this hypothesis,[22] and my intuition is to concur, I remain unconvinced that this is necessarily the direction of causation, and certainly the theoretical result is ambiguous. For example, the typical unskilled worker who migrates quits his job in one city, and following relocation, searches for new employment in the new region. Presumably the worker was responding to wage differentials in the two locations. If the same family has two earners, the gain from such a move will be greater upon the reemployment of both workers. Of course, costs have also risen with higher family opportunity costs due to foregone earnings.

Professional workers more frequently already have new jobs prior to relocation. Thus, if both earners are professionals, mobility may be hindered by the need to secure two jobs. However, upward mobility in a corporate society is dependent on willingness of individuals to move to various locations as they progress up the business hierarchy. Therefore, the existence of two such workers in a single family may increase the frequency of opportunities for the family to transfer while one member receives a promotion in the same firm and the other searches for new employment. The most significant result of the increasing incidence of dual career families as it relates to Roger's paper may be the tendency of such families to locate in major metropolitan areas where job opportunities are more diverse and more suitable to accommodate two workers from the same family.

NOTES

1. Larry Sjaastad, "The Costs and Returns of Human Migration," *Journal of Political Economy Supplement* (October 1962).

2. Expected earnings are a function not only of the prevailing wage rate but also the probability of obtaining employment. See, for example, M.P. Todaro, "A Model of Labor Migration and Urban Unemployment in Less Developed Countries," *American Economic Review* (March 1969), pp. 139-48.

3. For developing countries, see Gian Sahota, "An Economic Analysis of Internal Migration in Brazil," *Journal of Political Economy* (March/April

1968); T. Paul Schultz, "Rural-Urban Migration in Colombia," *Review of Economics and Statistics* (May 1971); Ralph Beals, Mildred Levy, and Leon Moses, "Rationality and Migration in Ghana," *Review of Economics and Statistics* (November 1967); and Michael Greenwood, "A Regression Analysis of Migration to Urban Areas of a Less-Developed Country: The Case of India," *Journal of Regional Science* (August 1971).

4. L.C. Thurow, *Investment in Human Capital* (Belmont, Calif.: Wadsworth, 1970), p. 33.

5. Michael Greenwood, "Research on Internal Migration in the United States: A Survey," *Journal of Economic Literature* (June 1975), p. 421.

6. J.V. Henderson, "Optimum City Size: The External Diseconomy Question," *Journal of Political Economy* (March/April 1974).

7. David Segal, "Are There Returns to Scale in City Size?" *Review of Economics and Statistics* (August 1976).

8. Gerald Goldstein and Leon Moses, "A Survey of Urban Economics," - *Journal of Economic Literature* (June 1973), p. 471.

9. Greenwood, op. cit., p. 417.

10. Simon Kuznets, *Modern Economic Growth* (New Haven: Yale University Press, 1966), p. 60.

11. L. Yap, "Internal Migration and Economic Development in Brazil," - *Quarterly Journal of Economics* (February 1976).

12. Joseph Spengler, "The Population Obstacle to Economic Betterment," *American Economic Review* (May 1951), p. 354.

13. Kuznets, op. cit., p. 67.

14. Discussion of paper by Goran Ohlin, "Economic Theory Confronts Population Growth," in Ansley Coale, ed., *Economic Factors in Population Growth* (New York: Wiley, 1976), p. 22.

15. Alfred Sauvy, "The Optimal Change of a Population," in ibid., pp. 68-69.

16. Joseph Spengler, "Economic Implications of Low Fertility," presented to the Conference on Social, Economic and Health Aspects of Low Fertility, sponsored by the World Health Organization and National Institutes for Health, March 1977.

17. T.W. Schultz, "Investment in Human Capital," *American Economic Review* (March 1961), p. 11.

18. Marcelo Selowsky, "On the Measurement of Education's Contribution to Growth," *Quarterly Journal of Economics* (1969), pp. 449-63.

19. Allen Kelley, "The Role of Population in Models of Economic Growth," *American Economic Review* (May 1974), p. 41.

20. Gary Becker and Gregg Lewis, "On the Interaction between Quantity and Quality of Children," *Journal of Political Economy* (March-April, 1973), Part II, pp. S279-88.

21. Robert Clark and Joseph Spengler, "Changing Demography and Dependency Costs: The Implications of New Dependency Ratios and Their Composition," presented to *Support for the Aged: Policy Options and Research Needs*, a conference sponsored by the Gerontological Society, April 1976; and Robert Clark, "The Influence of Low Fertility Rates and Retirement Policy on Dependency Costs," prepared for the American Institutes for Research in the Behavioral Sciences, July 1976.

22. Larry Long, "Women's Labor Force Participation and the Residential Mobility of Families," *Social Forces* (March 1974). In examining data from the United States, Long finds increased intracounty mobility but decreased interstate mobility when the wife works. However, he finds that "a working wife thus appears to have little effect on her husband's long-distance migration in the early years of his career—the years when long-distance migration is most likely to occur." (p. 346).

Chapter Twelve

Discussion of "Migration, Urbanization, Resources, and Development," by Andrei Rogers

William J. Serow

As a discussant, one is usually faced with the choice of carefully reviewing the major paper for one of two primary reasons: (1) to unearth relatively minor details for purposes of not necessarily constructive criticism; or (2) to find points that permit further elaboration or extension of the major paper. This paper reflects the second approach, and may be viewed as an extension of Dr. Rogers's fine paper in that it focuses on issues relating to rural development and some of the policy implications for this sort of development.

As the title indicates, the paper initially views issues of rural development from a demographic perspective, treating separately the questions of fertility and migration. The aim in doing so is to preserve the notion of demographic transition, with its separate natural increase and mobility components, as outlined previously by Dr. Rogers.

FERTILITY

It is a demographic axiom that fertility in rural areas will, as a rule, exceed that of urban areas. Because of a paucity of reliable fertility data in most portions of the Third World, one is forced to seek confirmation of this assertation by examination of relatively crude measures such as the child-woman ratio. While this is a far from perfect measure,[1] it is about the only tool available for our purposes. It is certainly clear from the imperfect and far from complete data in Table 12-1 that fertility among both the rural and urban residents of developed countries is substantially lower than that in developing countries. Continuing high fertility in the rural portions of developing countries will only continue to add, as Dr. Rogers has suggested, to continued population growth in urban areas through inmigration from rural areas in search of employment opportunities. These rural dwellers swell the urban population both directly (through their inmigration) and indirectly[2] (through reproduction).

As a consequence, declines in rural fertility will enhance development by reducing population pressure in both the rural and urban portions of a country. The mere fact of population growth, it might be argued, aids as a deterrent to economic and technological advance, simply because it requires a larger share of investible resources to be devoted to equipping the new entrants to the labor force (that is, maintaining a constant capital-labor ratio), rather than increasing the amount and quality of capital available per worker.[3] Additionally, a high rate of population growth necessarily implies a very large share of young dependents in the population. Not only do these persons consume but not produce (thus decreasing the share of total income that can be saved), but given current levels of infant mortality, many of them will die prior to reaching labor-force age.

Perhaps the major question that has confounded persons interested in the roll of population growth in the development process is whether reduced population growth is a precondition to economic development, or vice versa. This latter concept is perhaps best stated by Kingsley Davis,[4] who forcefully argues that family planning programs per se (that is, programs aimed at reducing population growth on the assumption that this will enhance development) ignore entirely the motives of individuals regarding their own reproductive behavior. Thus, a successful family planning program will allow the individual to attain desired family size but, according to Davis, this size may well be consistent with fairly high rates of population growth.

Economic development, therefore, might be supposed to reduce fertility, by affecting the motivations of individuals to reproduce. Consider some of the possible motivations for desiring a fairly large family in a developing society: the additional social pressure to insure a male heir; the need for old-age security; and the supply of relatively inexpensive labor to assist in cultivating the family holding. The process of economic development is likely to mitigate all of these pressures to some extent. Along with economic development is likely to come a sharp decline in infant mortality; as this ensues (given time for recognition of this change), fertility will decline, simply because fewer children will be required to ensure the survival of a male child to adulthood. This factor, along with the growth and development of some sort of social welfare system, should also mitigate the old-age security issue. Finally, if improvements in agricultural technology are sufficiently diffused, the need for additional farm labor becomes proportionally less.

As the situation stands at present, it is frequently argued that the marginal productivity of farm labor in many developing countries approximates zero, and this fact alone contributes substantially to rural-urban migration in these nations. This might make the rural sector better off in the sense that their own output might be shared by fewer persons (or, at least, that per capita income or consumption would rise), but—as Todaro has demonstrated—not have much effect on the well-being of the migrant, given the possibility of a low probability of finding employment. Indeed, Todaro suggests that it is difficult to reduce substantially "the size of the urban traditional sector without a concentrated effort at making rural life more attractive."[5] One means of doing this is to allocate capital funds for improving rural amenities, thus increasing the real income of rural residents relative to urban residents, and reducing the relative strength of the rural push or urban pull.

The role that improvements in income or other measures of well-being actually have on reproductive ideals and performance is another topic that has been the subject of considerable debate among scholars over the past decade. While time and space do not permit an analysis of the differences between the so-called Becker and Easterlin "schools" of the economic determinants of fertility, a recent study by Sanderson concludes that agreement on two major points (role of bequests or expenditures per child as fertility determinants, and the role of intergenerational perceptions of income as a determinant of fertility) has been reached.[6] In other words, according to Sanderson, "It is possible to entertain both the hypothesis that parents' aspirations for their own standard of living and bequests for their children depend, in part, on their background and the hypothesis that the parents' aspirations for their children's standard of living as well as their own depend, in part, on their current income."[7]

Through what might be termed a critical minimum effort thesis, it may be alleged that fertility will decline as development progresses. The United Nations describes this hypothesis as follows: "In a developing country where fertility is initially high, improving economic and social conditions are likely to have little if any effect until a certain economic and social level is reached; but once that level is achieved, fertility is likely to enter a decided decline and to continue downward until it is again stabilized in a much lower plane."[8]

This hypothesis suggests that a minimum threshold of development must be attained as a precondition to fertility diminution and the subsequent reduction of population growth rates, in the manner of the natural increase component of the demographic transition described previously by Dr. Rogers.

An important addendum to this hypothesis has recently been advanced by Kocher,[9] who suggests that a wide diffusion of rural development and equality in the distribution of the development process and its benefits will lead to more rapid modernization among a relatively larger share of the rural population, which will lead to a more widespread desire for smaller families and earlier, more rapid, and sustained declines in fertility. The overall framework is outlined by Kocher as follows:[10]

1. Population growth, whatever the level, is not an obstacle to growth of per capita agricultural output.
2. In most developing countries, new agricultural technology is a precondition for agricultural growth and development.
3. The degree to which diffusion of technology and other developmental processes will be widespread depends on government policies and domestic institutions.
4. If these diffusions are widely diffused so that the distribution of the benefits of development is fairly widespread, the standard of living will rise and a more modern life-style will be adopted by a majority of the rural population. Based on the reasoning of the economics of fertility outlined above, this will cause an increase in parents' aspirations for themselves and their children, which should lower desired family size. It is at this point that an effective family program can hasten and facilitate a spontaneous decline in fertility.
5. Finally, if the diffusion of innovation is limited by institutions, policies, or both, then a dualistic pattern of rural development will ensue, with the bulk of developmental efforts being shared by a privileged few, while the majority of rural dwellers will continue their traditional mode of life.

If the diffusion of rural development is not widespread, then there is no incentive for the disenchanted rural resident to remain at home. Hence, nondiffused rural development only adds to the rural-urban migration movement.

MIGRATION

As noted above, rural-to-urban migration customarily occurs because of some combination of what demographers call push and pull forces. As Everett Lee has described it: "In every area there are countless factors which act to hold people within the area or attract people to it, and there are others which tend to repel them."[11] These factors vary with individuals, but each weighs the positive and negative factors of the current place of residence vis-á-vis those of competing places of residence and, theoretically, decides: (1) whether to move; and if so (2) to which competing area.

For the case of developing countries the rural resident will be faced with a substantial (and probably growing) differential in urban-rural income (pull), and the prospect of little advance in economic status within the rural community (push). Even given the low probability of employment in the urban area, the individual might decide that, from a private perspective, the benefits of migration outweigh the costs. From the viewpoint of society, however, the public costs of this migration might well outweigh the public benefits.[12] A substantial portion of the cost was alleviated in the past through emigration,[13] but for presently developing countries such a mechanism has effectively ceased to operate.

It has proved somewhat difficult to measure private and public costs and benefits of internal rural-urban migration in developing countries. Yap, in her review of the literature on the subject, finds that "though there is a wide variation in the quality of the jobs obtained, migrants seem to receive higher incomes in their destination than in their place of origin."[14] On the other hand, a summary report by the National Academy of Sciences notes that studies usually indicate that the costs of providing jobs for rural-urban migrants in developing countries are so high that it is better (from a cost-benefit point of view) to reduce drastically the volume of rural-urban migration and make all possible efforts to keep prospective migrants in their (rural) place of origin. However, the Academy notes that while "it is difficult to argue with the arithmetic of these studies . . . it can be asked if they are attuned to the reality of the situation. A similar study in the period of intense urbanization of now developed countries would probably have yielded the same conclusions."[15]

Rural-urban migration, then, might be a phenomenon which is an integral part of the development process.[16] As such, the question that might appropriately be asked is not whether steps should be taken to curb this flow, but rather, Should it (and how should it) be rechannelled? It should be noted that some claim that developing countries are presently "overurbanized." Abu-Lughod summarizes the argument:

> Many students of urbanization have suggested that countries in the early stages of industrialization suffer an imbalance in both the size and distribution of their urban populations, implying primarily that they have a higher percentage of people living in cities and towns than is "warranted" at their state of economic development.[17]

Although this thesis, at least that portion dealing with the size of the urban population, has been refuted by Sovani,[18] Kamerschen,[19] and others, there remains the question of the maldistribution of the urban population and the possible need to rechannel its growth.

RESOURCES AND RURAL DEVELOPMENT

The urban pattern of most developing nations can be best characterized as that of the "primate city," that is, one which is overwhelmingly large in comparison with all other cities in the country "Commonly, within developing countries there is no hierarchy of cities of various sizes such as that found in developed nations, and primate cities most frequently occur in countries with relatively low overall levels of urbanization."[20] Hoselitz notes that such a system may be all that most developing countries are capable of supporting, but that the system of the primate city has harmful overall effects for several reasons: (1) the depletion of valuable personnel from rural areas; (2) the consumption of nearly all investment monies; (3) the subsequent prevention of the development of other urban areas; and (4) a tendency toward relatively high consumption and relatively low production.[21] While in the course of urbanization the development of an urban hierarchy in developing countries is probably inevitable, much can be done to shape the mode of this new urban development.

The logical means for this planned pattern of urban development is to concentrate resource allocation in the presently rural sector, on the theory that economic change in the rural sector will eventually create a demand for urban-type development through specialization of labor and increased demand for services. As Dr. Rogers notes in his paper, this state of urban development customarily comes at a relatively late stage in economic development—indeed, as he notes, it seems to be presently occurring in the United States.

In order for such a program to succeed, it would seem that rural development efforts, while based on agriculture, must go beyond this into rural multisectional development. An example of this approach is that presently taken by the World Bank, in what they term integrated rural development projects. The ultimate aim is to improve the standard of living of rural residents by improving their productivity, usually by introduction and expansion of technological change at the micro level. In order to accomplish this, the World Bank believes that three basic conditions must be met:[22] (1) producers must know how to increase their output; (2) they must have access to the means of increasing their output; and (3) they must have the incentive to make the effort and accept the risk associated with increasing their output. In order to facilitate this process, bank projects are concentrated on effective means of delivering to farmers all necessary goods and services. This includes not only capital inputs, but also such infrastructural items as irrigation and transportation. While such a venture may prove relatively costly in the short run, the long-run effects are likely to see a balanced growth and development of rural and urban areas, with a true urban hierarchy developed to service the needs of all residents. This is a requirement in many developed, as well as developing, countries.[23] The latter, however, have the opportunity of coping with, and shaping their future, in a manner that will reflect and avoid the mistakes made by now developed countries at similar stages of their development.

NOTES

1. "The Child-woman ratio is an imperfect tool for the study of fertility differentials, as it is affected by differential infant and child mortality as well as by differential completeness of enumeration of the child population. More particularly, when used to study differences between urban and rural fertility, the ratio may also distort the rural-urban fertility differential because of age-selective migration from rural to urban areas." United Nations, *The Determinants and Consequences of Population Trends* (New York, 1973), p. 97.

2. This twofold contribution is made clear in William J. Serow, "The Potential Demographic Impact of Migration, *Review of Regional Studies* (Fall 1974), pp. 16-28; and Campbell Gibson, "The Contribution of Immigration to the United States Population Growth: 1790-1970," *International Migration Review* (Summer 1975), pp. 157-77.

3. See Joseph J. Spengler, "Agricultural Development Is Not Enough," in *World Population—The View Ahead*, ed. R. N. Farmer, J. D. Long, and G. J. Stolnitz (Bloomington: Indiana University, 1968), pp. 104-26.

4. Kingsley Davis, "Population Policy: Will Current Programs Succeed?" *Science*, November 10, 1967, pp. 730-39.

5. Michael P. Todaro, "A Model of Labor Migration and Urban Unemployment in Less Developed Countries," *American Economic Review* (March 1969), p. 147.

6. Gary Becker and Nigel Tomes, "Child Endowments and the Quantity and Quality of Children," *Journal of Political Economy* (August 1976), pp. S143-62; and Richard A. Easterlin, "Population Change and Farm Settlement in the Northern United States," *Journal of Economic History* (March 1976), pp. 45-75.

7. Warren C. Sanderson, "On the Two Schools of the Economics of Fertility," *Population and Development Review* (Sept.-Dec. 1976), p. 474.

8. United Nations, "Conditions and Trends of Fertility in the World," Population Bulletin No. 7 (1963), p. 143.

9. James E. Kocher, *Rural Development, Income Distribution and Fertility Decline* (New York: The Population Council, 1973), p. 143.

10. Ibid., pp. 56-57.

11. Everett S. Lee, "A Theory of Migration," *Demography* (1966), p. 50.

12. This distinction stems from Larry A. Sjaastad, "The Costs and Returns of Human Migration," *Journal of Political Economy* (October 1962) (Supplement), pp. 80-93.

13. The particularly interesting case of emigration from Ireland as an alternative to rural-urban internal migration is analyzed in Robert E. Kennedy, Jr., *The Irish: Emigration, Marriage, and Fertility* (Berkeley: University of California Press, 1973).

14. Lorene Y. L. Yap, *Internal Migration in Less Developed Countries: A Survey of the Literature*, International Bank for Reconstruction and Development Staff Working Paper No. 215 (Washington, 1975), p. 25.

15. National Academy of Sciences, *Rapid Population Growth*, Vol. 1: *Conclusions and Policy Implications* (Baltimore: Johns Hopkins Press, 1971), p. 46.

16. This is probably true not only for nations as a whole (witness the Industrial Revolution), but also for segments of national populations that are relatively disadvantaged. For a discussion of this phenomenon among an economically disadvantaged group in the United States, see Calvin L. Beale, "Rural-Urban Migration of Blacks: Past and Future," *American Journal of Agricultural Economics* (May 1971), pp. 302-307.

17. Janet L. Abu-Lughod, "Urbanization in Egypt: Present State and Future Prospects," *Economic Development and Cultural Change* (April 1965), p. 313.

18. N. V. Sovani, "The Analysis of Over-urbanization," *Economic Development and Cultural Change* (January 1964), pp. 113-22.

19. David R. Kamerschen, "Further Analysis of Over-urbanization," *Economic Development and Cultural Change* (January 1969), pp. 235-53.

20. J. John Palen, *The Urban World* (New York: McGraw-Hill, 1975), p. 328.

21. Bert F. Hoselitz,"The City, the Factory, and Economic Growth," *American Economic Review* (May 1955), pp. 166-84, cited in ibid., p. 331.

22. Montague Yudelman, "Integrated Rural Development Projects: The Bank's Experience," *Finance and Development* (March 1977), pp. 16-17.

23. The need for such rural development in the United States is spelled out in Luther Tweeten and George L. Brinkman, *Micropolitan Development: Theory and Practice of Greater-Rural Economic Development* (Ames: Iowa State University Press, 1976).

Index

About the Contributors

P. Buringh, research scholar, educator, author. Presently Prof. Buringh is a member of the Dept. of Soil Science, Agricultural University, Wageningen, The Netherlands. He served as President of the Landbouwhogeschool (Agricultural Univ.) from 1970-1973 when he elected to return to his chair as Prof. of Tropical Soil Science. His current research deals with potential food production as limited by climate, water and soil, and he is author of *Computation of the Absolute Maximum Food Production of the World.*

Glenn W. Burton, Research Geneticist. Presently Dr. Burton is an Agricultural Research Service, USDA Research Geneticist at the Coastal Plain Station, Tifton, Ga. He is a Distinguished Alumni Professor in the Agronomy Division, University of Georgia and served as its Chairman for 14 years. His many awards include the USDA Superior Service Award and membership in the National Academy of Science. He has consulted on food production in many countries and was a member of a plant science team invited to the People's Republic of China in 1974 to help improve their plant science and agriculture.

Robert Clark, economist, educator, author. Presently Asst. Professor, Department of Economics, North Carolina State University; Senior Fellow, Center for the Study of Aging and Human Development, Duke University and Project Director, National Science Foundation Grant, "Age Structure and Economic Change." Formerly, Post-doctoral Fellow, Center for Aging and Human Development, Duke Univ.; Investigator, National Science Foundation Grant, "Economics of a Sta-

253

tionary Population: Implications for the Elderly," directed by Juanita Kreps. Coauthor (Juanita Kreps), *Sex, Age and Work: The Changing Composition of the Labor Force.*

Benjamin C. Dysart III, civil engineer, educator, conservationist. Presently Professor of Environmental Systems Engineering, Clemson University; Director and Executive Committee member, National Wildlife Federation. Formerly, Scientific Advisor for Civil Works, Office of the Secretary of the Army; site visitor, National Science Foundation; Civil Works Advisory Committee, Dept. of the Army; staff engineer, Union Carbide Corp.; member, S. C. Heritage Advisory Board; President, S. C. Wildlife Federation; Director, Water Resources Engineering and Water Resources Research Institute, Clemson University.

James E. Helpin, administrator, research pathologist, educator. Presently, Dr. Halpin is Director-at-Large, Southern Agricultural Experiment Stations; member, National Planning Committee (USDA) for Agricutural Research; member, Agricultural Research Policy Advisory Council (USDA) and Fellow-American Association for the Advancement of Science. Formerly, Professor of Plant Pathology, Clemson University; Assoc. Director, S. C. Agricultural Experiment Station; Assistant Agronomist with The Rockefeller Foundation Program of Agricultural Research (Columbia, Mexico, Chile). Research interests: soil-borne organisms and the diseases they incite in forage crops.

Gordon J. MacDonald, government official, geophysicist, educator, author. Presently Henry R. Luce Professor of Earth Sciences and Director of Environmental Studies and Policy at Dartmouth College. Prof. MacDonald is also consultant to the U.S. State Dept., Chairman, Commission on Natural Resources, National Academy of Sciences, and a member of the Dept. of State's Advisory Committee on Science and Foreign Affairs. The author of *The Rotation of the Earth,* he has been a consultant to the U.S. Geological Survey; a member of the President's Council on Environmental Quality; consultant to NASA, member, President's Science Advisory Committee; and director of the Atmospheric Research Laboratory, University of California.

John J. McKetta, Jr., educator, chemical engineer, author. Presently, E.P. Schoch Professor of Chemical Engineering at the University of Texas-Austin where he was Dean of Engineering and Executive Vice Chancellor-Academic Affairs for the entire University of Texas system. Formerly, Chairman, National Energy Policy Committee and the National Air Quality Control Committee; president, Chemoil Cons., Inc. Director of 11 companies and author of the 10 volume *Advances in Petroleum Chemistry and Refining* and the new 25 volume encyclopedia on chemical processing.

Harvey J. McMains, executive, engineer, educator. Vice President and Executive Director, National Bureau of Economic Research; Professor of Management, U.S. Army War College. Formerly, Director, Corporate Planning, Data Communications Planning, Analytical Support, American Telephone and Telegraph; Adjunct Professor, Management Philosophy, Pace University; member, technical staff and Chief Engineer, Bell Telephone Company.

John R. Meyer, economist, educator, author. Presently, Professor, Harvard University; President, National Bureau of Economic Research; Chairman, National Academy of Sciences Committee on the Benefits and Costs of Automobile Emissions Control; member, Commission on Law and the Economy, American Bar Association; Director, Dun & Bradstreet Companies, Inc., Consolidated Rail Corp., Rainier Bancorporation; Trustee, Mutual Life Insurance Co. of New York. Formerly, Professor, Yale Univ.; Committee on Population Growth and the American Future. Author, *The Urban Transportation Problem* and *Local Public Finance and the Fiscal Squeeze.*

John R. Pierce, engineer, educator, author. Presently Professor of Engineering at California Institute of Technology, Dr. Pierce formerly was Executive Director of Research-Communications Sciences, Bell Telephone Labs; a member of the President's Science Advisory Committee, and recipient of the National Medal of Science, the Valdemar Poulsen Gold Medal, and the Morris Liebmann Memorial Prize. He is author of *Man's World of Sound* and *Symbols, Signals and Noise.*

Andrei Rogers, research scholar, educator, author. Prof. Rogers is Research scholar and Area Chairman, Human Settlements and Services Area, at the International Institute for Applied Systems Analysis in Laxenburg, Austria. Formerly, Dr. Rogers was Professor of Civil Engineering and Urban Affairs at Northwestern University and the University of California-Berkeley. He is author of the following books: *Matrix Analysis of Interregional Population Growth and Distribution, Matrix Methods in Urban and Regional Analysis,* and *Introduction to Multiregional Mathematical Demography.*

William J. Serow, demographer, research director, author. Presently, Research Director, Population Studies Center, Tayloe Murphy Institute; Associate Professor, Department of Sociology, University of Virginia; member, Executive Council, Southern Regional Science Association. Formerly, Assistant Director, Bureau of Population and Economic Research; Lecturer, Colgate Darden Graduate School of Business Administration, Univ. of Virginia; and Demographic Interne, Demographic Division, The Population Council. Author, *Potential Influences of Zero Population Growth on American Society.*

H. Guyford Stever, educator, engineer, government official, author. Until January, President Ford's Science and Technology Advisor; Director, Office of Science and Technology Policy; Federal Coordinating Council for Science, engineering, and Technology; U.S. Chairman, US-USSR Joint Commission on Scientific and Technical Cooperation; First Chairman, US-Israel Bi-National Science Foundation. Previously, Director, National Science Foundation; President, Carnegie-Mellon University; Professor of Aeronautics and Astronautics, Massachusetts Institute of Technology; Head, Mechanical Engineering and Naval Architecture and Marine Engineering Departments; Chief Scientist, U.S. Air Force. Author, *Flight.*

Lyle C. Wilcox, author, educator, researcher. Dean of the College of Engineering and Professor of Electrical and Computer Engineering at Clemson University, Clemson, S.C. Principal investigator/director of research projects for the National Science Foundation, NASA and the Department of the Army in Instrumentation and Controls, Computer Applications, Circuits and Systems Design. Listed in National Register of Prominent Americans and International Notables; member American Association for the Advancement of Science.

T. Bruce Yandle, Jr., economist, educator, author. Presently, Senior Economist, Executive Office of the President, The Council on Wage and Price Stability; Head, Department of Economics, Clemson University. Formerly, Dr. Yandle taught at Georgia State University; was Sales Engineer for Austin Brown Associates, and Executive Vice President, Bearings & Drives, Inc. His research interests are in price theory, housing and environmental quality. He is coauthor of *The Economics of Environmental Use.*